Europe, Policies and People

Also by Sue Hatt

GENDER, WORK AND LABOUR MARKETS

MARKET, STATE AND FEMINISM (*co-author with Graham Dawson*)

WOMEN, RESEARCH AND CAREERS (*editor with Julie Kent and Carolyn Britton*)

Europe, Policies and People

An Economic Perspective

Edited by

Sue Hatt
Principal Lecturer in Economics
University of the West of England
Bristol

and

Frank Gardner
formerly Principal Lecturer in Economics
University of the West of England
Bristol

Consultant Editor: Jo Campling

First published 2002 by
PALGRAVE
Houndmills, Basingstoke, Hampshire RG21 6XS and
175 Fifth Avenue, New York, N. Y. 10010
Companies and representatives throughout the world

PALGRAVE is the new global academic imprint of
St. Martin's Press LLC Scholarly and Reference Division and
Palgrave Publishers Ltd (formerly Macmillan Press Ltd).

ISBN 0–333–94550–6

This book is printed on paper suitable for recycling and
made from fully managed and sustained forest sources.

A catalogue record for this book is available
from the British Library

Library of Congress Cataloging-in-publication Data
Europe, policies, and people: an economic perspective/edited by Sue Hatt
and Frank Gardner.
        p. cm.
    Includes bibliographical references and index.
    ISBN 0–333–94550–6
    1. European Union countries – Economic policy. 2. European Union
countries – Economic conditions. 3. European Union countries – Social
condition. 4. European Union countries–Economic integration. I. Hatt,
Sue, 1946– II. Gardner, Frank, 1935–
    HC240 .E8185 2002
    338.94–dc21   2001054597

10   9   8   7   6   5   4   3   2   1
11   10 09 08 07 06 05 04 03 02

Printed and bound in Great Britain by
Antony Rowe Ltd, Chippenham, Wiltshire

Contents

Part II People and Business

Part III People, Workers and Welfare

List of Boxes, Figures and Tables

Acknowledgements

We would like to thank all the students, friends, family and colleagues who have encouraged us to write this book. A project like this involves the work of a large team of people to give advice, lend computing facilities, help with references and so on, and we are grateful for all the support we have received without which the project would never have been completed. The editors and the authors are especially indebted to John Hatt, whose idea it was to focus the book around the people of Europe – a theme that has unified the book and made it more than simply a collection of disparate contributions.

In particular we would like to mention Jo Campling, who, as consultant editor, has provided a great deal of timely advice and support. We are also grateful to colleagues at the University of the West of England for providing access to the resources without which the book would not have been possible. This book has been substantially improved by the comments and suggestions of our colleagues and by the anonymous reviewer whose constructive comments have helped us to revise our earlier draft. Our friends, family and colleagues have had to live with the fact that completing this book has absorbed a great deal of our time and energy over the last two years and we are indebted to them for their forbearance.

Sue Hatt
Frank Gardner

Notes on the Contributors

Brian Ardy is Research Fellow at the European Institute South Bank University. He is currently working on an ESRC 'One Europe or Several' project on 'Adjustment to EMU'. He is also visiting lecturer at the Department of Agricultural Economics and Management at the University of Reading. In addition to EMU Brian's research interests include the EU budget and agriculture, particularly in relation to enlargement. These research interests have had practical results with work on projects funded by the EU, the Westminster Foundation for Democracy and the Department for International Development in Bulgaria, Croatia, Hungary, Latvia, Lithuania and Poland.

Jonathan Bradley is Principal Lecturer in International Business Economics at the University of the West of England (UWE). He is the author of several publications concerned with economic change in Europe, Eastern and Western. He has wide experience of European business, especially in connection with investment projects and privatisation. He is non-executive Chair of Perpetual European Investment Trust PLC, of Regent Magna Europa Fund PLC, and of the Balkan Fund.

Peter Cullen is a Senior Lecturer in Economics at UWE. He teaches European integration studies at undergraduate and master's degree levels within the Economics and Social Science Faculty and the Bristol Business School. His research interests include various aspects of European integration, but particularly monetary union and the air transport sector. He is also his faculty's international links coordinator and examiner in Economics (English) for the European Baccalaureate (but he would really like to be a professional pilot).

Frank Gardner was formerly a Principal Lecturer in Economics at UWE. He is a member of Chatham House, Royal Institute for International Affairs, and is an examiner in Economics for the European Baccalaureate in European Schools where the multilingual children of the civil servants of the 'New Europe' are educated. He has over thirty years' experience teaching Economics and International Relations at all levels.

Sue Hatt is Principal Lecturer in Economics at UWE. She is the author of *Gender, Work and Labour Markets* (Macmillan – now Palgrave, 1997) and joint editor of *Women, Research and Careers* (Macmillan – now Palgrave,1999) and *Market, State and Feminism* (Edward Elgar 2000). She has extensive teaching experience at undergraduate level and her main research interests lie in students' experience in higher education and in feminist economics.

James Korovilas is an Associate Lecturer in Economics at UWE. His research interests include economic developments in post-communist Albania, migrant labour and the Greek informal economy, and the formation of an independent economic system in Kosovo, and he has published articles on these topics. With the help of the Westminster Foundation, he is currently researching the role of the Deutschmark in providing a stable economic platform for the Kosovan economy.

Sahand Panah is an Associate Lecturer in Economics at UWE. Previously, he was managing director of an export company and worked as the Middle East export facilitator and consultant for a number of European enterprises. His research interests include international business economics, business strategy and cultural convergence. He has taught on a wide range of courses at undergraduate and postgraduate level and he has supervised a number of MSc dissertations.

Martin Sullivan is Senior Lecturer in Economics at UWE. Before coming to UWE, Martin worked in local government as an Economic Development Assistant, producing reports on the local economy, industrial sector studies and labour market analyses. He teaches the Economics of the European Union and international business economics at undergraduate and postgraduate level and he is a member of the Institute for Teaching and Learning in higher education. His specialist research interests are the analysis of public and private pensions provision and the regulation and governance of financial services activities, and he is currently writing a book on pensions.

List of Abbreviations

ACP	Africa, the Caribbean and the Pacific
ADA	Airline Deregulation Act
BSE	Bovine Spongiform Encephalopathy
CAP	Common Agricultural Policy
CCT	Common Customs Tariff
CEE	Central and Eastern Europe
CET	Common External Tariff
CFP	Common Fisheries Policy
CJD	Creutzfeldt–Jakob Disease
CMD	Capital Movements Directive
CTP	Common Transport Policy
DETR	Department of Environment, Transport and the Regions
EAGGF (FEOGA)	European Agriculture Guidance and Guarantee Fund
EBRD	European Bank for Reconstruction and Development
EC	European Community
ECB	European Central Bank
ECJ	European Court of Justice
ECOFIN	Council of Ministers of Economics and Finance
ECSC	European Coal and Steel Community
ECU	European Currency Unit
EDC	European Defence Community
EEA	European Economic Area
EEC	European Economic Community
EFTA	European Free Trade Area
EIB	European Investment Bank
EIU	Economist Intelligence Unit
EMCF	European Monetary Cooperation Fund
EMU	Economic and Monetary Union
EPOS	Electronic Point of Sale
ERDF	European Regional Development Fund
ERM	Exchange Rate Mechanism
ESCB	European System of Central Banks
ESF	European Social Fund

EU	European Union
FDI	Foreign Direct Investment
FEOGA (EAGGF)	*Fonds Européen d'orientation et de guarantie agricole*
FT	*Financial Times*
GATT	General Agreement on Tariffs and Trade
GDP	Gross Domestic Product
GMO	Genetically Modified Organism
GNP	Gross National Product
G7	Group of Seven (USA, Canada, UK, Germany, France, Japan and Italy)
G8	Group of Eight (as above plus Russia)
MNC	Multinational Corporation
MNE	Multinational Enterprise
MU	Monetary Union
NATO	North Atlantic Treaty Organisation
PAYG	Pay As You Go
PMPS	Prefunded Money Purchase Scheme
PPP	Public–Private Partnership
PPS	Purchasing Power Standard
OCA	Optimum Currency Area
OECD	Organisation for Economic Cooperation and Development
OPFS	Occupational Pension based on Final Salary
R&D	Research and Development
SME	Small and Medium Enterprises
STEP	Social, Technological, Economic and Political
TAC	Total Allowable Catch
TENs	Trans-European Networks
TEU	Treaty of the European Union
TGV	*Train à grande vitesse*
TOR	Traditional Own Resources
UK	United Kingdom
UN	United Nations
UNFPA	United Nations Population Fund
USA	United States of America
WTO	World Trade Organisation

1
Introduction

Sue Hatt and Frank Gardner

Throughout Europe people are beginning to appreciate that the European Union (EU) can have far-reaching effects upon their daily lives. Decisions taken by the EU have, for example, affected interest rates, the length of the standard working week, the pension rights of part-time workers and the ability of British farmers to export their produce. This book considers economic developments in the European Union and will assess their significance for the people in the member states. The focus of the analysis is on the consequences of Europe-wide developments for particular groups of citizens or for those located in certain member states. In this way, we try to reflect the diversity of European countries within the overarching structure of the Union while considering the often conflicting, but sometimes complementary, interests of the different groups. A Europe which offers profitable opportunities for business, for instance, might not necessarily work in the interests of its people as workers, shareholders, consumers, taxpayers, parents and so on.

In the early stages of its development, the stated aim of the European Community was economic integration. During the 1960s progress was substantial but the low rate of economic growth and the high inflation of the 1970s delayed further initiatives. The launch of the Single Market programme in the 1980s was designed to complete the creation of a large and unified market providing opportunities for firms to become more competitive and take advantage of economies of scale. At the end of the twentieth century, the introduction of the single currency and the advance to economic and monetary union has offered businesses a chance to reduce transactions costs and to plan with confidence for the future. Each of these economic developments has offered firms the chance to expand in a wider market but, as the

European market-place has become more integrated, concern has grown that, while some groups might be profiting, others might not. Large firms, for example, might be able to expand and diversify but these activities tend to reduce regional variety for consumers and threaten the survival of small local producers.

This book analyses the consequences of European economic integration for the citizens of the member states. Using the word 'Europe' can become confusing. It is often used to refer to the idea and process of West European integration. The word is also used to denote the institutions that have structured this process – that is, the European Economic Community, the European Communities, the European Community and, finally, the European Union. Strictly speaking, Europe defines a geographical entity – the continent as a whole, including a large number of non-member states to the east. We have not adopted a standard usage in this book. The evolution of living language reflects the complexities of this debate and we have left contributors free to employ the words and terms that they feel best convey the sense of their argument.

The focus of this book is primarily economic policy and economics. Writing from the perspective of this discipline, each contributor examines an issue and highlights the effects for particular groups of people in Europe. While not all contributors agree about the extent to which the policies of the EU have benefited the peoples of Europe, nevertheless the combination of economic analysis and a people-centred approach provides a coherent theme to these contributions.

The impact of Europe-wide policies on the people depends upon the particular conditions in the various member states. While economic integration in Europe has gone ahead, social policy has remained the responsibility of the member states each of which has developed its own particular blend of welfare capitalism. For the people of Europe, the effects of Europe-wide developments with respect to the single currency, immigration, business strategy and the regulation of working hours, for example, has therefore depended on the balance between market institutions, non-market institutions and state support. Historical factors take their place alongside political and economic developments in shaping the extent to which EU legislation affects the ordinary citizen. Each country, and indeed each region, displays considerable diversity in terms of policies, institutional structures, social norms and other cultural influences; these factors set the context within which European integration is enacted. In some countries the introduction of minimum standards makes very little difference as higher standards have already been set while others struggle to comply with the EU benchmarks. Some chapters consider the impact of European developments within the context of one or two member states whereas other contributors prefer a Europe-wide survey.

This book is intended to serve a wide audience. The editors have ensured that the text is accessible to the general reader, to business-people and to public policy-makers. Specialist journalists and researchers in European issues, as well as to academics from a range of discipline areas, will, we hope, find something of interest here, but our main objective is to place before a wider audience some of the 'people' issues too often ignored in the 'Europe debate'. Although all the contributors have a background in economics, their analysis explores the interface between economics, business, politics, sociology and social policy. While some will read the whole book, others might be interested in one or two chapters or, indeed, in just one part of the book. Anyone interested in the making of the new Europe, however, should find something of interest within at least one of the three parts into which the book has been divided.

In Part I 'Concepts and History' the contributors consider themes and issues within a historical context. Gardner outlines the history and development of European integration in the second half of the twentieth century. The contrast between the founders' vision of an integrated Europe bringing peace, prosperity and stability to the people and the prosaic realities of a bureaucracy which regulates and threatens to stifle enterprise is discussed. Within Europe, it is argued, economic and political integration have been inextricably interlinked and the political elites have sometimes been more concerned with maintaining cooperation, and thus protecting their own power base and lifestyle, than with promoting economic growth and improving the economic well-being of all the peoples of Europe. The fifteen member states come from different traditions and have varied social and market structures and these different perspectives have affected the speed with which the EU has been able to move forward in particular areas. While agriculture has been accorded considerable attention due to the importance of this sector within the six founder member states, fishing has not attained a similar status. The EU has thus been far more advantageous for farmers than for the fishing community in general. The power balance within the EU has influenced the development of policy and the priority accorded to each sector. This in turn has had profound effects upon the lives of the different groups of people within Europe.

Bradley provides an overview of European capitalism(s) in Chapter 3. He surveys the current literature and relates theoretical debates to the empirical evidence, arguing that, as the economies of Europe become more integrated, traditional distinctions between different modes of European capitalism are becoming outdated. *French dirigisme*, the *German Sozialmarktwirtschaft* or British *market-based capitalism* have had different implications for the people as workers, shareholders, entrepreneurs, taxpayers and consumers. In many respects, however, these categories no longer represent appropriate distinctions within the context of European integration. This detailed and carefully reasoned chapter examines whether a genuinely European style of capitalism is emerging, discusses the key features of this new model and assesses the extent to which it is 'popular' in that it brings widespread benefits to the people of Europe.

Part II 'People and Business' examines different aspects of European policy. As the third largest trading block in the world, the Single European Market has provided opportunities and threats for both EU and non-EU firms operating in the region and Panah explores the implications of a Europe without borders for business strategy in Chapter 4. This chapter portrays the dynamic process of change and competition created by the Single Market and affecting the strategic choices of multinational enterprises. He examines the impact of the new European business environment on people living in Europe in terms of employment, pricing policy and consumer choices. The nature of the company response to these changes in Europe is illustrated by two illuminating case studies. The first of these explores the entry of Wal-Mart into the European retail sector, while the second focuses upon the merger between Daimler-Benz and Chrysler which has been instrumental in changing traditional attitudes towards business strategy in Europe. Many multinationals are developing strategies to accommodate the technical, demographic and social changes taking place within Europe. In their respective roles as consumers, employees, entrepreneurs of small and medium size companies and pensioners, the people of Europe might benefit in the long term but, in the more immediate future, some groups might find themselves under pressure. The chapter concludes that the management of such profound change and the consequent frictions will pose challenges to the business elite, public policy makers and the people of Europe in the years ahead.

Turning to the single currency, Cullen considers whether the introduction of the euro is primarily intended to serve the interests of business or the consumer. The implications of the single currency for people in two states is compared. The British and Italian economies are similar in size but, while the UK has been sceptical about the EU in general and the single currency in particular, Italy has been an enthusiastic participant in the project. The Italians have used the Maastricht criteria and the run up to the adoption of the euro to tighten macro-economic policy and bring the public finances under control. These unpopular measures have generally been accepted by the Italian people who consider membership of Euroland to be in their long term interests. No such consensus has developed in the UK. The brief participation in the Exchange Rate Mechanism in the early 1990s was unsuccessful. The high interest rates needed to control inflation in a reunified Germany were not appropriate for the depressed British economy of 1991 and yet, with a fixed exchange rate, the ability to set a different interest rate was limited. This experience convinced many people that joining the single currency would constrain the freedom of the UK government to pursue an economic strategy which was in the best interests of the British people. The improvement in the performance of the British economy subsequent to leaving the ERM led many to be wary of further engagement in Euroland. Cullen attributes these different stances to the political and economic experiences of the two populations.

The European Union affects many people's lives through its expenditure and taxation policies and yet these activities are often unrecognised and unacknowledged by the citizens of Europe. In Chapter 6 Ardy analyses EU data to explore the sources of revenue and the direction of expenditure within the EU. He argues that the budget performs poorly on many of the key criteria for assessing tax systems. The EU budget is reasonably efficient but it is not very equitable, nor is it transparent. Many people are often unaware that the benefits they are receiving arise from expenditure by the EU. Although the Commission argues that the citizens of Europe derive benefits from EU membership which are far more extensive than an analysis of the budgetary flows suggests, nevertheless the budget will be an issue of political concern as long as the key issues of equity and transparency remain unaddressed.

The business theme is developed further in Chapter 7 with respect to the financial services sector. When people or companies purchase financial services products, such as insurance and pensions, they expose themselves to the risk of losses arising from fraud, negligence and incompetence. The task of financial regulation is to reduce such risks and thereby preserve consumer confidence in the financial system. Sullivan examines the new European regulatory environment for financial services and considers whether the risk to which consumers are being exposed has increased as a result of new structures that have evolved. In a clear and succinct analysis, he argues that the single European licence approach to regulation is fundamentally flawed and suggests that, if cross border trade becomes widespread, a Europe-wide regulatory agency can be expected to offer better protection to consumers of financial services.

The next chapter turns attention to the transport sector. The Treaty of Rome identified the need for a Common Transport Policy to promote efficiency and achieve wider aims, such as economic development, cohesion and free movement of goods and people. This policy which is explored by Cullen in Chapter 8 looks at the harmonisation of national transport policies, the creation of infrastructure networks and the promotion of competition through deregulation. While private transport has increased rapidly, the cost of this development for people's daily lives is hard to estimate. New roads facilitate the distribution of goods but also bring increased risk of accidents and add to environmental pollution. Cullen discusses some of the major issues with respect to the conditions of employment, the development of outlying regions and the promotion of tourism which arise out of the development of a Common Transport Policy.

The Common Agricultural Policy (CAP), the subject of Chapter 9, contrasts sharply with the Common Transport Policy. It has developed as an all-inclusive Union-wide policy and Hatt analyses its consequences for producers, consumers and taxpayers. The reform of the CAP during the 1990s has shifted the cost away from consumers towards taxpayers, making it more transparent and equitable. However, she argues that CAP remains an expensive policy which serves the interests of food producers rather than those of food consumers or users of the countryside. This chapter considers the reasons why a common agricultural policy was a priority in the early stages of the Community's development, examines the political interests which have shaped the development of that policy and evaluates the ways in which it has affected, and is affecting, the people of Europe.

The final section of the book focuses upon people rather than policies. Each of the three chapters considers a particular group of people at a significant point in their life history and evaluates the impact of the policies of the EU upon their lives. In Chapter 10, Hatt focuses upon families and the provision of care. She examines the ways in which national governments' welfare policies interact with markets and the provision of care, especially for children. The implications of these policies for women and for men as they seek to reconcile their parental obligations with paid employment is discussed with particular reference to Italy, the UK and Sweden. The measures which the European Union has taken to establish minimum standards are considered and their impact is evaluated in these three countries. Hatt draws upon the work of feminist economists to argue that the EU policies have had the most significant effects in the UK where women have participated extensively in the labour market but national regulations are weak.

In Chapter 11, Korovilas switches attention to the working age groups with a focus on migrant workers and their experiences within the EU. While free movement of labour within the EU has always been central to the European ideal, policy with respect to immigration from non-member states has been less clearly defined. Greece was once a donor country providing migrant workers for the more northerly states and, perhaps for this reason, has in practice adopted a more open approach than many of her neighbours towards inward migration, chiefly from Albania. This chapter draws on interview data to explore the experiences of Albanian workers within Greece and considers their reasons for migrating, the costs and benefits of working in Greece and their future plans. Korovilas argues that many Albanians in Greece might like to move to other EU countries and assesses their chances of so doing against the background of the Schengen Agreement.

In Chapter 12 Sullivan considers the final phase of the life cycle – old age. He explores the link between changes in the population age structure and the reform of public pensions provision. Three types of pension structure are analysed. He reviews the ubiquitous Pay-As-You-Go schemes and considers prefunded money purchase pensions and occupational pensions as alternatives. The difficulty of balancing redistribution and equity on the one hand with efficiency and affordability on the other is explored and he emphasises the importance of pensions as a Europe-wide concern.

In the concluding chapter, the editors draw together some of the themes developed in the body of the book and evaluate the developments taking place within the new Europe. While the other chapters have focused primarily upon people within the EU, this final chapter discusses some of the implications of EU policies upon insiders and outsiders. In an increasingly global economy, policies and developments within the EU interact with events in the rest of the world to affect the lives of people in Europe and beyond. This theme of insiders and outsiders strikes the concluding note in the book.

We hope that in this volume we have achieved a measure of coherence through a clear focus on a unifying theme – that is, *people*. Each of the contributors has brought a particular perspective to the analysis, and the book therefore reflects diverse viewpoints. It has been the task of the editors to find a textual compromise between the enthusiasm of the authors for a particular topic and the need to accommodate each chapter within a meaningful synthesis. Discussions between editors and authors have been lively and fruitful as the drafts proceeded. The most frequent request made to contributors was for 'economics as if people mattered'. We asked ourselves how the progress of integration both in terms of numbers of members and in depth of activities has affected different groups of people. The economics and the politics of the new Europe have made a big impact on people as consumers of goods and services, but we have sought to look beyond consumption and concern ourselves with people as carers, pensioners, savers, migrant workers, and even employees facing job loss. We have tried to identify those people who gain and those who lose as policy competencies are developed, providing, we hope, a useful addition to the literature on the European Union.

Part I

A People's Europe: Concepts and History

2

From Customs Union to People's Europe?

Frank Gardner

> The last world war ended half a century ago. Under American influence in particular, Western European rivalries have been pacified and converted into benign economic competition and co-operation.
>
> (Kapteyn, 1996, p. 170)

Europe: the context

During the latter half of the twentieth century, a dollar-dominated world, within which the United States of America (USA) sought to create a liberal economic order managed by international institutions, replaced the economic nationalism, trade wars and competitive exchange depreciation that characterised the Europe of the 1930s. It was US leadership within a Cold War context that set European elites on their path to integration – accepting the risk that a regional bloc might not fit easily into an open global system. The unease and ambivalence voiced by the British weighed less with US policy-makers than the need to fortify, unify and strengthen Europe against the Soviet Union. In establishing the European Economic Community (EEC), the politicians of the centre parties within Europe created what was in Kapteyn's (1996) words ' a market without a state'. It is this use of economic means to political and social ends that will be explored in this chapter.

The basis of the liberal international trade order was the General Agreement on Tariffs and Trade (GATT) and under Article XXIV there were two permitted routes to regional integration – the free trade area and the customs union. The first was intergovernmental and limited in scope, but the second was much more ambitious, wide-ranging and supranational, in that a common external tariff (CET) and agriculture were involved, thereby implying political as well as economic cooperation. The USA favoured the customs union approach as appropriate for Europe.

Within the market economies of mainland Europe too, there was a strong preference for a customs union as the basis for the relaunch of integration in the mid-1950s. This preference owed much to the political experiences of those countries during the Second World War. Unlike British elites, the political class on the Continent had become persuaded of the need for a new Europe. Fascism and war had shattered civic society across the Channel, so it was the reconstruction of a democratic and civilian polity, not the mere elimination of economic nationalism, that was the central preoccupation of centre party politicians on the Continent. The failure of the elite in British government circles to understand this simple fact led directly to the creation of the Franco-German axis that has defined the nature of the European project since the 1960s.

The customs union approach was no more than an economic means to a political end. Indeed, this is the quintessential nature of the new Europe. Economic goals are more easily understood and accepted by ordinary people than grand political designs. For this reason, economic objectives are set and pursued and these become the steps by which political ends are achieved. Economic cooperation between the nations of Europe was vital in the chaotic conditions of the mid-twentieth century and remains important at the beginning of the twenty-first. However, it was always the reconstruction of democratic, peaceful society – a political objective rather than the achievement of more prosaic economic ends – that lay at the heart of 'Europeanism'. These issues remain better understood in mainland Europe than in Britain.

European integration: economics or political economy?

It is, of course, very difficult to disentangle economics from politics and even more difficult to define 'political economy' – a linguistic term that has lost favour in an age of fragmented social science disciplines. European integration is indeed about political economy. Since most people outside Britain judge it to be more about politics than economics, one must, of necessity, explore the untidy borderlands between these two disciplines. Efficiency, stability and equity are the three criteria that political economy can deploy to evaluate both the analytical propositions of positive economics and the policies implemented by government. Economic analysis can deal quite happily with the first two criteria, but finds greater difficulty when it addresses issues of fairness and justice.

The emergence of an economics profession claiming scientific status for the discipline pushed the study of economic issues away from value judgements and philosophy towards positivism. Mathematics, logic and models were elevated above political economy and history. Many economists sought to enhance the status of their subject by the self-conscious avoidance of normative statements and policy prescriptions. In practice, this proved impossible in many applied areas. The study of European integration is such an applied area and concerns for regulation, redistribution and welfare make it a field where political economy, history and philosophy need a place.

The customs union route led directly to the politicisation of economics. A free trade area does not need a great many administrative staff but a customs union requires a supranational bureaucracy for negotiating with the rest of the world. Jean Monnet, one of the 'founding fathers' of the EU, was himself every inch the bureaucrat. He did not seek elected office and his skill was as a behind-the-scenes facilitator, never seeking to compete with the nationalist charisma of someone like de Gaulle. Both men shared a profound distaste for electoral politics and for parliaments but, whereas de Gaulle represented the strand in French culture which saw great merit in strong presidential leadership, Monnet represented the tradition of the powerful, long-lived bureaucracy. Monnet and his allies set out to build institutions where benign bureaucrats would regulate affairs without interference from nationalist politicians or squabbling parliaments. They were, in large measure, successful.

The European Commission achieved its first recognition as an actor on the international stage when it negotiated on behalf of its member states at the various GATT rounds that liberalised world trade in the 1960s and 1970s. Of even greater importance was the opportunity, within the customs union framework, for the Commission to take over the regulatory responsibility for the agriculture sector. Agricultural trade, thanks to American policy in the immediate postwar period, lay, in general, outside the purview of the GATT. The Commission grasped the opportunity with enthusiasm. A highly protectionist system of market support, intervention buying and export subsidy was put in place and became, as Chapter 9 explains, the 'political glue' to hold the community together. One of the most serious of the many crises of

European integration was that of the 'Empty Chair' in the mid-1960s. This arose because the Commission sought to move integration forwards by linking the financing of the Common Agricultural Policy (CAP) to more supranational decision-making. The Luxembourg Compromise of January 1966 resolved the immediate crisis but left important questions unanswered with regard to the respective roles of the Commission and the member states.

During the late 1950s and 1960s the integration of Europe moved forward with confidence as postwar reconstruction gave way to new growth and a new vitality. The Rome Treaty gave expression to this feeling, taking in its stride the success of the European Coal and Steel Community (ECSC) and the failure of the European Defence Community (EDC) in 1954. The belief took hold that the way forward was to be found through creating a common European regulatory framework for one sector after another, rather than attempting to deal directly with political and security issues of great urgency. It was the North Atlantic Treaty Organisation (NATO), with US presence on the front line in the Cold War, that allowed the six founder members the luxury of pursuing their integration strategy through cooperation to devise a CET and a CAP. Little changed over the years and US power both within the European region and in the wider world has rarely been appreciated and has often been resented. Nevertheless US power has been the essential foundation upon which the Europeans have been able to build their project.

The economics of European integration became a subsidiary matter, wholly subordinated to questions of social and political renewal. The nation states of mainland Europe were perceived by the generation of postwar leaders of centre right and centre left alike to have failed their peoples. Defeat in war, Fascism, Naziism, practice of or complicity in genocide, destruction of civic dignity as well as buildings – these were the shared experiences of the belligerent states of the mainland. Within the core of Europe the central ambitions were to avoid Fascism and war. Britain did not lose its democracy or its war. In Monnet's words:

> I never understood why the British did not join this, which was so much in their interest. I came to the conclusion that it must have been because it was the *price of victory* the illusion that you could maintain what you had without change. (Charlton, 1983, p. 307, original italics)

A lesson from history

Economics was always the means, never the end. In many respects the story of European integration resembles a strange replay of Europe's economic history. During the two or three centuries within which the modern nation states of Europe emerged, the theory and practice of mercantilism dominated economic affairs. It was, in brief, the manipulation of economic activity in order to serve the nation and the nation's ruler. Protection of home markets, increasing national holdings of precious metals through achieving a trade surplus, encouragement of strategic industries, the exploitation of colonies through trade monopolies and the close regulation of any activity which might increase the financial and military power of the ruler; such were the policies indicated by mercantilist theory. Internal barriers to trade which hindered the growth of the power of the state were abolished to be replaced by tariffs and monopolies directed at outsiders.

It was Friedrich List, a German political economist developing his ideas in response to Adam Smith, who provided a coherent version of mercantilism as a tool for nation building. His major work became the intellectual blueprint for the *Zollverein*. This Prussian-led customs union provided, during the middle decades of the nineteenth century, the economic foundation upon which Bismarck and Kaiser Wilhelm built a powerful Reich. Although he accepted that sometimes state action was desirable, Adam Smith, in contrast to List, held that free markets should be the rule. List took issue with this analysis. In his view the established economic power of England could only be effectively challenged by protecting the infant industries of a united Germany. His chief complaints against Smith were that his political economy was all economy and no politics and that he propagated a doctrine designed to condemn Germany to be a nation of cuckooclockmakers, unable to learn the industrial arts of which England was the master. Just as Germany needed unity in order to meet the technological challenge of Britain in the nineteenth century, so Europe needs unity now to meet the competition from the USA and the emerging powers in Asia.

List was not altogether wrong; the *Zollverein* was a success. Economic growth in Europe in the nineteenth century was rapid in Western Europe even in areas outside the *Zollverein*. It was slow in the East even for areas within the *Zollverein*. This would suggest that the removal of trade barriers is a necessary but not a sufficient condition for economic improvement. Other factors have a part to play, as Landes points out:

> If we learn anything from the history of economic development, it is that culture makes all the difference. (Landes, 1998, p. 516)

The historical comparison is instructive and can suggest some lessons for the new Europe. In the short run, the abolition of internal barriers often yields good results. Trade expands and economic growth can be very rapid indeed. This was the experience of European integration in the 1960s. It is very likely, however, that in the longer run the politicisation of economic affairs will not only slow down growth, but might well generate some very undesirable consequences for civic society and political institutions. More and more resources are diverted from productive investment into political persuasion as lobbyists flock to the political centre to play the regulation game. The result, within quite a short time, is the growth of a regulatory bureaucracy which hinders economic growth, speedily becomes corrupt, and destroys faith in democracy. The mandarins of the Ming dynasty in China and the officials of the Ottoman and Byzantine empires all ruled large, rich territories. These were impressive empires but lacked the dynamic of the disunited nineteenth-century Europe which outpaced them in terms of economic growth. The core of the Eurosceptic case (Connolly, 1995) is that a byzantine Brussels bureaucracy will strangle enterprise, eliminate national individuality, and follow the pattern of decline that characterised the non-European empires of the past.

Markets or regulation

The balance between politics and economics, and between dynamic enterprise and stifling bureaucracy is hard to achieve. The membership of the EU has increased and the institutional structure has developed considerably since the early years. Broadly popular, well-supported by a passive consensus among electorates, it was enthusiastically endorsed by almost all the politically active groups within Europe. Whilst European institutions and policies may be subjected to criticism, the 'idea' of Europe, the idealism that created the project in the early postwar years, remains as powerful and popular as ever. Clearly the people of Europe are inclined to credit the European Union with the dignity, peace and prosperity that they have enjoyed in the postwar era. Economic growth was particularly rapid amongst the founder member states in the 1960s immediately after the EEC was established. Living standards continued to rise, albeit more slowly and fitfully, throughout the latter half of the twentieth century. This is indeed an achievement. However, the extent to which this economic prosperity should be attributed to the existence of the EU is debatable. Perhaps too little importance has been given to the role of the United States of America, defending Western Europe during the Cold War, maintaining an open liberal world economic system and providing essential public goods at very low cost to the Europeans. By and large though, it is reasonable to conclude that the people of Europe are correct in their endorsement of the EU. It is better to dispute the safety of beef than the frontiers of nations.

This conclusion must, however, be heavily qualified. In two important respects – institutional structure and economic philosophy – the EU has proved to be ineffective and, more importantly, totally unable to move towards self-improvement. The institutional structure of the adventure from EEC to EU has, over the second half of the twentieth century, failed to move away from bureaucracy and secrecy towards democracy and accountability. In economics, the *dirigiste* tradition of French economic history and the *Zollverein* experience of Germany have been the framework for policy-making with serious adverse consequences for efficiency, growth, stability and equity within the European region and in the wider world. These two weaknesses are interdependent. In Britain to some degree, in the United States to a considerable extent and in the emerging global economy in Asia, there is limited regulation of markets – at least in economic principle if not always in political practice. This is not the conventional wisdom within Continental Europe. To pose the issue in Kapteyn's (1996) terms, for most Europeans, the market does require the influence of a powerful regulatory state.

It is not simply a matter of contrasting Adam Smith's views with those of Colbert and List, nor a question of counterposing the French preference for strong state direction with the British belief in free enterprise and, perhaps, fitting the German social market philosophy somewhere in between. Not at all: modern capitalism is more complex than that, as the next chapter will argue. The institutional framework of the European project, however, and its early evolution during the period before British entry have predisposed policy-makers towards constraints on market freedom. Regulation and bureaucracy have become the norm. It remains to be seen whether or not the Lisbon summit of March 2000 constitutes a real change of direction. A rational choice to trade off some economic growth for greater social stability may be acceptable, but, if regulatory systems arise as the unintended outcome of poorly structured and undemocratic institutions, dominated by a mixture of sectional interests and the self-interest of office holders, then citizens are wise to question the legitimacy of the enterprise.

The policy process in Brussels

> The European Community was born to end divisions in Western Europe. It has succeeded. With NATO, it has given us peace and prosperity in our part of the Continent, and made war unthinkable. The determination of the founding fathers has succeeded far beyond the estimations of most people in their time. Their vision was proved right for its age. But it is outdated. It will not do now. (John Major, cited in Reading, 1995, p. 207)

These words encapsulate an important idea. The new millennium requires different institutions from those created in the aftermath of mid-century conflict. Policy-making within Monnet's construction of Europe has been more in the hands of the Commission than anywhere else; of this we may be sure. It is the right of initiative which gives the Commission its preeminent place within the policy-making process. National ministers and their civil servants can amend, shape, even reject proposals but it is from the Commission that these proposals must originate. It, like all bureaucracies, has the inestimable power of permanence. Even in 1999 when an adverse report from the European Parliament on fraud and corruption within the Commission caused all the Commissioners to resign, they were subsequently reinstated to ensure executive continuity. These events have demonstrated the virtual indestructibility of the Commission. No amount of scandal, dishonesty, corruption, abuse of power or inefficiency can touch it. From this defective foundation at the heart of Europe all sorts of other defects follow (Connolly, 1995). The death of democracy and honesty in the prevailing climate of corruption is the most important of these defects and provokes visceral anti-Europeanism. For Eurosceptics, the existence of an unelected, unaccountable, unremovable and unreformable Commission is such a central failing that they reject the whole edifice constructed thereon.

For economists of a more pragmatic turn of mind, the question of how the machinery of the EU can produce bad economic policies which are like granite monuments in their capacity to resist reform is a much more immediate issue. Economic policies can be adjudged bad when they work against the criteria of efficiency, stability and equity. If policies waste or misallocate resources, they fail the test of efficiency. If they seem likely to store up troubles for the future, they can be judged to fail the stability test. If they are widely seen to be arbitrary and unjust in the redistributive effects, they can be condemned as inequitable. Because the main purpose of the Commission is to act as an engine of growth for the integration process, it gives less attention to the narrow economic criteria than to the effects it hopes to achieve with respect to the wider goals of integration.

When the Commission first considers a policy, its salience with respect to furthering integration is central. In the language of international institutions, it is 'task expansion' that is sought. If the EU, or any other agency for that matter, can develop more competencies, raise its profile with new publics and hopefully expand its budget and its personnel, such gains are deemed to be progress. Two factors feed this drive for growth. According to neo-functional integration theory popular in the 1960s and 1970s, the best way to build a new Europe and undermine nationalism was to take control of sectors of economic activity so that gradually the people looked to Brussels rather than to their national government for the solution to their problems. The other factor is the tendency for administrators to expand their own numbers. Such expansion allows them to do a better job and also secures them higher status and salaries.

No better example of the bad economic outcomes can be adduced than the hasty fabrication of a Common Fisheries Policy (CFP) in the period just before British entry into the EEC. It was only in the early 1970s on the proposed entry of the maritime states – Denmark, Norway, Ireland and the UK – that a CFP was speedily conceived and prematurely brought to birth. Its congenital defects are the Total Allowable catch (TAC) concept and the awarding of national quotas within a Community Pond. The objective of furthering integration is well served since control of fishing is taken from the nation state and given to the EEC. The rationale is to prevent overfishing and the destruction of fish stocks by rationally planned exploitation of a Community resource. In their haste to preempt discussion with new members who might delay or abort the enterprise, a very bad policy was adopted.

Writers have dealt with this policy problem in very different ways. Nicoll and Salmon (1994) deal only with aspirations. Under the CFP,

> over-fishing is prevented by the comprehensive allocation to interested member states of quotas within the Total Allowable Catch and

by regulating fishing areas and fishing equipment such as mesh sizes. (Nicoll and Salmon, 1994, p. 137)

Barnes's (1988) view was not dissimilar but, writing more recently, Barnes and Barnes (1995) talk of a failure of implementation and cite some revealing facts about the real world. As Tables 2.1 and 2.2 indicate, Spain, with a much larger fishing industry than the UK, has relatively few inspectors and recorded no inspection days at sea. It is hard to see how they could ensure effective compliance with the policy while remaining on dry land. One must conclude that, in practice, they carried out very little enforcement activity. The UK, on the other hand, with a smaller fishing industry, devoted considerable resources to enforcement activity. They had a larger inspectorate which spent a total of 2500 days at sea. This disparity of enforcement activity between the two countries is very marked.

The problems of enforcing the CFP are compounded in practice. The TAC is shared out, species by species, between the nations who then award quotas for each species to each fishing enterprise. Catching fish is not an exact science. The catch is almost certain to include fish for which no quota is held and fish which meet the quota requirement but will not command a good price. Small and non-quota fish are either discarded or are landed in secret and sold on black markets. It is impos-

Table 2.1 The structure of the EU fishing industry

	Number of vessels	Gross registered tonnes	Landings (ECU million)	Percentage of GDP
Spain	20 759	619 329	1764	0.518
UK	8283	206 934	622	0.083

Source: Commission of the EC (1992) *Community Structural Policy: Assessment and Outlook* (adapted from Barnes and Barnes, 1995).

Table 2.2 Comparison of member states' enforcement

	Shore-based inspectors	Inspection days at sea	Inspection planes	Aerial surveillance hours
Spain	12	0	–	50
UK	152	2500	5	4800

Source: House of Commons Agricultural Committee, Sixth Report 1992–3, *The Effects of Conservation Measures on the UK Sea Fishing Industry* (adapted from Barnes and Barnes, 1995).

sible to quantify the waste precisely but it is estimated that some 40 per cent of the catch may be discarded dead.

This policy does not therefore conserve stocks; in practice it results in wasteful depletion. The foolishness of this approach is so obvious that the good faith of those who devised it has been questioned. This policy has operated for more than two decades because bureaucrats will not initiate action and national politicians are less concerned with global wastefulness than with appearing to support their own fishermen. To make matters worse, the costs of policing and enforcement are high and the state with the biggest fleet – Spain – makes little effort to meet its responsibilities and contents itself with maximising its catch, irrespective of the damage done to fish stocks. So far from dealing with the 'tragedy of the commons' (Hardin, 1977), EU policy exacerbates it.

The Common Fisheries Policy is an illustration of the pattern of policy-making within the EU. First, the value of the proposals in the context of promoting integration is considered. Next, the political constraints of the member states are fed into the process and great attempts are made to reach a consensus. In this bargaining process, member states seek to protect the vested economic interests of important national groups (Moravcsik, 1998). Economic criteria are less important than bargaining leverage. Spain gained concessions on early admission to fishing grounds by threatening to veto the progress of enlargement. The deliberations of the Council of Ministers are secret and one must assume that such secrecy is maintained because politicians wish to conceal the nature of the bargains that are struck. To summarise, the main features of the decision-making process require a policy to:

1. Expand or consolidate Commission competencies
2. Accommodate the current political and economic interests of the most powerful actors
3. Recognise economic criteria merely as constraining parameters

All too often, the dynamism of economic forces challenges the rigidities of the policy framework, and yet establishing this framework has been defined and publicised as a great success. Everyone can see the need for reform; everyone has special interests to defend. Neither member states nor the Commission can cut through the tangle of mutual concessions that has been secretly agreed. Any reform at all is difficult; radical reform is impossible. Reform that does occur – such as the recent modification of the CAP – invariably leads to greater expenditure and to the enlargement of the EU budget; such an outcome is not unwelcome in Brussels. The reform of the CFP may well follow a similar route.

The people's Europe

Having considered economics and policies, attention must now be turned to the question of 'people' and the 'people's Europe'. The general benefits of peace, prosperity and civic reconstruction that the people of Europe have enjoyed have already been mentioned and these must never be forgotten. The economic case, however, is not so clear. The removal of barriers to trade – both the tariff-cutting of the early period and the removal of non-tariff barriers during the late 1980s – has been beneficial, but the flood of regulations that accompanied the creation of the Single Market have been a burden to small businesses. The gains from negative integration – that is, the sweeping away of barriers – are now being negated by the losses of positive integration – the overregulation of economic activity at the European level. Big business can cope with regulations and is proactive in Brussels, vigorously defending its interests, but small and medium enterprises find the costs of compliance high and the paperwork burdensome.

The people who suffer from the slowing down of economic growth and the scarcity of jobs which small businesses and service trades provide are the marginal members of the labour force. If you are immobile, poorly qualified or a woman, new local jobs are of greater importance to you than the subsidised protection of those already employed. Even within sectors such as agriculture, where the EU has direct responsibility, one cannot say that the small producer enjoys much support. The winners from the CAP tend to be big farmers and agribusiness. The irony whereby the European ideal centres itself on civic values, social progress and political reconstruction but, in practice, has taken its most important initiatives by seeking to regulate people, as producers, is quite striking. As it moves to deal more directly with people, rather than with economic actors, the EU faces a challenging agenda.

Over the last half of the twentieth century, the process of European integration within the western part of the Continent has conferred benefits on some people and made life a bit more difficult for others. The new Europe is a pleasant place for people who speak other languages than their own, are disposed to move from place to place, have the personal and professional qualifications valued by large organisations and are alert to the new opportunities that are being created. One group of people is very alert to these new opportunities. The politicians, civil servants, functionaries, journalists, lobbyists and communicators who inhabit the new corridors of power in Brussels have gained most from the new Europe. Salaries are attractive, expenses very generous, and the lifestyle and cuisine pleasant. For the great majority of the political elite and the 'chattering classes', the new Europe is the good life. If you have a sharp intellect and a puritan conscience, however, you must not speak out. From time to time, well-informed insiders have expressed doubts about the wisdom and integrity of the Commission's activities. The response from the authorities has been swift and sharp. The attempts to silence Connolly (1995) and van Buitenen (2000) exemplify the high priority which the Commission places on conformity.

The people and European law

At the present time, the European Union has passed from its idealistic formative stage of intergovernmental cooperation and customs union, but has not yet arrived at a democratic federation of peoples. It is a ramshackle confederation with an entrenched bureaucracy whose ambition is greater than either its competence or its honesty. The balance of the institutions is very poor and there is an overrepresentation of the small states that the Nice summit failed to address.

Policies are unevenly enforced and some states make no pretence of obeying European law. The actual making and implementation of European law is worth noting. A huge corpus of law has been built up from Commission initiatives, through bargaining in the Council of Ministers and by interpretation in the European Court of Justice (ECJ). For example, the Bosman Ruling, which upheld freedom of movement for soccer players, is a well-known judgement that illustrates the power of the ECJ. This case meant that the arrangements for the transfer of soccer players operated by FIFA (*Fédération internationale de football association*) up to the summer of 2000 contravened European law. Since national courts must defer to and enforce decisions of the ECJ, it is clear that the legal structure of all member states has been fundamentally altered.

The extent to which and the speed with which people's rights are enforced is an interesting issue. It is true that certain types of judgement can produce changes in behaviour – especially corporate behaviour – quite quickly. States, however, are less amenable than companies and may resort, in the words of Hamlet, the Prince of Denmark, to 'the law's delay'. This prolongs the period before compliance. The French response to the BSE findings provides a good example of this practice. Even after a ruling by the Commission, they refused to permit British beef to enter their country prior to the outcome of a decision by the ECJ. As a result, British beef producers continued to suffer prolonged exclusion from the market.

Similarly, there is, in theory, a legal right of free movement for individuals throughout the EU. However, in late August 2000 movement across the channel from France to Britain was restricted by the action of French protesters. Holiday-makers and other travellers depended on the French police force to ensure the exercise of their right and, in this particular instance, those rights were not speedily enforced. British holiday-makers endured prolonged delays as their departure from French ports was prevented by blockades. In this instance, people were frequently unable to exercise their rights and legal remedies are often slow and weak. Neither hauliers nor holiday-makers are likely to get effective redress by using the corpus of European law. Perhaps in the fullness of time, legal process – or the threat of it – may protect people and ensure that their right to travel freely is always respected. At the time of writing, however, this seems far in the future.

The immediate response is more likely to be a reversion to traditional diplomacy. Protests will be made and discussions will be held on an old-fashioned intergovernmental basis. The relevant EU institution – in this case a meeting of foreign ministers – will simply be the forum for the bargaining of interests and, hopefully, the peaceful resolution of difficulties. This is a much older form of bargaining and international relations than the rules-based modern image of the EU as a legal entity. The EU as such was not able to deliver even the right of freedom of movement across national boundaries. In the case of the BSE dispute, the role of the EU has been to constitute itself as a forum for bilateral diplomacy rather than taking *communautaire* action to enforce the legal rights of citizens.

Conclusion

The European Union is but one of many international institutions created to build a better world in the second half of a violent century. It is now time to look at all these new creatures in international society, these actors that share the world stage with states. During the first half of the twentieth century, wars, Fascism, ethnic hatreds and economic misery disfigured Europe. Fanatical nationalism was identified as the root cause of the troubles and a great many people concluded that the best hope for the future was to tame the nation state by setting up institutional structures for cooperation. The institutions, both the European ones and the global ones, have helped contain bad behaviour and given some encouragement to the growth of a more civilised international order.

Unfortunately, many of the institutions set up in the aftermath of the Second World War are at the end of useful lives and stand in need of renewal. This should not surprise us. Nothing lasts for ever. Two destructive agents of decay have undermined international institutions. They are intergovernmentalism and bureaucracy. The first leads to the elevation of particular interests above the community interest and the second destroys democracy. Politicians choose to present themselves as defenders of the national interest within the forum of the international institution. They calculate, probably correctly, that this patriotism is more likely to win support at home than the thankless task of exercising proper control over the detailed implementation of policies that have drifted into the hands of permanent officials.

If the political elite fails to persuade the people of the need to move the European enterprise forward, they are likely to lose the support of ordinary people. The Danish people were not persuaded of the need to participate in monetary union and rejected this in the referendum in September 2000. The Irish voters did not endorse the Nice Treaty in the referendum of June 2001. The passive consensus which underpinned the creation of a new Europe cannot last for ever. Monetary union and proposals for a more federal structure recognise this need to move forward – the metaphor that has been coined in the past is that of a bicycle: 'if you don't move forward you fall off'. Those who oppose such policy initiatives stress the threats to democracy and economic welfare that will be generated as an ill-balanced institution seeks to drive itself forward without first securing more active support from its people.

References

Barnes, I. with Preston, J. (1988) *The European Community* (Longman, London and New York)
Barnes, I. and Barnes, P. (1995) *The Enlarged European Union* (Longman, Harlow)
Charlton, M. (1983) *The Price of Victory* (BBC, London)
Connolly, B. (1995) *The Rotten Heart of Europe* (Faber, London)
Hardin, G. (1977) *Managing the Commons* (Freeman, San Francisco)
Kapteyn, P. (1996) *The Stateless Market* (Routledge, London)

Landes, D. (1998) *The Wealth and Poverty of Nations* (Little, Brown, London)
Moravcsik, A. (1998) *The Choice for Europe* (UCL, London)
Nicoll, W. and Salmon, T. (1994) *Understanding the New European Community* (Harvester, Hemel Hempstead)
Reading, B. (1995) *The Fourth Reich* (Weidenfeld, London)
Van Buitenen, P. (2000) *Blowing the Whistle – One Man's Fight against Fraud* (Politicos, London)

3
In Search of Euro-capitalism

Jonathan Bradley

Introduction

Capitalism grew up in Europe and has colonised many parts of the world. This chapter examines several issues relating to its current development in its birthplace. First, it considers the extent to which the various European economic systems are tending to converge on one conceptual or historical model. The differences between them are deeply rooted in history, and yet changes in the global environment may be encouraging them to become more like each other. Second, it looks at whether a clearly identifiable supranational 'Euro-capitalism' is emerging to replace or overlay the national variants. As the European Union has developed politically and economically, policy has been made cooperatively and common bodies of law have been created. It is worth considering whether these together amount to a new kind of capitalist system. Third, this chapter discusses the extent to which any of the European varieties of capitalism are 'popular' in nature; in particular, in pursuit of the main theme of this book, it asks whether the identified changes in the broader European political economy are taking capitalism closer to or further from the wishes and control of its citizens. Fundamentally, if Euro-capitalism exists, does it empower the people?

Definitions of capitalism

This chapter will work on the assumption that, despite the many criticisms of it, the concept of capitalism is still useful for understanding the development and configuration of economic systems. As Gardner has noted in the previous chapter, contemporary capitalism is highly complex and varied, encompassing, as it now does, most of the rich world. It may be seen as, for example, a historical social system (Wallerstein, 1983), the vital underpinning of a political destination (Fukuyama, 1992), or as an essentially economic arrangement (Seldon, 1990). Capitalism is a concept used by several academic disciplines, and is not easy to define in terms of only one of them. Similarly, the diverse origins of capitalist systems are difficult to explain entirely in terms of economic theory (Crouch and Streeck, 1997). The analysis of political, social and historical phenomena integral to capitalism may require ideas drawn from their respective fields of study. Hence, the regulationist perspective stresses institutional change and associated modes of regulation (Boyer, 1997).

In a broad context, all contemporary capitalist economies share some basic defining characteristics – the sine qua non of capitalism. The two most central are the institution of private property and the prevalence of market mechanisms. They also display dynamic tendencies that are evidenced in frequent change and profit-seeking creation of wealth: attributes summed up in Keynes's reference to 'animal spirits' (Keynes, 1973). A system reliant on political decision would, by and large, have opposite characteristics.

In the wider literature relating to the comparative political economy of capitalism it is possible to identify a number of diagnostic variables that may be used to distinguish different capitalist variants. Each of them can be measured on a notional scale of their dependence on market or political decision-making for their allocative outcomes. On this basis, the most market-based capitalism would have the following features:

- A low share of the public ownership of productive assets
- Labour markets characterised by low union density and little collective bargaining
- Corporate governance arrangements serving shareholders, rather than 'stakeholders'
- Little government involvement in the determination of prices and wages
- Low or non-existent international trade barriers
- An unequal distribution of wealth and income
- High levels of industrial and commercial concentration, in the absence of regulation
- An economy open to external competitive influence
- A social and cultural acceptance of capital

Convergence in European economic structures

Conventional analysis of comparative economic systems has focused on several key features of an ostensibly European model (Gregory and Stuart, 1999) of capitalism. These include well-developed social welfare arrangements, a substantial role for the state, progressive taxation regimes, a measure of public ownership of the productive and financial systems, strongly entrenched universal banks, and a tradition of state intervention in economic activity, to protect strong vested interest groups. For the sake of convenience this combination of features could be called the 'Continental model', and is sometimes described as the Rhenish or Rhineland model. Germany has been held up as an example of this kind of economy, but France and Italy would often be thought to have shared many of its features.

Whatever name it is given, this kind of controlled capitalism is frequently contrasted with a 'market-based' or American model, which is characterised by a less interventionist state, by low levels of collective ownership, by tax systems favouring personal wealth creation, by more specialised financial institutions and by the exercise of stock market discipline on economic agents – especially underperforming managers. The only European economy coming close to this model has been the United Kingdom, although some of its characteristics have been visible in other states, such as Ireland and the Netherlands.

Albert (1991) has referred to the European Union as the 'battlefield' between these two capitalisms, and the arena in which a new *modèle européen* may be fashioned. In this case it is very clear that the model envisaged by him is not the American one, but a version of Rhineland capitalism. This chapter finds that the traditional continental versus market distinction is becoming less relevant as all European economies respond to the pressures of globalisation.

Public/private ownership

Before the Second World War the public sector was large in many European economies, and it continued to grow in almost all countries for several decades after the war. During the 1980s and 1990s, however, this trend was reversed. Starting in Britain, state authorities throughout Europe began the privatisation programmes that have continued for a number of years and have resulted in tangible reductions in the size of the public sector, even in countries such as France where it has traditionally been strong. Germany, Italy and Spain all have privatisation programmes for remaining public assets stretching into the twenty-first century. Privatisation has been a major contributor to systemic convergence amongst capitalist economies, not just in Europe but globally.

Labour market characteristics

Throughout most of Western Europe, labour markets are still heavily regulated, and employee remuneration is determined in imperfect markets. Academic analysts have long drawn attention to contrasts between Europe and America in their attitude towards employment issues (Emerson, 1988). Many members of the EU have long traditions of interventionist social policy and this is reflected in the aspirations of the Protocol and Agreement on social policy that accompanied the signing of the Treaty of Maastricht (Tsoukalis, 1997). This is the Social Chapter that the UK refused to sign. Furthermore, at the level of the member state, public spending on social protection, such as unemployment, sickness and disability benefits, is much higher in Europe than in either the United States or Japan (European Commission, 1995) and is strongly supported by the people of Europe. To the extent that convergence is occurring, it is not towards any single existing model, but towards arrangements that combine features from different systems. All countries are affected to some extent by broad shifts in working patterns involving more short-term contracts, more part-time work, increased home-working and multi-occupation employment, and associated changes such as the diminution in trade union membership. These changes tend to impel economies more towards so-called flexible labour markets, and therefore towards market-driven capitalism. On the other hand, EU agreements are tending to reinforce social protection in such matters as parental leave, unfair dismissal, minimum wages, or work by young people in ways reminiscent of the 'continental model' identified above. In this respect, therefore, the changes in labour markets are ambivalent, providing evidence of the development of both market-based capitalism and the Continental model.

Corporate governance

The conventional wisdom has been that Great Britain was an exemplar of a market-based corporate governance regime and that the Continental European countries had bank-based or institution-based systems. In the first of these types, the shares of most large businesses are listed on a stock exchange, and can be traded freely and easily. Shareholders who become unhappy with the performance of the company in which they have invested can vote with their feet, by selling the shares. Shareholders and managers tend to keep each other at arm's length. The ultimate punishment for failing managers is that the share price is driven down to such a low level by dissatisfied investors that another company makes a takeover bid and they lose their jobs. In the institution-based, or Rhenish, system, stock markets are much less important. Shareholders such as banks have large and long-term shareholdings and discipline is exercised over corporate managers by engaged insiders who represent shareholders and bring about change from within rather than through hostile takeover.

This traditional distinction, never wholly accurate, became more blurred during the 1990s. In Britain, many pension funds have become very long-term holders of certain shareholdings, and some institutions have become less passive in their attitude towards intervening in the affairs of the companies in which they have shareholdings. These changes have taken the British system a little closer to the so-called Continental model. Conversely, the securities markets have become more important in Germany, France and Italy as investment resource allocators and institutional shareholdings have become less heavily concentrated, taking those countries a little closer to the so-called market model. The evidence for this has been the growing value of stock market capitalisation as a proportion of national income and the decreasing number of medium and large companies that have remained private and unlisted on a stock market. The successful hostile takeover in early 2000 by the British company, Vodafone, of the German company, Mannesmann, was a dramatic illustration of the change. Here again, some convergence is taking place but it is not towards either a pure 'Continental' or a pure market model, but rather towards a combination of both systems.

Government involvement in prices and wages

This comes in many forms, but all of them represent some departure from a model of unbridled capitalism. Governments place restrictions on levels of pay in terms of their maxima and their minima. Long-standing minimum wage regulations in most EU countries place a downward limit on wages, and the government's role as employer – or provider of finance in health, education and other public services – acts as an upper limitation on pay levels in the public sector. Major price distortions exist as a result of government manipulation through taxation – for example, vehicle fuel, tobacco and alcoholic drink prices. By contrast, if one considers the formal prices and income policies of the 1970s and 1980s, governments throughout Europe appear to have drawn back from overt intervention in such matters, bringing their economies closer to a market-orientated model.

International trade tariffs

Ever since its inception, the European Union and its predecessors have followed a policy that amounts to the principle of free trade at home and more managed trade abroad, as the Common External Tariff was erected around the member states and trade barriers were gradually reduced within the Community. Even if non-tariff barriers persisted, the rhetoric has favoured a free single market internally. The EU has been more frankly protectionist in its external relations, for example in agriculture, aerospace and automobiles. Within the inevitable constraints of the General Agreement on Tariffs and Trade (GATT) and the World Trade Organisation (WTO), the EU has contrived to face both ways, giving it the luxury of being able to draw on a wider range of arguments to support its case internally or externally. The EU stance, however, does not denote a position of uncompromising attachment to free market capitalist ideals, but rather an expedient pragmatism. As all member states of the EU are subject to the same tariff system, they have, by definition, converged on the same pattern of trade management.

Distribution of wealth and income

Wealth and income distribution, already very unequal in many Western European states, tended to become even less equal during the 1990s. Regional inequality has also tended to remain static or to rise (Dunford, 1999). The global market for professionals has led to a widening of income differentials whilst reduced taxes on savings have had a similar effect. In this respect, all of the economies of Europe have been forced to move towards market-based capitalism. Some of these emerging inequalities are discussed in more detail elsewhere in Chapters 10 and 11.

Industrial concentration

In a number of industries increased consolidation has already taken place, and is still continuing, as a result of two main factors. The first is external to Europe, namely the increased competition arising from the globalisation strategies of multinational corporations. The second is associated with the economic effects of the European Union Single Market and competition rules. Examples include banking, telecommunications, news media and publishing, aerospace and defence manufacturing. European companies have often combined to meet challenges from the USA or Japan, or have sought external alliances to maximise scale efficiencies, particularly in purchasing and marketing. Whether this consolidation represents concentration, in the strict economic meaning, depends on how the relevant industries are defined. In its implementation of Union competition policy the European Commission increasingly takes a global view. European capitalist enterprises, and their managers, are responding to the dynamics of the world capitalist system. Some of these issues are discussed further by Panah in Chapter 4.

Economic openness

European countries, like other developed nations, have been subject to the worldwide increase in capital flows. This is by no means a recent development. Facilitated by the Bretton Woods arrangements and a shortage of capital in Europe, direct investment by American corporations burgeoned from the 1950s onwards (Scammell, 1983). They also took a full part in the moves towards global free trade orchestrated by the GATT. Whilst European trade has grown overall, intra-European trade has developed faster than trade with the rest of the world. The stock of investment held by non-Europeans in Europe and the stock of investment held by Europeans in non-European states have also increased faster than output (Dicken, 1992) This overall picture of openness must be qualified by the continued involvement of national governments in foreign direct investment (FDI) decisions, by the operation of EU tariff rules, by entire institutions such as the Common Agricultural Policy and by covert industrial championing. Within this context, the differences between Western European economies are unimportant compared with what they have in common.

Social and cultural underpinnings

There have been few cultural barriers to the pursuit of profit in the United States of America. Not only has money-making been an acceptable activity, but the educational system has been supportive of this philosophy. Many European countries, by contrast, have placed considerable constraints on the uncompromising pursuit of business success. These have been evidenced in different ways: in France the, intellectualism of some *énarques* and the tradition of strong state intervention; in Spain and Italy, a strongly embedded social fabric; in Britain, a tradition of disdain for 'trade' on the part of aristocrats and academics (Snow, 1959). This was notably true in the former communist states where, at least officially, private money-making was regarded as at best a tolerable vice and at worst a crime. Such cultural factors are difficult to measure, but, in the 1980s and 1990s, various pointers have hinted at a more capitalist-friendly environment. Perhaps the most important of these are the growing numbers of students studying for business degrees and the eagerness of governments to encourage small and medium enterprises.

Economic supranationality in Europe and the birth of Euro-capitalism

The previous section has demonstrated that the European economies have been converging but not on the kind of system favoured by Michel Albert or Jacques Delors. The European capitalist model clearly requires some redefinition. The attempt at redefinition starts with an examination of European economic supra-nationality, moves to a discussion of the common elements in national European capitalisms and, finally, considers whether these two, taken together, constitute a new Euro-capitalism.

In principle, this can refer to a number of economic phenomena that occur above and beyond policy-making in nation states. These fall into three main categories: first, the creation of economic regimes, applying in principle throughout the areas covered; and, second, specific and partial interventions by international institutions, which, in this context, are mainly those of the EU. These first two categories are broadly concerned with public sphere economic rules and policies. The third factor relates to non-governmental organisations, such as multinational corporations. In this sense, economic supranationality could be seen as an aspect of the wider process of economic globalisation. The distinction is very important, nevertheless, because European economic integration, while connected with globalisation, is distinct from it.

The extent of European economic supranationality

Since 1951, when the Treaty of Paris began the formal process of integration in Europe, there has been a gradual accretion of economic supranationality as the institutions and policies of the European Union have evolved. This has been complemented by developments in the public and private sectors at national level and has been reinforced by the external forces of globalisation (Dyker, 1999). The three issues in the European Union that impinge most directly on the character of Europe's capitalism are monetary integration, competition and market regulation policy, and the role of state ownership of industry. Each of these will be examined in turn.

The new currency arrangements in Europe are clearly supranational. They may have had to be agreed by the governments of member states, but they are now substantially beyond their reach. The eleven states that initially adopted the euro have ceded control over monetary policy to the European Central Bank (ECB) in Frankfurt and have also voluntarily constrained the conduct of domestic macroeconomic policy, as Cullen explains in Chapter 5.

The application of EU competition rules by Brussels is a supranational activity that has led to a relative strengthening of the Commission compared with national governments and private companies. As the ability of member states to intervene was constrained by the creation of a single market, so the EU has begun to take on greater powers. New merger legislation has given the Commission additional powers that it has used to considerable effect.

So far, there is no supranational state ownership of business. Privatisation has been widespread in European nations since the early 1980s, and is still continuing even in countries traditionally having a large public sector, such as France and Italy. In such an atmosphere, it is unlikely that 'Euro-nationalisation' could occur in the foreseeable future.

Whether the Common Agricultural Policy is seen as a structure or a long–term subsidy intervention, it still constitutes a major supranational arrangement standing above the European nations. The same is true of regional, or 'cohesion', policy (Church and Hendriks, 1995). Although the Commission has been actively engaged, along with national governments, in the promotion of European champions in, for instance, aerospace, defence, engineering and electronics, the development of supranational industrial policy has been hampered by the lack of available funds.

Many multinationals are based in European countries and take strategic decisions such as where to locate a new factory, how to optimise the company's international taxation burden, or where and how to raise new capital. These decisions can no more be bounded by national borders than the companies taking them, and are in effect economically supranational. In Europe, they will be subject to national law in any individual state, but they will also be subject to European regulation and law through the Commission and European Court of Justice. Thus economic supranationality in Europe already exists and the next section will examine its character.

The systemic orientation of European economic supranationality

At first sight, monetary integration does not seem to be a process that is necessarily capitalist in nature. The European reality is different because the manner in which integration is occurring reinforces one mode of capitalist organisation at the expense of another. The European Central Bank, guardian of the new euro, was created largely in the image of the German Bundesbank, and it operates in a monetary regime that is founded on an assumption of the beneficial effect of the separate conduct of monetary and fiscal policy (Tsoukalis, 1997). Notwithstanding its German inspiration, this is not *Rhenish* capitalism but essentially a market-orientated vision because 'independent' monetary policy is outside the day-to-day discretionary control of democratically elected government.

Multi-speed economic integration is causing some features of the supranational sphere to become more highly developed than others, with no clear expectation as to whether, or when, the balance will be redressed. Clearly, the conduct of monetary policy within Euroland has become the concern of an independent supranational institution. No similar institution has come into being to oversee the development of macroeconomic policy and thus monetary policy lacks proper boundaries (Barratt Brown, 1995).

The increased role for supranational entities in the pursuit of competition policy, far from preserving a Continental capitalist identity, has resulted in opening European markets more extensively to global pressures. Once again, European capitalism has been drifting in a market-orientated direction (Cox and Watson, 1995). Euro-capitalism seems to be developing without a public business sector and, therefore, appears to be more in tune with liberal economic thought than the economies out of which it has grown. Whilst significant areas of supranational intervention remain, confirming the Continental European, rather than market-orientated, character, these features are persisting rather than developing. The Common Agricultural Policy provides a good example of this trend and is explored in greater depth in Chapter 9.

The behaviour of non-government organisations also illustrates the changing nature of capitalism in Europe. For instance, the influence of market-based models on European-based multinational corporations seems to have been increasing. An example of this is the decision of several large German corporations to list their shares on foreign stock exchanges. The evidence offered shows that just as, at a national level, traditional notions of a distinct continental European model need to be redefined, so too, at a supranational level, European economic structures and policies are assuming an altered hue. Traditional ways survive, and yet the chill wind of globalisation is felt here also. Euro-capitalism is born, but under a liberal star.

Popular capitalism

Although this term is used, it is with some reluctance, given the contentious overtones associated with it, particularly in the United Kingdom in connection with Margaret Thatcher's vision of a 'share-owning popular capitalism in Britain' (Thatcher, 1993). In a more empirical sense it is worth looking at how far the beginnings of Euro-capitalism tend to strengthen or weaken the position of the citizen as an economic agent. Since Euro-capitalism is unavoidably influenced by the forces of globalisation, an enquiry into the viability of popular capitalism on a European scale becomes also an examination of its compatibility with global capitalism. The analysis could, in principle, relate to citizens in many of their roles – as employees, producers, employers, consumers, savers, property owners, or as indirect contributors to economic policy-making through the political process.

Some of the most prominent thinkers about capitalism would no doubt regard the very concept of popular capitalism as a contradiction in terms. For Marx, 'Capitalism' was the means by which 'Capitalists', 'the owners of the means of social production and employers of wage labour', withheld power and wealth from the proletariat (Marx and Engels, 1967). Since he, and most neo-Marxian intellectual successors, would regard capitalism as inherently unstable in the long run, they would find it difficult to imagine how capitalism could be made 'popular'.

On the other hand capitalism, albeit protean and variegated, has proved remarkably durable, as predicted by many of its apologists (von Mises, 1951). Taking an eclectic view of what makes capitalism 'popular', it would be possible to construct a theoretical model of what popular capitalism would be like. It could be expected to have some or all of the following features:

- Widespread ownership of stocks and shares.
- Financial institutions responsive to their stakeholders
- Controls on producer market power
- Strong and effective consumer protection groups
- Labour markets that are both flexible and fair

- Equitable distribution of wealth and income within a property-owning democracy
- Freedom of market entry

In each case, the focus is on the relationship between capital and people, in their various roles.

Individual shareholding

The ownership by individuals of ordinary equity shares in companies declined in the major Western European states in the postwar years until the privatisation programmes of the 1980s and 1990s caused a resurgence. First of all in Britain, and later in other countries, millions of citizens became the owners of shares in newly privatised enterprises. During the communist era in Central and Eastern Europe, individual share ownership was either impossible or discouraged but, after 1990, there too new pro-market governments were keen to encourage wide distribution of company shares in an attempt to underpin the new capitalist systems. Nominally, at least, share ownership is very wide in Poland and the Czech Republic, for instance.

Ironically, increases in the nominal ownership by private citizens of equity shares has not contributed to a significant economic empowerment of the masses. Most shares continued to be owned by institutional investors such as banks and pension funds. Even in those companies where large numbers of private citizens bought shares, such as British Gas in Britain or Telefónica in Spain, share ownership has been so diffuse that investors would have found it difficult to bring much influence to bear on company management even if they had shown any real sign of wanting to do so. Acting alone, small shareholders have no influence; they have infrequently been involved in voting on any major issue and there has been little sign of attempts to organise shareholders to act collectively. There are no shareholder referendums on senior management competence, no votes at annual meetings on executive pay levels, and only limited shareholder consultations. Whilst shareholder representative organisations do exist, their influence is negligible. So far, at least, the EU authorities have been no more successful than national governments in ensuring that popular ownership brings popular power. In this respect, Euro-capitalism is not popular capitalism.

Responsiveness of financial institutions

Many of the assets managed by the institutional shareholders are indirectly held for the benefit of individuals in their capacity as pensioners, policy-holders, unit-holders and other investment stakeholders. Even though individuals might not be able to exercise much influence as direct shareholders, they might be able to do so through the intermediation of the institutions in which they invest. In order to serve this function the institutions would need to be highly responsive to the wishes of their customers. Pension funds, for instance, would take note of the views of their beneficiaries about such matters as overseas investment, executive pay, and venture capital for small businesses. Unit trust managers would be clearer about their policy relating to voting in takeovers and mergers and perhaps be prepared in key instances, like, for example, the Vodafone/Mannesmann takeover, to consult their unit-holders.

Although 'ethical' and 'environmental' investment funds are available to the public, they are somewhat exceptional in that they only represent a very small proportion of total funds under management. On the whole, European investment institutions do not act as conduits for the views of their investors and stakeholders about the investments made on their behalf. They content themselves with marketing financial products that promise consumers the delivery of a financial return without any opportunity to influence the manner in which it is achieved. Moreover, many investment funds are run by self-perpetuating groups of professionals who have little more interest in the preferences of their clients than the size of the cheques they will write.

There is absolutely no evidence that financial institutions feel under any greater obligation to be responsive to their stakeholders in a Euro-capitalist milieu than in other capitalist systems. Given that most of the personal financial wealth held by individual people is held through financial institutions, this must be seen as a major weakness in the credentials of popular Euro-capitalism.

Producer market power

In this respect, the evidence on popular capitalism is contradictory. Industrial concentration, by creating larger commercial units, potentially reduces the influence of both individuals and social groups. This occurs through the lengthening of lines of communication within companies, the reinforcement of the bargaining position of large corporations or 'organised capital', and the remoteness of strategic decision-making from a large number of employees. The production line workers at Longbridge would always have been the last to hear of any further shift in the fortunes of the Rover Group, but ownership by a foreign automotive giant such as BMW ensured that they would be lucky even to read about it in the newspaper before their next-door neighbours.

As this chapter has pointed out, in Western Europe industrial concentration has tended to increase. The increased discretion over pricing policy gives companies greater power over the end-users of their products and services and this has been poorly counterbalanced by the effects of market contestability and regulation. Yet privatisation and deregulation of many industries have increased consumer choice and competition.

It is difficult to view the net effect of these various developments as firm evidence of increased consumer sovereignty and, therefore, of 'popular' capitalism. The enhanced consumer choice derived from deregulation appears to be a once-only event, whereas the concentration process associated with globalisation is likely to continue for the foreseeable future. In these circumstances, capitalism will only become more 'popular' to the extent that consumer interests are strengthened at least as much as corporate market power. The European Commission could claim to be helping in this direction through its competition policy, for example.

Consumer protection

There are two main ways in which consumer interests in Europe are actively promoted, as opposed simply to being served by the operation of the forces of supply and demand in the marketplace: by EU or national government action and by the action of pressure groups organised by or for consumers.

The European Commission has been issuing regulations concerning food labelling, consumer education and public health from an early stage in its history (Randall, 1997). By the year 2000, there was a substantial body of legislation and the intervention of the Commission was very much in evidence. Its role was most notable in the notorious 'beef crisis' of the late 1990s, in which the debate over consumer protection more closely resembled a political wrangle among national interests than a disinterested application of legal rules. Governments manoeuvred in the Brussels committee rooms to protect their own interests and to gain market advantage. The role of the Commission has been paternalistic, though benign, rather than 'popular'.

Sui generis consumer organisations in Europe have been less well-developed and less visible than their counterparts in the United States. Although bodies such as the Office of Fair Trading and the Consumers' Association in the UK and the *Verbraucherschutzverein* in Germany have existed for some time, they are not crucial in the working of consumer markets and their limited importance does not offer much support to a view of European capitalism as 'popular'. Private and public sector action would have to go much further for it to be possible to conclude otherwise.

Labour markets

The dilemma at the heart of the notion of 'popular capitalism' is nowhere so clear as in its theoretical approach to labour issues. Which value should its popular nature put first – the economic standing of individuals or the right to organise in pursuit of negotiating power with employers? Should it stress security of employment or freedom of contract and freedom of movement? This ideological ambiguity is echoed in the contradictory practical influences that have been at work in the European labour markets. On the one hand, both global and regional factors have been encouraging mobility and openness. The use by multinational companies of low-cost labour in less-developed countries has, in effect, exposed employees to labour market competition from outside Europe. Within the European Union, the application of Single Market rules has, in theory, permitted free movement of people within one Union-wide labour market. On the other hand, EU policy has been extending socially protective regulation in ways that benefit those affected but do not further systemic liberalisation. Moreover, in practice migration has been more notable from non-EU countries into the Union than from one EU country to another, as Chapter 11 illustrates. This indicates that workers within Europe have not been rushing to make use of their new freedom to move (Tsoukalis, 1997). In summary, labour market conditions in Western Europe are shaped by tensions between powerful global economic forces and embedded European social instincts. They are not the consequence of a putative popular capitalism.

Distribution of wealth and income

To be 'popular', capitalism does not, in principle, entail a more equal distribution of income and wealth than would otherwise be the case. Some theorists would argue that developed mass market capitalism has tended to reduce inequality compared with less-developed forms of economic organisation (Friedman, 1982). The notion does, though, surely hint at meritocracy, albeit elitist, and at the widespread opportunity for property ownership. It might postulate, for instance, an economy in which the operation of the market would perpetuate large inequalities, but in which the lowly could better themselves through hard work and ability and in which the dispossessed could realistically aspire to modest capital accumulation. On a measure of this kind, although it has already been observed that income and wealth inequalities have not diminished in Europe, a case may still be made that some limited movement has taken place towards a more 'popular' version of capitalism. Several pieces of evidence might be offered in support of this contention: educational opportunities have widened, with many more students entering higher education, share ownership and home ownership are wider and social mobility has increased. Even if true, however, none of these are peculiarly European phenomena, and could not justly be claimed by enthusiasts for European supranational policy-making as evidence of its success.

Freedom of entry for new businesses

It must be axiomatic of popular capitalism that people may become capitalists, in particular by creating their own business. In most of Europe, East and West, governments of all political persuasions have enthusiastically promoted small business creation, motivated usually by the hope that it would help to contain unemployment. Tax incentives have been granted, venture capitalists have been encouraged, and 'second' and unofficial stock markets have been founded. Whether or not coincidentally, these measures have been accompanied by rapid growth in the number of businesses, especially of sole traders. At the end of the twentieth century, there was a luxuriant flowering of Internet and communications-related businesses, such as lastminute.com in Britain, Bidlet in Sweden and Ricardo in Germany. Many of them were rapidly listed on new stock exchanges designed for new businesses. Again, however, these events have very little to do with collective European action but much more with intellectual fashion among policy-makers and with the exigencies of global competition in a liberal economic environment.

Summary of 'popular capitalism'

The 'seven pillars' of European popular capitalism have been tested for strength. Only three of these can truly be accounted strong enough to support such a great temple: individual shareholding, control of producer market power, and the facility to start new businesses. All of them put at least some economic power in the hands of ordinary people. Of these three, the only one where European supranational agency can claim any credit is the second, through the implementation of competition policy by the European Commission. The other four pillars – responsive financial institutions, effective consumer protection, enabling, but humane, labour markets, and the wide distribution of wealth – are simply too weak to underpin the edifice of Euro-capitalism. This is not a strong advertisement either for the popular nature of Euro-capitalism or for the capability of existing European supranational activity to uphold it.

Conclusions

This chapter set out to discover whether Euro-capitalism really has been born, and if so whether it is popular Euro-capitalism. This would be a political economy in which more economic decisions would be taken by ordinary people and fewer by bureaucrats, or Eurocrats, and in which large numbers of people could have a share of the rewards and a stake in the system. In other words, it would empower rather than enslave, liberate rather than oppress.

To try to find an answer, three key questions were investigated: whether national capitalist systems in Europe have become more like each other, whether a European capitalism with its own character is developing at a level above the nation state, and whether any part of European capitalism is people-orientated.

The analysis showed that, in significant respects, European economies have come to resemble each other more closely. They have not, however, been converging on established conceptions of European capitalism but on a more market-orientated version influenced by global forces. While not quite 'red in tooth and claw', like the American capitalism of the railroad pioneers and the Wall Street bond dealers, this version is more liberal and more ruthless than traditional European variants. Second, it was concluded that supranational economic structures and policies are indeed arising above the nation state and that these too are different from traditional European practices. They seem to be evolving into hybrids of Albert's Rhenish and American market-based systems. If an incipient Euro-capitalism can be identified, therefore, it is not the one anticipated by proponents of a distinctively European way. Euro-capitalism has been born, but it is not the creature that many might have expected. Third, the practice of this emerging Euro-capitalism was examined against a theoretical yardstick of what 'popular capitalism' might look like. Some evidence was found of movement towards greater people-orientation, but overall the verdict was not positive. Of the seven main criteria, Euro-capitalism appeared partially to satisfy only three. Although Euro-capitalism gives the outward appearance of being more popular in some ways, the inner reality is disappointing.

If this analysis is correct, European economic policy-makers will face the difficult task of reconciling potentially conflicting aims. European citizens, having sniffed just a little of the fresh oxygen of popular capitalism, are likely to want more rather than less control over their economic lives. Ironically, the very national and Eurocratic elites who have so far maintained the civilising constraints on global capitalism are themselves remote from the people. If the peoples and governments of Europe wish it otherwise they will have to cooperate actively to make it so.

References

Albert, Michel (1991) *Capitalisme contre capitalisme* (Editions du Seuil, Paris)

Barratt Brown, Michael (1995) *Models in Political Economy* (Penguin, Harmondsworth)

Boyer, Robert (1997) 'French Statism at the Crossroads', in Crouch and Streeck (1997)

Church, Clive H. and Hendriks, Gisela (1995) *Continuity and Change in Contemporary Europe* (Edward Elgar, Aldershot)

Cox, Andrew, and Watson, Glyn (1995) 'The European Community and the Restructuring of Europe's National Champions' in Hayward, J. (ed.), *Industrial Enterprise and European Integration* (Oxford University Press, Oxford)

Crouch, Colin, and Streeck, Wolfgang (1997) *Political Economy of Modern Capitalism* (Sage Publications, London)

Dicken, P. (1992) *Global Shift* (Paul Chapman Publishing, London)

Dunford, Michael (1999) 'Geographical Disparities, Economic Development and European Union Structural Policies', in Dyker (1999)

Dyker, David (1999) *The European Economy* (Longman, Harlow)

Emerson, Michael (1988) *What Model for Europe?* (MIT Press, Cambridge, Mass.)

European Commission (1995) *Social Protection in Europe 1995* (Office for Official Publications of the European Communities, Luxembourg)

Friedman, Milton (1982) *Capitalism and Freedom* (University of Chicago Press, Chicago, Ill. and London)

Fukuyama, Francis (1992) *The End of History and the Last Man* (Penguin, London)

Gregory, Paul R. and Stuart, Robert C. (1999) *Comparative Economic Systems* (Houghton Mifflin, Boston, Mass., and New York)

Keynes, John Maynard (1973) *General Theory of Employment, Interest, and Money*, 2nd edn (Macmillan – now Palgrave, London)

Marx, Karl, and Engels, Friedrich (ed.) (1967) *The Communist Manifesto*, ed. A. J. P. Taylor (Penguin, Harmondsworth)

Mises, Ludwig von (1951) *Socialism – an Economic and Sociological Analysis*, English edn (Jonathan Cape, London)

Randall, Ed (1997) 'Health Policy and the European Union', in Symes, Levy and Littlewood (eds) (1997)

Scammell, W. M. (1983) *The International Economy since 1945* (Macmillan – now Palgrave, London)

Seldon, Arthur (1990) *Capitalism* (Blackwell, Oxford)

Snow, Charles Percy (1959) *The Two Cultures and the Scientific Revolution* (Cambridge University Press, Cambridge)

Symes, Valerie, Levy, Carl, and Littlewood, Jane (eds) (1997) *The Future of Europe: Problems and Issues for the Twenty-First Century* (Macmillan – now Palgrave, London)

Thatcher, Margaret (1993) *The Downing Street Years* (HarperCollins, London)

Tsoukalis, Loukas (1997) *The New European Economy Revisited* (Oxford University Press, Oxford)

Wallerstein, E. (1983) *Historical Capitalism with Capitalist Civilization* (Verso, London and New York)

Part II
People and Business

4
European Business Strategy

Sahand Panah

Introduction

From the very start, the construction of Europe concerned itself with economics and with business. The idea of an economic community within a common market signalled that West Europe would be 'open for business'. Economic forces and firms from outside were welcomed into a capitalist reconstruction protected from Eastern communism by American military power, as Gardner argues in Chapter 2. Both European and American versions of capitalism continue to shape the policies, people and business firms within the new Europe, as Bradley demonstrates in Chapter 3.

According to Mintzberg (1987), strategy is about winning and gaining control, and business strategy is concerned with the match between the internal capabilities of the company and its external environment (Grant, 1998). In this sense, strategy can be viewed as a set of plans, decisions and actions for adjusting a firm's resources and capabilities to the opportunities that arise in the external environment in order to achieve a sustainable competitive advantage over rivals within an industry and market. This chapter outlines how the dynamic process of change and competition created by the advent of the Single Market has affected the strategic choices of multinational enterprises (MNEs). It will begin by evaluating the social, technological, economic and political environment in which firms operate to identify the opportunities and threats facing businesses in Europe. The strategies that businesses have adopted in response to these challenges will be examined with particular reference to two case studies of Wal-Mart and DaimlerChrysler. Finally, the impact upon consumers, workers and stakeholders will be explored to conclude the chapter with a people-centred approach.

Social, technological, economic and political (STEP) analysis

To identify the key forces of change within a market that affect the firm's strategic opportunities and threats, the firm should scan its external environment. STEP analysis is a popular method of carrying out an environmental audit of social, technological, economic and political opportunities in order to assess the likely impact of these factors on the firm's relationship with its customers, its suppliers, its competitors and the governments of the countries within which it operates. These interactive triggers within the Single Market have encouraged MNEs to reformulate their long-term strategy to operate effectively within the European environment (Ellis and Williams, 1995). At the beginning of the twenty–first century the pace of change is accelerating.

The social dimension

Whilst consumers are becoming less loyal and more volatile than before, the Single Market extends their range of choice. Multinationals need to be responsive to the changing demands of their customer base. Social and demographic factors are important to firms as family patterns alter and spending power shifts between age groups. Sullivan discusses the effects of the rise of the 'grey generations' in social and political life in Europe in Chapter 12. This change in demographic trends and other social factors have had significant implications for firms' long-term planning. The Internet is homogenising consumers' tastes and preferences across the Continent, thereby shortening the life cycle for many products. As a result, regional product harmonisation becomes possible, reflecting the emergence of common consumer trends. While some elements of the product and service offered may continue to be customised for an individual market, differences will be accommodated within an overall policy of standardisation.

The technological dimension

European countries have technological excellence in different industries. Germany, for example, excels in chemicals, engineering and automotive products; France leads in food, chemicals and automotive products; Italy is famous for textiles, clothing and fashion products;

and the UK's strengths lie in fuels, chemicals, machinery and service industries. Firms enjoy opportunities for relocating into areas where the technological base is well-developed so that they can implement long-term research and development (R&D) strategies (Hymer, 1976). Advances in information technology, telecommunications, satellite broadcasting, the Internet and interactive services via television and mobile phones will also provide firms with an important mechanism to overcome country-based restrictions. Companies in Europe will be able to use similar marketing campaigns in different European countries. As more businesses move to the web, on-line customers will find more choice, and better-quality and cheaper products; those without access to the web may, however, be disadvantaged.

The economic dimension

The economic aspects of integration dominate the concerns of most multinational enterprises. The convergence of the business cycle and the hopes for strong growth, low inflation and a stable monetary framework regulated by the European Central Bank (ECB) together provide a sound platform for MNEs to formulate and implement medium to long term investment planning. The provision of training and vocational education together with greater flexibility in labour markets should encourage growth and trade.

For large firms, the most significant implication of these developments is their expanding business opportunities but, for people, the most important element is the expansion of their life chances, through education and training. These two are not necessarily in conflict and there may even be a considerable degree of complementarity. As the free flow of capital, goods and services within the community creates more efficient resource allocation, resources shift to the efficient producers. These companies will be able to expand output to take advantage of the large market and will reduce the monopoly power of indigenous firms. Less efficient businesses, on the other hand, will decline and shed labour. Firms in Europe will be able to supply the whole market from a single location instead of having to produce fifteen different products in the member states. Harmonised product standards, stable exchange rates, a single currency and simplified tax regimes will make life easier for businesses.

The political dimension

The Single Market has brought greater stability and unity to Europe (Hill, 2000). It has diminished MNEs' exposure to political risks and has reduced the complexity arising from interactions with different governments, regulatory bodies, trade unions and consumer groups. The political culture within Europe has resulted in the development of a legal framework which has shaped the ways in which privatisation and deregulation have taken place. Privatisation programmes and deregulation of markets have created new opportunities in the region. Recent examples of large-scale privatisation include France Telecom, Telecom Italia, the Portuguese motorway operator, Brisa, the Spanish energy group, Endesa, and Lufthansa, the German airline. Liberalisation policies have not only led to increases in trade but, more importantly, have encouraged wider share ownership by Europeans.

Since 1999 one important change has been the introduction of the euro. In addition, the completion of the Single Market has made it possible for firms to integrate their functional activities. This has involved greater investment in such areas as technology, production processes, marketing and distribution. Moreover, in pursuit of long-term growth, mergers, business acquisitions, joint ventures and alliances have all been stimulated.

Strategy implementation

STEP analysis provides firms with a useful checklist against which to evaluate and forecast the changing nature of the external forces influencing the industry and market in the medium to long term. The Single Market is having a profound effect on the strategy and operations of businesses in terms of pricing policy, corporate finance, legal contracts and internal systems (El Kahal, 1998). For example, price transparency is forcing retailers to put an end to differential pricing across the region. The development of the market in corporate bonds allows even medium-sized companies to access funds directly. These forces create significant opportunities and threats for both European and non-European companies and have encouraged them to reformulate their business strategies to consider how best to use their resources and capabilities within this changing environment. More and more people are faced with profound changes in their working lives.

American multinationals

The dominant culture of the large business firm and its strategies are influential throughout the world. American multinationals follow customer-based strategies. This is done through vertical segmentation of the market in terms of costs and demand, and identification of potential customer subsets within the entire market. As a result, European firms face powerful competition because many American firms do not believe in merely searching for a niche market. In a hostile environment, their preferred strategy is adopting a 'glocal' approach – that means 'think global, act local'. In this way, the company will satisfy the needs of specific customers at competitive prices. Customers will find it rewarding to switch from incumbent suppliers. These ambitious and aggressive long-term strategies will bring benefits to Europeans by accelerating organisational learning, through effective communication and management of human resources.

Many American companies such as Wal-Mart, Procter & Gamble, Colgate-Palmolive and Intel, are able to create a network structure to eliminate inventory pile-up. They connect with suppliers who deliver goods only when they are needed, thereby enabling a swift response to changing external circumstances. The philosophy of these companies is to establish relationships and contracts with their local suppliers, distributors and retailers, which enable them to benefit from economies of scale in marketing and logistics. An example of this strategy is the contract between Compaq and Packard Bell NEC to supply their PCs only to Dixons Group in the UK. The key success factor for American companies is to implement a consumer-oriented strategy by learning about their customers and the products they want. These companies are then able to tailor the product to meet customer tastes and preferences and to incorporate customer feedback at the product design and manufacturing stage. In 1998, for example, while European and Japanese companies spent 8 per cent and 6 per cent of their revenues on innovative R&D, their American counterparts spent 16 per cent. In the information technology and software industry, IBM and Microsoft lead their sectors with investments of $5.8bn and $2.8bn respectively. In the automobile industry, General Motors (GM) allocated $7.9bn, Ford $6.3bn, and DaimlerChrysler $5.8bn to these activities. In the pharmaceutical sector, Merck stands out as the largest US drug company with investment of $2.9bn (*Financial Times*, 15 October 1999). This indicates the significance of achieving a competitive advantage through investment in intangibles, such as research, skills and knowledge.

The market entry or expansion strategy of US firms has mainly been through horizontal acquisitions of indigenous firms to achieve the corporate objectives of gaining and retaining customers' loyalty. American companies rely on intensive marketing to create a brand identity. Strategies that transcend national and international boundaries are typically at the top of most American companies' agenda. This is enhanced through effective vertical and horizontal communication, improving accountability and knowledge-sharing and an adaptation of a learning culture that involves local, regional and international managers in decision-making processes (Day and Wendler, 1998). Innovative leadership is the key to success in global business, as Henry Ford, Sam Walton and Bill Gates have shown. The case study of Wal-Mart in Box 4.1 provides an insight into how such strategies were developed and implemented to achieve a competitive position in the European retail sector.

Box 4.1   Wal-Mart's Arrival in Europe

The impact of external triggers depends, to a great extent, on the firm's ability to respond swiftly to external changes and achieve first-mover advantage. Responsiveness to environmental change requires information and flexibility of response. Information is essential to identify and anticipate external changes, while flexibility of response requires that a firm be able to redeploy its resources swiftly to meet those changes.

Wal-Mart, the world's largest retail group with an annual turnover of $150bn (1999), has achieved its market leadership position through its low cost distribution system and its differentiation strategies. Founded in 1962 by Sam Walton of Bentonville in Arkansas, USA, the strategy of the company has been based on a business system that responds quickly and effectively to changes in demand by replacing inventory with point-of-sale information backed up by efficient distribution and purchasing networks. By adopting sophisticated logistics, it becomes easier to maintain supply efficiency even when demand varies. In this way economies of operation are achieved and preserved. Wal-Mart's approach enables it to provide the appropriate mix of goods to meet changing customer tastes. The company offers its customers shopping round the clock, personalised products and service. Clothes, toys, cosmetics, DIY goods, food and grocery are all on offer at competitive prices in its 1861 Discount Cities or Supercenters. The company's 'Ten Foot Attitude' requires all employees within ten feet of customers to provide them with help.

Technology has been another vital ingredient in Wal-Mart's success. In electronic point-of-sale (EPOS) technology, Wal-Mart is IBM's biggest customer. Continual monitoring of sales data enables the management to balance product mix and promotional activity, by linking its computers with those of its suppliers. Thus, it avoids running out of popular items or carrying excess inventories. The company operates the world's largest commercial data warehouse with the equivalent of six billion pages of text to gather and analyse detailed information on a daily basis. This has made it possible for the company to scrutinise all aspects of its business and to make product decisions swiftly. In terms of technology alone, Wal-Mart would seem to be well ahead of other major retailers.

The internationalisation of the company began in 1991 and since then it has acquired 726 stores in locations like Canada, Mexico, Argentina, Brazil and Puerto Rico, and has joint venture or franchise operations in China, Indonesia and Korea. In December 1997, Wal-Mart entered the fragmented and oligopolistic European retail market by taking over Germany's Wertkauf hypermarket chain and, in late 1998, by acquiring the Interspar hypermarket from the Spar Handels group. The company has now 95 stores in Germany each offering a minimum of 100 000 product lines. On 14 June 1999, Wal-Mart acquired Asda, the third largest retail store in the UK, for an all-in-cash offer of £6.72bn ($10.8bn), outbidding Kingfisher's offer of £5.8bn ($9.3bn) which was all-in-paper.

Asda enhances the group's expertise in fresh groceries, small-store operation, fashion merchandising and product development and will benefit from Wal-Mart's far-reaching experience in global outsourcing and inventory replenishment technology. At the same time, it aims to localise itself in the market to prevent excessive standardisation of its products, a development which may alienate local customers, vendors and governments. Such a transfer of competencies is likely to enhance the capabilities of merging companies in their respective markets.

Wal-Mart's arrival in Europe has caused a major shake-up in the retail industry and stimulated competition in the supermarket sector by providing products offering better value for money. Its radical price cuts are threatening European retailers, whose strategies in the 1980s and 1990s were to expand activities into emerging markets, somewhat neglecting their home markets. Wal-Mart has reduced the enthusiasm of European retailers for any further expansion in international markets and made them realise that they can no longer afford to 'sit back and take it easy'. It has forced them either to embark on consolidation through mergers and alliances – such as Karstadt, Germany biggest department store, and Quelle, the country's second largest mail order group – or else to restructure themselves to focus on core strengths and improved service. For example, in 1999, Metro, Germany's largest retailer and the world's second biggest after Wal-Mart, moved to strengthen its own hyper-market business with the acquisition of the Allkauf and Kriegbaum networks and announced a massive restructuring of its core cash-and-carry operations, while shedding four of its non-core businesses. In France, the friendly takeover of Promodes by Carrefour in late 1999 has created the world's second largest retail group. Ahold, a Dutch supermarket operation, announced its U-turn strategy in the late 1990s. It sought expansion through consolidation by cooperating with other European retailers – with Carrefour, Promodes and Casino. The success of this strategy, however, is still in doubt.

Since its arrival in the UK, Wal-Mart has begun to transform the retail sector. The UK retailers have found themselves facing price wars on everything from food to cosmetics and from clothing to household goods. By offering shoppers a web-based service to assist them in the hunt for the cheapest products, Asda has been winning customers from rivals such as Sainsbury and Safeway. In 1999, Somerfield announced the closure of 500 of its stores, some 350 of which were sold at less than their book value. Sainsbury's, Marks and Spencer, Safeway, Kingfisher and Great Universal Stores are all under pressure. As a result, these companies are undertaking far-reaching reviews of their business strategies. Tesco, the UK's largest supermarket chain, has been trying to compete with Asda through price-cutting. Wal-Mart has a considerable advantage in terms of sheer size in any such struggle.

Wal-Mart's corporate business approach highlighted here represents a vivid illustration of an American company implementing a global strategy. The pace of change within the retail sector has been rapid and shows no sign of slackening.

Source: *Financial Times*, 1997–2000, various issues.

European multinationals

Another response to increased competition following the advent of the euro is to implement a corporate-based strategy in order to control costs carefully. This can be done in several different ways and rationalisation or 'downsizing' has been as significant as national consolidation. The removal of middle-management layers brings cost reduction, redundancies and a reexamination of the organisational heritage.

Performance is enhanced through improved internal communications and a better mix of skills, facilitating knowledge-sharing and shorter organisational response times (Hamel and Parahalad, 1994). The human costs of such changes are, however, often high.

Increased decentralisation in operational and strategic decision-making and effective communication between senior managers and the workforce are the essential elements of successful internal restructuring (Kay, 1993). Companies such as Nestlé, Unilever and Danone have recently reduced the number of plants, increased operational integration and consolidated production into larger plants to achieve greater scale economies and revenue growth. In 1999 Shell, with operations in 130 countries, restructured its top management to incorporate those from diverse backgrounds. The company had come to believe that Shell had failed to identify opportunities and adjust its business strategy because of a mismatch between the diverse background of the executives in subsidiaries and the cultural homogeneity at headquarters.

For European banks, competition is intensifying. US investment banks, such as Merrill Lynch and Goldman Sachs, are competing vigorously with indigenous banks such as Deutsche Bank. The consolidation of the Swiss Bank Corporation and the Union Bank of Switzerland in 1998 to form the United Bank of Switzerland (UBS) has revolutionised consolidation activity in the European banking sector. In Britain, France, Italy and Spain, the consolidation of the banking sector has been marked. As consolidation continues, sheer size and power will dominate the market; medium-sized banks will have to merge or seek niche markets.

Many European companies are beginning to recognise that they cannot go it alone. The Vodafone bid for Mannesmann in 2000 is, for example, the biggest and most vivid example of the growth in stakeholder power that promises to change the shape of the European business environment, as Bradley notes in Chapter 3. The unlikely amalgamation between Chrysler and Daimler in 1998 illustrates the changing perspectives of European business elites and this is discussed in Box 4.2.

Box 4.2 Revamping traditional culture (DaimlerChrysler)

After many months of negotiation, the world's biggest manufacturing merger of $38bn occurred between Daimler-Benz of Germany and Chrysler of the USA in late 1998. As a result, Daimler has become the only European car manufacturer with a substantial presence in the USA car market. The merged group vies with GM, Ford and Toyota for global leadership in the automotive sector.

During 1990s, the overall profitability of the automotive industry was low. The industry has come under pressure to provide better returns for its shareholders. The force of increased competition has put severe pressure on many firms and produced international rivalry among car-makers. At the global level, industry concentration has been growing for some time, as many small and medium-sized producers are the subject of merger and acquisition activity. For example, Peugeot merged with Citroën; VW acquired Seat, Skoda and Rolls-Royce; BMW acquired Rover; and Ford acquired Jaguar. The result has been a downturn in the fortunes of many major producers, in the face of a chronic overcapacity due to world-wide investment in new plants and process technologies.

The situation has left the auto-makers with two alternatives. The first is to consolidate through further merger and alliances; the second is to seek a new niche market. Daimler's partnership with Chrysler offers a viable solution to the sluggish European car-market and the long-standing dilemma of whether to develop a second brand or to expand into volume car making. The benefits of merger include synergy through the sales of Mercedes-Benz in the buoyant US market and extra sales of Chrysler models in Europe.

So far, the merger may be regarded as successful on three fronts. First, from a financial point of view, the share prices of both companies have increased during the first three years. Second, from an economic perspective, the merger did not result in job losses, for blue- or white-collar workers. Third, strategically, the merger has enabled the new corporation better to manage the engineering process and to produce a wider variety of cars, while preserving distinct brand identities. People, as shareholders, enjoy better returns; people, as workers, keep their jobs; and people, as consumers, have more choice.

Although Daimler is the world's biggest maker of trucks, a leading van manufacturer and one of the world's largest builders of buses and coaches, it is best known as a producer of luxury saloon cars. Chrysler, on the other hand, has a particular strength in light trucks, multi-purpose vehicles and sports utility vehicles, and also makes a wide range of saloon cars under the Dodge, Plymouth and Chrysler brands. The merger has built upon the complementary activities of the two companies and its success will depend upon achieving effective collaboration between American and European business philosophies.

Chrysler is renowned for its cost-cutting strategy. Its cost-leadership is derived from ready access to capital and a wide portfolio of diversified engineering skills. From 1992 to 1994, the company was the most profitable of the world's largest auto producers, primarily because it had gone furthest in slashing its costs during the 1980s. The new corporation hopes to gain competitive advantage through the combination of effective differentiation of its products with low-cost strategy. The merger also increased the marketing potential of the group globally as the intention has been to keep individual brands distinctive. This required the corporation to restructure its internal and external organisation. As a result, several hundred senior executives were reassigned to head the main departments whilst areas such as finance, strategy and purchasing were amalgamated into one department for the whole group. This has been made possible by a reorganisation of engineering and production staff into 'platform teams', freeing them from corporate bureaucracy and allowing them to produce imaginative designs faster than ever before.

German companies have traditionally pursued either an international or an organic strategy. The international strategy has involved manufacturing products at home and then exporting them whilst the organic strategy means acquiring existing businesses in other countries. Core competencies in the form of intellectual value-added and product design have all been firmly retained in the home country, while overseas subsidiaries have been responsible for sales, distribution and customer support. Daimler has been the first German company to abandon this tradition and to share its creative technical know-how with engineers from an entirely different culture. The company has accepted American norms and has changed its practices accordingly. More importantly, the two companies have managed to adapt their respective cultures in terms of language, aesthetics, markets, work tradition and governance. DaimlerChrysler has not only conducted a business merger but, more importantly, they appear to have overcome cultural diversity: a remarkable achievement in the art of management.

So far, the indications are positive. In 1999, the group delivered its first joint statement, showing a 29 per cent rise in full-year net profit. Consequently, the dividend to shareholders was significantly higher than either Daimler or Chrysler had paid before the merger. American and German employees received profit-related payments of about $4200 each, following the company's introduction of a workers' profit-sharing scheme in 1998. These figures seemed to confirm the earlier pledges of Daimler's management that the amalgamation would result in increased sales, profits, market share and stronger synergy. Only time will tell whether the DaimlerChrysler merger can deal appropriately with the ferocious competition in the automotive industry. Its success will, to a great extent, depend upon achieving effective collaboration between American and European business philosophies.

Source: *Financial Times*, 1998–2000, various issues.

Emerging corporate strategies

Collaboration and outsourcing of non-core functions – an activity which requires trust between partners – is becoming a common operational practice amongst European multinationals. Companies in sectors as diverse as telecom, energy, utilities and information technology are moving away from the conglomerate model of diversification to concentrate on value chain activities that are the source of competitive advantage. Outsourcing non-crucial operations and reducing backward integration increases stability, flexibility and the responsiveness of the firm in the market place. It also flattens the organisational structure and eliminates bureaucracies and overhead costs. All of these positive outcomes enable the company to focus on its core functions and to promote organisational innovation. In recent years, outsourcing both non-core functions and those activities where specialist partners can bring expertise has become important.

The willingness to team up with outsiders to acquire and retain intellectual assets has moved higher and higher up the corporate agenda. European firms have been slow to adopt outsourcing but now see advantages in a practice which increases their capacity for flexible response in volatile markets. For example, Corus, Nokia, Siemens and ICI have outsourced some of their operations to small and medium-sized companies. As a result, SMEs specialising in activities such as consultancy, catering, cleaning, security and couriers have been growing very rapidly. The growth of these small firms provides employment for many people throughout Europe.

Another fashionable justification for growth is the pursuit of synergy. Many companies which have gone through restructuring and downsizing are now concentrating on establishing a wide network of alliances and relationships. In 1996 Roche, one of Europe's largest pharmaceutical companies, turned one of its subsidiaries, Protodigm, into a 'virtual' company. The company subcontracts its work to as many as twenty suppliers for each of the three drugs it produces and the entire business is supervised by a handful of people. By striking hard bargains with its suppliers, keeping overheads and bureaucracy to a minimum and processing the product quickly, Protodigm has achieved substantial scale economies. In 1999, Roche's total pharmaceutical sales rose by 12 per cent, more than twice as fast as the market rate of growth (*Financial Times*, 15 October 1999). Schumpeter (1950) contends that an organisation will achieve a competitive success by adjusting its resources to enter a new market while also preserving its old market through innovation. In this respect, many large MNEs operating in Europe have adopted competitive-based or multibrand strategies to defend their existing positions whilst attempting to overturn the competitive advantage of new entrants. For instance, VW, European's largest vehicle-maker, creates highly differentiated products to address particular market sectors. Audi is at the top end of the market; VW is the volume brand; the relaunched Skoda serves the economy sector and Seat projects a sporting image. These strategies have enabled VW to remain ahead of its competitors.

To remain competitive in the Single Market, companies need to be inventive and innovative and to facilitate the speedy transfer of knowledge within their workplace. The sharing of knowledge within the firm has now become a critical factor for growth and expansion. Rising consumer incomes and technological advances have enabled many firms to provide innovative products, thereby creating new market segments (Ducker, 1999). This process can be regarded as a 'new way of doing business' exemplified by such firms as Ikea, Dyson and the Body Shop.

Pettigrew *et al.* (1999), in a survey of 450 European businesses, found that although many are carrying out changes within their organisations, these have been 'piecemeal' rather than systemic. Very few companies combine their discrete changes into a comprehensive system and yet this is necessary for future success. In Unilever, for example, an ambitious programme known as 'Restructuring for Outstanding Performance' gave a newly created executive committee responsibility for the strategic oversight of product areas, while decentralised profit and operating responsibility was given to 'business groups', organised on a regional basis. Responsibilities were clear, layers were taken out and decisions could be taken in an integrated fashion at the level of regional markets. Unilever became a 'multi-local multinational'. Since

1997, Unilever's performance has improved faster than that of its competitors on all the main measures. It was not structural changes alone that achieved this. The structural changes relied on better processes and a focused strategy at work. The Unilever example emphasises that higher performance requires the full set of complements, but that putting them all together can take years of careful foundation-building.

The impact on people

The strategic choices already outlined have a fundamental impact on the survival and success of multinationals operating in the Single Market. The consequences for the people of Europe are also far-reaching. The people of Europe – or at least some of them – have become very discriminating consumers. Those who can access information via the net can compare prices in euros and seek employment in the Europe-wide labour market stand to gain; others are less fortunate and may even be disadvantaged by these new developments, at least in the shortrun. The balance of bargaining strength has shifted away from producers and towards well-informed consumers. Whenever regional and quasi-monopolies are replaced with more competitive structures, then customers will benefit. Firms in Europe will be confronted with both internal and external challenges that require them to conform to the testing norms of management to achieve and sustain a competitive edge within their respective industries and markets. Competition will require a firm to innovate, to extend its product range and to retain shareholder value.

Enhanced economic growth arising from new business strategies should benefit people in a variety of ways. Low interest rates and wider access to equity markets tend to encourage share ownership by the Single Market's citizens. They will also increase the availability of risk capital, essential for growth in technology-oriented European companies enhancing employment opportunities in the region. Low interest rates also bring about low mortgage rates which will speed up cross-border activity in real estate and lending; European citizens will have more choices in the Continent's housing market. Although liberalisation in many areas – energy prices, telephone calls, Internet connections and shop opening hours – will stimulate competition and create new jobs, the impact of these developments on the quality of people's lives might, however, be more debatable. Weekend working, night shifts and unsocial hours have become more common in this brave new world of work. The part-time jobs are often insecure or temporary, introducing uncertainty into people's lives and offsetting some of the benefits of growth. These changes create flexibility in economic structures but entail social costs.

Nevertheless, these changes set in train improvements in living and working conditions through tax and social insurance harmonisation and the provision of education and vocational training by both the governments and the private sector, developments that might improve the productivity of the existing and future workforce. The expansion of service jobs in areas such as distribution, education, health and social work, hotels and catering has made a positive contribution to reducing long-term unemployment in many of the member countries. SMEs, benefiting from the outsourcing of larger companies, can make a substantial contribution to job creation. However, the terms and conditions of employment in these expanding sectors might be more insecure than jobs in the manufacturing sector, and the ability of the EU to protect marginal workers from exploitation remains questionable, as Hatt notes in Chapter 10.

Since the beginning of 1996 there have been signs that Europeans have been taking their savings out of bonds and banks and investing in shares as the gap between the respective returns has been widening. In many cases, these savers have been investing in new American MNEs entering the European market. By the end of 1998, there was more money in equity funds than any other type of fund (Barrett, 2000). The shift has been due to several factors. First, since 1996, the European Union has been both the world's largest source and recipient of foreign direct investment (FDI). In 1998, the net inflow was $644bn. Second, shares are becoming more attractive as companies are committing themselves to long-term investment in Europe. Third, thanks to market liberalisation, firms can engage in diversified investments without incurring substantial transaction costs. Fourth, the merging of national markets into one large European equity market has broadened the investment horizons for small investors. Fifth, changes in demographic trends have increased the need to build up pension funds for retirement, a proposition which Sullivan evaluates in Chapter 12. The harmonisation of taxes within Euroland and the development of a Single Market in financial services would imply still further standardisation. If costs are thereby reduced, pensioners should benefit. Moves towards a regulatory framework for a unified market in financial service products are discussed by Sullivan in Chapter 7.

Conclusion

The most important economic argument for completing the Single Market was the opportunity for economic growth. Several specific sources of increased growth have been identified in this chapter. Hopefully, economic growth will be stimulated by the internal and external economies of scale that might be created by centralised production facilities by firms within the region. These opportunities will encourage both European and non-European enterprises to implement long-term growth strategies and to find ways to serve customers and empower employees. Many multinationals have developed and are still developing pan-European strategies to exploit the situation as the new Europe adjusts to technical, demographic and social change. Europeans, in their respective roles as consumers, employees, entrepreneurs of small and medium-sized companies and pensioners, might benefit in the long term. The management of such profound change will pose challenges to the business elite, public policy-makers and the people of Europe. The long-run benefits of growth may indeed be considerable but the short-term frictions will require both nerve and judgement in the years ahead.

References

Barrett, S. (2000) *'Foreign Direct Investment in the USA'*, PhD thesis, University of the West of England, Bristol.

Day, J. D. and Wendler, J. C. (1998) 'Best Practice and Beyond: Knowledge Strategies', *McKinsey Quarterly*, no. 1, pp. 19–25

Ducker, P. (1999) *Management Challenge for the 21st Century* (Butterworth-Heineman, Oxford)

Ellis, J. and Williams, D. (1995) *International Business Strategy* (Pitman, London)

El Kahal, S. (1998) *Business in Europe* (McGraw-Hill, Maidenhead)

Financial Times, various issues, 1997–2000

Grant, R. M. (1998) *Contemporary Strategy Analysis*, 3rd edn (Blackwell, Cambridge)

Hamel, G. and Parahalad, C. K. (1994) *Competing for the Future* (Harvard Business School Press, Cambridge, Mass)

Hill, C. W. L. (2000). *International Business: Competing in the Global Marketplace*, 3rd edn (McGraw-Hill, New York)

Hymer, S. H. (1976) *The International Operation of National Firms: A Study of Direct Foreign Investment* (MIT Press, Boston, Mass)

Kay, J. (1993) *The Foundation of Corporate Success* (Oxford University Press, Oxford)

Mintzberg, H. (1987) 'Crafting Strategy', *Harvard Business Review* 65, July/August, p. 70

Pettigrew, A. *et al.* (1999). 'New Notions of Organisational "Fit"', *Financial Times,* 29 November
Schumpeter, J. A. (1950) *Capitalism, Socialism and Democracy*, 3rd edn (Harper & Row, New York)

5
Money for the People: Economic and Monetary Union

Peter Cullen

Why EMU? The theory

Perhaps the most supranational initiative within Europe has been the move towards monetary union, as Bradley argued in Chapter 3. To clarify these issues, the theory of monetary union will be explored in this chapter and the policy responses of Britain and Italy will be compared. Full economic and monetary union (EMU) requires two or more regions or states to adopt common macroeconomic policies and a universally acceptable currency. Within most states of the EU, the euro is that currency. Although various institutions are developing economic responsibilities and competencies, they appear to be insufficiently powerful and wide-ranging to perform the functions demanded for true EMU. The economic arguments for and against monetary union in Europe rest on one very simple proposition. Under what circumstances is it advantageous for a particular geographical area to have one currency? Unfortunately, while the question is simple, the answer is complex.

There is no conceptual reason why one currency should not serve the entire world economy, and in many global markets the US dollar is the standard measure of value and means of exchange. Providing buyer and vendor are happy to accept any product as 'money', then it acts as a currency. National currencies are political statements as well as economic tools, and it is no coincidence that cash is virtually always adorned with images of the state, be they monarchs, presidents, notables, or national symbols such as flowers. They give the currency the backing of the state and its institutions. They convey confidence, and confidence is the key to the value of money. The design of euro notes carefully avoids anything which might be identified as national. The name, therefore, has no connections with the *ancien régime*, thus 'euro' rather than crown, franc, or mark.

The 'one state, one currency' model has a very long history with clear economic benefits: a strong currency enhances national status and identifies the boundaries of the state. For governments, monetary policy is a major macroeconomic tool, and the external value of the currency influences trading relations and competitiveness. If the exchange rate rises, exports become more expensive abroad, while if the exchange rate falls, imports become less competitive. Thus, despite the theoretical possibility, there are compelling reasons from the perspective of political economy why the whole world does not share one currency; were that to happen economic autonomy and exchange rate flexibility would disappear.

Nonetheless there are circumstances where removing autonomy and flexibility might bestow benefits of reduced costs and closer integration, and possibly reinforce the political structure. During the 1990s, Western Europe developed a single market and that brought calls for a single currency. But did a single currency imply a single state, a federal structure and attendant institutions, all of which did not exist in the EU when the euro was launched? This paradox forms the background to economic and monetary union in Europe.

Economic theory has attempted to evaluate the benefits of single and multiple currencies. By defining what constitutes an Optimum Currency Area (OCA), Mundell (1961) stated that fixed exchange rates between two countries would impose no economic costs when one or both of the following conditions are met:

- Wage rates and prices in both countries are perfectly flexible – that is, real exchange rates can change despite fixed nominal rates.
- Perfect mobility of labour and capital exists between the two countries – that is, changes in demand will cause factors to flow to the area of higher return, causing a return to equilibrium.

In the latter case, fiscal policy can counter the impact of demand changes on output and employment. In a monetary union emphasis is placed upon fiscal policy as the ability of national governments to use monetary policy to control the economy is substantially removed. However, there is a danger that one country's fiscal policy may adversely affect other members, causing them to adjust their own fiscal policies. Thus, a further requirement of an OCA is that individual states must maintain their ability to counteract shocks, and not be more vulnerable to them than before (Kenen, 1995).

Clearly, the European Union does not constitute a 'perfect OCA': labour is not perfectly mobile, and prices and wages display 'stickiness'. Interestingly, on the same criteria, the UK, Italy, and probably most other West European economies, are not perfect examples either. The UK and Italy possess governments with the power to redistribute resources between growing and declining regions, or wealthy and disadvantaged groups in society, through fiscal policy. The EU does not. Regions such as south-east England or Lombardia can subsidise Northern Ireland and the Mezzogiorno: the EU budget's redistributional impact is far more limited, and overall it must balance, as Chapter 6 shows.

The degree to which the EU approximates to an OCA has prompted extensive debate (Kenen, 1995). A great deal centres on the issue of *asymmetric shocks*; that is, the degree to which changes in aggregate demand or supply make an impact upon regions. A great deal also depends upon how responses to them are transmitted. If nominal and supply shocks are symmetrical and are becoming more so, then the single currency is likely to be beneficial. If, however, demand and labour market shocks display a considerable degree of asymmetry, then fiscal autonomy must be maintained in a European Monetary Union. It may be that there is greater symmetry in the 'core' countries, such as Belgium, Denmark, France, Germany and the Netherlands, than elsewhere, leading to the conclusion that a two-speed approach to EMU is feasible and desirable, economically, if not politically.[1]

Some argue (European Commission, 1990) that monetary union itself influences the frequency of shocks and their impact. States lose some of their ability to create demand shocks, either autonomously, or in response to external factors. Shocks, when they do happen, will be more symmetric where integration has promoted economic convergence, less so if it has intensified specialisation and diversification. The challenge for the European Central Bank (ECB) was to coordinate monetary policy so as to minimise the asymmetry problem. The independent ECB is responsible for setting the interest rate for Europe. Upon inception in January 1999, it set a low interest rate in response to the depressed nature of the economies of many member states. Although a base rate of 3 per cent was intended to stimulate investment and encourage economic growth, it was not appropriate for all states. Germany needed an even lower rate and put political pressure on the ECB to reduce rates. On the other hand, the Republic of Ireland, which had been experiencing rapid growth and labour shortages, was concerned about the effect of a low interest rate on house price inflation. The asymmetry problem was real and immediate.

Monetary union: the economic impact

A monetary union is likely to promote microeconomic efficiency through lowering transactions costs, greater transparency and better resource allocation. From a macroeconomic perspective, however, the gains are more debatable (Hansen and Nielsen, 1997). Political supporters of EMU argue that it should deliver both, but with some loss of autonomy over policy-making.

The microeconomic gain from removing exchange rate costs was estimated to be only 0.25–0.50 per cent of GDP (European Commission, 1990), with further savings arising from the elimination of uncertainty, price discrimination and market segmentation. However, exchange rates will still vary against non-member currencies, possibly restricting trade outside the area and exacerbating trade diversion effects. A single currency and interest rate do not guarantee identical inflation or productivity rates across Euroland, and the lack of exchange rate flexibility as an adjustment mechanism puts even more pressure on other variables, such as wages.

The impact of monetary union upon the regions of Europe is disputed. On the one hand, it might aid the convergence process but, on the other hand, economies might diverge. The former hypothesis rests on the assumption that capital and labour flow to reduce regional differentials in wage rates and returns on capital, equalising the capital–labour ratios. Monetary union becomes part of the integration process, not a result of it. Opponents cite 'cumulative causation' effects; that is, marginal returns to capital in abundant regions can exceed those in deficient regions, particularly once the risk element is taken into account. Capital-abundant areas attract capital, whilst deficient regions lag further behind.

In the period preceding the establishment of the euro on 1 January 1999, evidence (Eurostat, 1999) suggests that most peripheral states performed better than the core, often as a result of inward foreign direct investment (FDI) attracted by low wage rates and/or currencies devalued during 1992–3. In 1998, FDI accounted for over 8 per cent of GDP in Ireland and Finland. Although capital was responding to deregulation and integration, the evidence was different for labour where mobility is traditionally low in Europe, often for social and cultural reasons. An incomplete convergence model with limited labour mobility still works, albeit slowly and imperfectly.

Comparison with the United States of America provides insights. America is generally more regionally diverse and specialised than Western Europe and asymmetric shocks do indeed occur, for example, in farming which affects the Midwest in particular. Unlike the EU, such problems are usually ameliorated through fiscal transfers from the federal government. The idea of an expanding German economy aiding a declining Portuguese economy may be attractive to integrationists, but it flies in the face of current political reality. If Euroland is to succeed it must follow the American model and simultaneously develop institutions with macroeconomic policy-making and resource redistribution powers.

Monetary union in Europe: winners and losers

The winners

A single currency area that removes the costs associated with the exchange of currencies and with the risks of fluctuations is clearly attractive in that it should allow markets to work efficiently and increase consumer welfare. Evaluating the distribution of benefits between the Union, national governments, businesses and the people is complex and rests on various assumptions. The EU and its larger firms should gain from greater competition and efficiency, tighter integration, and increased economic power and influence in global markets. National governments can reduce reserves and pursue policies without regard for their exchange rate implications. Businesses face fewer risks and reduced costs when trading within the MU and, potentially, outside it too. Consumers should benefit from transparency of pricing, greater choice, and lower retail prices prompted by increased competition and dynamism. Many of these issues are explored in greater depth by Panah in Chapter 4.

Assuming that a single currency delivers low interest rates over an extended period, then borrowers can expect gains from cheaper loans. It was estimated (Sherwen and Jones, 1999) in late 1999 that joining Euroland then would reduce the average UK mortgagee's monthly repayments by over £100 (160 euros). The resulting income effect should boost expenditure in other sectors, despite fears that house price inflation would nullify the impact for new buyers. Other business and personal lending rates should be correspondingly lower, bringing benefits to consumers and encouraging investment. There is no guarantee that MU rates will always be lower than those of non-members but the expectation is that on average over time, ceteris paribus, they should.

The losers

Low interest rates may benefit borrowers, but, of course, savers lose out. In mid-1999, real interest rates for savings in some Euroland states were only just positive. In the longer term, lower interest rates reduce annuity rates, with serious consequences for those with money purchase pension funds.

National governments use monetary policy for various purposes, and handing over this major economic tool to a European institution deprives them of considerable power; there is a loss of economic sovereignty. Even though many European governments have adopted the German 'Bundesbank model' and delegated the setting of interest rates to a committee of bankers and experts, removal of the ability to pursue an independent monetary policy imposes real costs. Governments at present retain competence over fiscal policy and, to date, the UK has firmly resisted suggestions of further fiscal harmonisation. When the German Finance Minister, Oskar Lafontaine, made such suggestions in late 1998 his comments were rejected, but national governments must face up to the rationale that, within a monetary union, subsidiarity requires that major policy tools are centralised.

For individuals too, the implications of a common currency are multifaceted. While lower prices and more choice increase consumer surplus and welfare, people are also employees and employers. Experience tells us that intensified competition and economic dynamism bring higher unemployment levels and bankruptcy rates, at least temporarily, as restructuring occurs. Many have an emotional attachment to their currency beyond its role as a means of exchange; it is an important symbol of national identity. The fear that a common European currency will diminish national and regional identity still further appears to be a real concern for many people. Any currency will only succeed if all accept it. Persuading the EU population that the euro would be advantageous and relevant to them was an important part of the preparations.

The process: creating a European monetary union

The Treaty of Rome makes no explicit reference to monetary union. The six founders had made sacrifices for postwar reconstruction, and there were many steps on the road to integration before such a radical step could be contemplated. Monetary union was not necessary in the 1950s and 1960s as the Bretton Woods System provided exchange rate stability but its demise in 1973 resulted in unstable, floating exchange rates. EEC states responded with a system of linked rates known as the 'Snake'.[2] Retrospectively the Snake is not regarded as a success but it did pave the way for a much more powerful structure.

In 1977, Commission President Roy Jenkins proposed a plan for EMU and the first real steps towards monetary union were instigated in 1979 with the creation of the European Monetary System.[3] It established:

- an exchange rate stabilising system – the Exchange Rate Mechanism (ERM)
- a central fund of deposits – the European Monetary Cooperation Fund (EMCF)
- a community-wide 'currency' – the European Currency Unit (ECU)

The ECU's value derived from a weighted average of EC member states' currencies in an attempt to reduce the possibility of Deutschmark domination; it is debatable whether it succeeded. It also acted as a 'divergence indicator' for misaligned currencies. Between 1979 and 1998 the ECU played an increasingly important role in European and global financial markets, paving the way for its replacement, the euro.

The ERM was constructed around a narrow band (+/–2.25 per cent) of fluctuation for stronger currencies, and a broad band (+/–6 per cent) for those likely to have difficulty in maintaining short-term stability – between 1979 and 1989 only the lira. Despite its flexible architecture, the ERM did little to stabilise member currencies in its early days. There were twelve realignments between September 1979 and January 1987; some currencies such as the Deutschmark and the guilder earned reputations for strength, and others, such as the lira and the French franc, for weakness. After 1987 the record improved considerably as confidence in the system grew and an improving economic climate emerged. Over the next four years, the Spanish peseta, sterling and the Portuguese escudo joined the ERM, on the broad band, and the only realignment was in January 1990 when the lira entered the narrow band.

Within an environment of stability and deepening integration engendered by the Single European Act and 1992 Programme, real progress towards a common currency and true MU occurred. Monetary union became both logical as a central component of the Single Market and achievable, or so political leaders believed. In June 1988, the European Council demanded that the Commission investigate economic and monetary union, resulting in the 1989 Delors Report.[4] Its main recommendations were incorporated in the Treaty on European Union (TEU) at Maastricht in 1991. This envisaged the achievement of MU through three progressive stages:

- *Stage 1* Completion of the Single Market and free mobility of capital were scheduled to occur on 1 January 1993.
- *Stage 2* The currencies of those states participating in the MU were to be within the narrow band of the ERM. The European Monetary Institute was established to manage transition to the third stage and act as a precursor to a European Central Bank (ECB). It would take over responsibility for gold and foreign exchange reserves from the European System of Central Banks (ESCB). Convergence criteria for Stage 3 were also established.
- *Stage 3* States deemed eligible for the Monetary Union were to proceed to the adoption of the new currency. Two possibilities were envisaged: a majority of states in January 1997, or any number in January 1999.

The programme was accepted by all member states, with the United Kingdom negotiating to delay a decision on Stage 3 participation to a later date.

The convergence criteria agreed at Maastricht required states to meet a number of monetary targets that were critical in determining the performance of EU economies over the next seven years. Briefly they were:

- Government deficit should not exceed 3 per cent of GDP at market prices.
- Total government debt should not exceed 60 per cent of GDP at market prices, or be converging with that level.
- Annual inflation rates should be within 1.5 per cent of the average of the three best-performing states.
- Long-term interest rates should be within 2 per cent of the average of the best-performing states with regard to inflation.
- Currencies should be stable within the ERM – not realigned for two years.

Within two years of Maastricht the ERM had encountered realignments, suffered two crises, lost two major currencies,[5] and only survived through restructuring bands to +/–15 per cent. By late 1993 meeting the fifth criterion meant something very different to when it was drafted. Despite its difficulties the ERM continued and the exchange rates of participating countries varied by far less than the +/–15 per cent permitted. It became clear early on that a majority of states would not meet all criteria by mid-1996. German reunification caused economic difficulties for many member states and strained the stability of the ERM.

The 1995 enlargement increased Union membership to fifteen, causing member states and the institutions to refocus on the 1999 deadline. Meeting the debt and deficit limits became the focus of attention. By 1996, only Luxembourg met both criteria. Many countries had comprehensive welfare systems that were partly funded by borrowing. Annual deficits well in excess of 3 per cent of GDP were normal for Mediterranean and Scandinavian members. Major adjustments to fiscal policy were required to meet the 3 per cent limit. The public debt ratio was an even greater stumbling block, as very few had levels below 60 per cent. Reducing public debt to any appreciable degree was difficult. It had grown over decades and could not be repaid without jeopardising monetary policy. Meeting the inflation and interest rate criteria looked impossible.

By 1997, all states except Greece met the inflation rate criterion and all but Greece and the UK the deficit criterion. Only Finland, France, Luxembourg and, ironically, the UK, satisfied the 60 per cent debt–GDP ratio requirement. Of the other states, several were close, but, with only months to go to the final decision date, Greece, Belgium and Italy all had figures of well over 100 per cent.

The need to reduce deficits, and maintain them at acceptable levels once Euroland was established, was recognised at the June 1997 Amsterdam European Council. A stability and growth pact was accepted by all member states. It required participants to maintain public deficits below 3 per cent of GDP or face sanctions of up to 0.5 per cent of GDP. The aim of the stability pact was to give confidence and credibility to the euro. Some critics (Buiter *et al.*, 1993) point out, however, that removing monetary policy from national governments' policy armoury places greater emphasis on fiscal policy, thus making budget deficit management more difficult.

As the final decision date approached, politics took precedence over economics. For the project to succeed, Euroland needed as many founder members as possible. Several governments had been pursuing austerity policies, with a depressing impact on public expenditure and welfare payments. Public sector workers and benefit recipients in France and Italy, where cuts were most severe, openly demonstrated their discontent. In addition, privatisation receipts and revaluation of assets delivered reductions in deficits and debt through 'creative accounting'.

By early 1998, eleven member states[6] had published change-over plans, indicating their intention to proceed to Stage 3. In early May 1998, the Commission stated that eleven states met the criteria,[7] views validated by the Economic and Finance Ministers' Council (Ecofin), the European Parliament, and the European Council. The setting of fixed bilateral exchange and euro rates, nominations for membership of the European Central Bank's executive board and conferring legal status on the new currency all followed immediately. The timetable for transition to the single currency was also agreed.

The people's view

During the convergence period, public support for the euro was lukewarm, particularly in states with a history of postwar prosperity based upon strong and stable national currencies. In early 1995, 53 per cent of EU citizens favoured monetary union, with significantly fewer in Germany, UK and Denmark (Eurbaro meter, 1998). It is easy to understand why the Germans were reluctant to relinquish the Deutschmark, or the Dutch the guilder, for the uncertainty of a untried currency. The enthusiasm of their leaders for further integration and esoteric arguments about the completeness of the European market took second place to personal interest.

Across the EU, opinions remained remarkably consistent throughout the period 1993–6 with over half in favour, and just over one-third against. With the approach of the deadline, support rose to new levels but with wide discrepancies between states as Table 5.1 shows.

Opinions varied markedly between different social groups:

- Men were more likely to be in favour than women.
- Professionals were more likely to be in favour than manual workers.
- The self-employed were more likely to be in favour than the retired and the unemployed.
- Support declined with age.

Table 5.1 Percentages for and against monetary union by state (spring 1998)

	For	Against
Italy	83	8
Luxembourg	79	18
Netherlands	73	23
Spain	72	17
Ireland	68	14
Belgium	68	23
France	68	25
Greece	67	17
Austria	56	27
Finland	53	38
Portugal	52	22
Germany	51	36
Sweden	39	50
UK	34	49
Denmark	34	57

Source: Eurobarometer 1998.

The impression is that, once it became inevitable, caution towards monetary reform was replaced by approval, albeit somewhat reluctantly. Supporters might suggest that this was a function of knowledge and understanding whilst sceptics see it as yet a further example of the EU forcing reform against the wishes of its people. The lack of support for the project in the UK is clear in Table 5.1. Germans, too, were rather unenthusiastic and in conflict with the desires of Kohl's government, which was keen to see Germany leading Europe. The German people, however, were not given a formal opportunity to express their views whereas on 28 September 2000, the Danish electorate rejected the euro in a referendum.

Preparing for EMU: a comparison between Britain and Italy

In the early 1990s, several currencies had difficulties maintaining their position within the Exchange Rate Mechanism (ERM). 'Black' or 'Golden' Wednesday 16 September 1992 witnessed the removal of both sterling and the lira from the ERM. Having negotiated the postponement of its decision on Stage 3, the UK would clearly be an unlikely candidate for early EMU entry. For the UK, meeting the Maastricht criteria became irrelevant. Italy immediately announced a determination to rejoin the ERM and be a founder member of the single currency area, and modified policy accordingly. The lira rejoined the ERM in

November 1996 and the race to conform to the other Maastricht criteria was on. The experiences of the two countries over the next few years make an interesting comparison.

The British and Italian economies are not dissimilar in terms of size and structure although the power of the unions and the size of the public sector differ considerably in the two countries. From 1992 to 1998, the period between the first ERM crisis and the decision on eligibility for MU, the two economies followed very different paths. The UK, with little intention of participating at Stage 3, or even of rejoining the ERM, had the freedom to pursue an autonomous policy, boosted by the depreciation of sterling. Italy chose the road to monetary union, and the austerity that it demanded.

Italy

The impact of meeting the Maastricht criteria on the Italian economy can be observed in Table 5.2. Bringing inflation, budget deficits and public debt under control demanded a tight macroeconomic policy that went against the grain. Growth throughout this period was modest, though higher than in some other aspirant members. Inflation was brought under control, along with nominal wage rates, increases in which fell from over 4 per cent in 1996 to 2.5 per cent by 1998

Table 5.2 British and Italian economic indicators, 1992–8

		1992	1993	1994	1995	1996	1997	1998
Change in GDP by	Italy	0.6	−1.2	2.2	2.9	0.7	1.5	1.4
volume (%)	UK	0.1	2.3	4.4	2.8	2.6	3.5	2.1
Consumer price	Italy	4.7	4.4	3.9	5.4	3.9	1.7	1.8
inflation (%)	UK	4.0	2.8	1.5	2.5	3.3	2.5	2.5
Unemployment	Italy	9.0	10.3	11.4	11.9	12.0	12.1	11.9
rate (%)	UK	10.1	10.4	9.6	8.7	8.2	7.0	6.2
Govt debt	Italy	108.5	119.1	125.6	124.8	124.0	121.6	118.8
(% of GDP)	UK	41.9	48.5	50.3	54.1	54.7	53.5	51.5
Budget deficit	Italy	−9.6	−9.6	−9.2	−7.7	−6.6	−2.7	−2.7
(as % of GDP)	UK	−6.5	−8.0	6.8	−5.8	−4.4	−2.0	0.4
Percentage change in	Italy	1.1	0.5	−0.6	−1.0	0.3	−0.8	1.4
real public spending	UK	0.5	−0.8	1.4	1.6	1.7	0	1.5
Long-term interest	Italy	13.7	11.3	10.6	11.8	9.4	6.9	4.9
rates (annual mean %)	UK	9.1	7.8	8.2	8.2	7.8	7.0	5.5

Sources: European Commission, 1999a; European Commission, 1999b; OECD, 1999.

(Economist Intelligence Unit, 1999), through a 'Social Pact'. Historically, Italy has been prone to unemployment and, under the austerity package, it rose to levels high even by its standards. Unemployment in Italy particularly afflicts the young and women, a point which is discussed by Hatt in Chapter 10. It also displays large regional disparities, with the rate in the south being about three times that in the industrialised centre–north.

Italy's main problem was to manage public finances within the levels agreed at Maastricht. In the 1970s and 1980s, total government expenditure rose from about a third of GDP to over a half, whilst revenues consistently lagged behind. This resulted in budget deficits of 10 per cent or more of GDP throughout the 1980s and an accumulated public debt in excess of 100 per cent of GDP by 1990. Convergence policies of expenditure cuts, tax increases and privatisation issues were introduced to rectify matters. Reductions in the reserves of gold and foreign exchange occurred between the end of 1996 and late 1998.

In May 1998, it was decided that Italy had fulfilled the Maastricht criteria and qualified to join Euroland on 1 January 1999. While there is little doubt that four criteria had been achieved, government debt was still 118 per cent of GDP. However, as the figure was falling – that is, converging with the 60 per cent target – it was deemed acceptable. To be fair, Italy was not the only country to have exceeded the debt target, though, with Belgium, it was the largest transgressor by some margin.

In short, Italy spent the post-1992 period reforming and stabilising its economy in preparation for MU. This was no mean achievement for an economy historically prone to short-term expediency measures, often as a result of unstable government. The cost in terms of employment and welfare cuts imposed a burden on many people. Dissatisfaction was manifest through public protest and industrial unrest but, none the less, it appears that most Italians were prepared to suffer in the short term in order to adopt the euro.

Having achieved its objective, the Italian government indicated its intention to continue with tough policies. They after all stood to gain from low interest rates that would reduce the cost of servicing their public debt. If preparing for Stage 3 was a matter of short-term pain for long-term gain, then Italy appears to be one state that has succeeded and has, so far, retained the support of its people.

The United Kingdom

For the United Kingdom, the removal of sterling from the ERM released it from any obligation to stabilise the exchange rate or meet other MU criteria. Interest rates fell, growth became positive following the severe recession of 1991–2 and, after peaking at over 10 per cent in 1993, unemployment fell to under 5 per cent by the end of the 1990s.

Budget deficits fell from about 7 per cent of GDP to a primary surplus by 1998–9; total debt in 1998 was 51.5 per cent of GDP. Britain pursued its own route with a considerable measure of success for its people. The pound was floated and stabilised at a lower level. Ironically, except for the fact that sterling had not reentered the ERM and that the interest rate was just outside limits, Britain met the Maastricht criteria and could have joined Euroland. Indeed, Britain would have had a stronger case for entry than some applicants that were accepted.

Attitudes towards monetary union differed significantly between the two countries as a Gallup survey published in January 1997 demonstrated (see Table 5.3).

Table 5.3 Responses to the single currency, January 1997 (percentages)

	UK	Italy
Should [your state] say now that it will definitely join a single currency, possibly in 1999?	12	37
Should [your state] say now that it will never join a single currency?	42	8
If there were a referendum about the creation of a single currency, how would you vote?		
In favour	26	71
Against	56	12
A single currency means that a sovereign government will soon become inevitable	33	18
or		
Even with a single currency, national governments can retain their sovereignty and autonomy	43	70
Are government spending and borrowing cuts to meet the Maastricht criteria worthwhile sacrifices?		
Worthwhile	17	54
Not worthwhile	59	33
What is your opinion on handing over decisions on interest rates to a European central bank, outside the control of national governments?		
In favour	15	46
Not in favour	69	34

Note: Some questions edited for brevity
Source: Gallup, *Political and Economic Index*, No. 405, January 1997.

Britain and Italy compared

Across the board, there is far greater support for the euro and fewer fears about its implications for the economy and governance in Italy than in Britain. Possible reasons are that:

- The Italian people are well-disposed towards the EU.
- Italian political parties display a positive approach to EMU.
- Italians perceive potential advantages in the euro.
- Italians distrust their national politicians.
- Italians prefer monetary policy to be determined exogenously.
- The lira has a history of instability.

Conclusions

A cynic might suggest that in a perfect Europe monetary policy would be German, industrial policy French, trade policy British and the lifestyle Italian. Under EMU, monetary policy is pseudo-German, industrial policy is shared between states and the Union, intra-EU trade policy is almost British and most people desire, but do not lead, an Italian lifestyle. Compromises have been made.

About 290 million people are undertaking a significant economic experiment. Time will tell whether a currency can be created to the mutual advantage of a number of structurally disparate economic areas. It is tempting to say that, with the power of three of the G7 states within it, a history of fifty years of integration behind it, and institutions of the European Union controlling it, the euro cannot fail. Sheer economic weight must ensure a good chance for success as the euro replaces national currencies and establishes a significant presence in the global economy. The creation of the euro should enhance economic efficiency and encourage optimism and dynamism across Europe.

Any benefits will not be achieved without costs. Fundamental questions arise about the sagacity of a single currency and the direction in which it may propel the European Union. Most people seem to have accepted the inevitable; they have offered grudging-to-reasonably-enthusiastic support. However, if things start to go wrong, it is not difficult to see on whom the people of Europe will focus their discontent. Euroland governments have delegated some of their ability to meet the economic aspirations of their electorates; that erosion looks set to continue. The power and accountability of EU institutions are simply not developed enough at present to assume these responsibilities, yet it will be these institutions that the people of Europe will blame should the project flounder. The people of Europe must have confidence in the euro, in the ideology and the institutions that back it, if it is to succeed. If not, the outlook for the European Union is bleak indeed.

Notes

1. The above empirical studies appear in Kenen, *Economic and Monetary Union in Europe*.
2. A detailed explanation of the 'Snake' is beyond this chapter's scope; for one, see Tsoukalis *The New European Economy Revisited*, pp. 141–2, and many other books.
3. All nine members in 1979 joined the EMS. However the UK kept sterling out of the ERM until October 1990.
4. The full title is *Report on Economic and Monetary Union (1989) from the Committee for the Study of Economic and Monetary Union*. It is commonly referred to by the title used in the text.
5. Sterling and the Italian lira were forced to suspend membership in September 1992.
6. Austria, Belgium, Finland, France, Germany, Ireland, Italy, Luxembourg, Netherlands, Portugal, Spain.
7. The debt criterion requiring states 'to be converging with 60 per cent' was interpreted liberally; see case study on Italy later.

References

Buiter, W. Corsetti, G. and Roubini, N. '1993 Sense and Nonsense in the Treaty of Maastricht', *Economic Policy*, vol. 37, pp. 63–84
Economist Intelligence Unit (1999) *Country Report: Italy*, 1st Quarter
Eurobarometer, (1998) *Eurobarometer*, 49, Spring, via http://europa.eu.int
European Commission (1999a) *European Economy Annual Economic Report No. 67* (EC, Brussels)
European Commission (1999b) *Eurostat Yearbook: A Statistical Eye on Europe*, 1998/9 edition (EC, Luxembourg)
Eurostat (1999) *Eurostat Yearbook*, Edition 98/99 (EC, Brussels)
Gallup (1997) *Political and Economic Index*, No. 405 (January)
Hansen J. D. and Nielsen, J. U.-M. (1997) *An Economic Analysis of the EU* 2nd edn. (McGraw Hill-London)
Kenen, P. B. (ed.) (1995) *Economic and Monetary Union in Europe: Moving Beyond Maastricht* (Cambridge University Press, Cambridge)
Mundell, R. A. (1961) 'A Theory of Optimum Currency Azas', *American Economic Review* 51, No. 4, pp. 657–65
OECD (1999) Main Economic Indicators, August 1999
Sherwen, P. and Jones, R. (1999) 'The Euro and You', *The Guardian*, 23 October
Tsoukalis, L. (1997) *The New European Economy Revisited* (Oxford University Press, Oxford)

6
The EU Budget and EU Citizens

Brian Ardy

Introduction

Government activity affects citizens in many ways. Most people, if asked, would probably specify health, education, social security expenditure and taxation as the government activities that impinge upon them most directly. The EU, however, is not so visible. In this respect, the impact of the EU's budget on people is less noticeable than EMU and the coming of the euro which were explored in the previous chapter. The most significant effect of the EU on people's lives has been through the construction of laws of which they are only dimly aware. The major purpose of this system of laws has been the creation of the Single Market and the Economic and Monetary Union. It is only in these areas that national governments have been prepared to pool sovereignty to obtain economic benefits.

The EU budget, therefore, reflects the extremely limited extent to which the governments of the member states have been prepared to relinquish control over their tax and expenditure policies – despite the efforts of the Commission to expand its competence in these matters. Thus, most EU expenditure is concentrated on two policy areas – agricultural and structural policy – and financed essentially by national budgetary contributions. This chapter examines these budgetary arrangements considering, first, the rules under which the budget operates. Next, the pattern of expenditure will be analysed, including a comparison between the EU budget and that of national governments. Then, the revenue sources of the EU will be examined and, finally, the overall impact of the EU budget on EU citizens will be considered.

Relative national prosperity in the EU

In order to evaluate the effects of the EU budget on member states and upon the 'average' national citizen, a measure of relative prosperity is required. Gross National Product (GNP) is used by economists as the basis for this measurement since it represents the gross income available to a country or, in other words, the value of the output produced by its resources. Figure 6.1 depicts two measures of GNP per head for the member states in the EU, indicating that Portugal has the lowest level and Luxembourg the highest level of prosperity.

The most straightforward measure is GNP at current market prices and, for the purpose of comparison between countries, this measure has, in the past, been converted into ECU at market exchange rates. This accounting process will be substantially altered by the advent of the euro. An alternative is to measure GNP, not by market exchange rates, but by purchasing power standard (PPS) exchange rates. Although PPS-measured GNP provides a better estimate of relative prosperity and is more stable than GNP measured at market exchange rates, it is the latter that will be used in this chapter. This is because GNP at market exchange rates is used as the basis of the EU budget. In Figure 6.1 and in the tables in this chapter, EU member states are

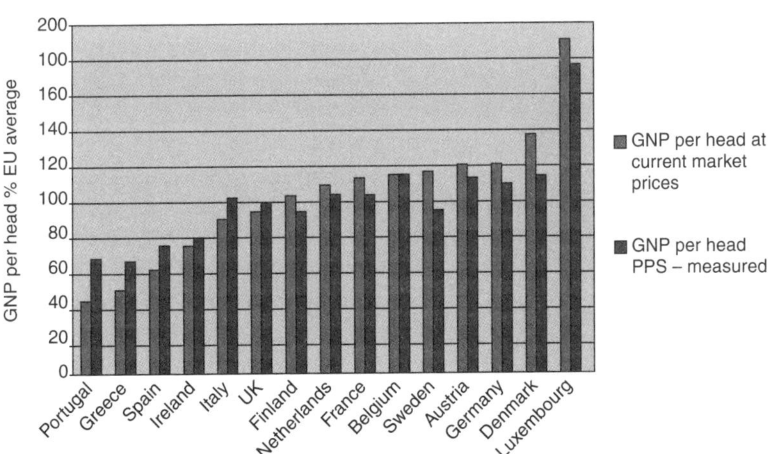

Figure 6.1   GNP per head, 1996–7 average
Source: European Commission (1998a) Annex 8.

arranged in the reverse order of the level of their GNP per head – that is, from the poorest to the richest countries.

EU budgetary rules

The rules under which the EU budget operates indicate the extent to which member states wanted to limit EU competence in this important area of government activity. There has been controversy in the UK over an EU-wide withholding tax on saving and over tax harmonisation, emphasising the sensitivity of this issue. Thus EU budgetary rules are designed to ensure maximum control by member states and minimum discretion of EU institutions over EU expenditure and revenue. In this respect, there are five basic principles derived from the Treaties (European Union, 1997): annuality, balance, unity, universality and specification. Annuality requires that the budget is only for the one year and authorisation cannot be given beyond this year. This prevents the build-up of long-term commitments but has caused problems because a great deal of EU expenditure is now on multi-annual programmes. The practical reconciliation of member state resistance and Commission pressure has been to make commitments for future years, which, strictly speaking, do not have to be honoured but which, in practice, are. Balance ensures that revenue covers expenditure and so deficit financing is not possible. If expenditure is going to exceed revenue, additional resources have to be raised in the current year. Any surplus is carried over as revenue for the following year. Unity requires that all expenditure is in a single budget document. Universality means that all EU revenue and expenditure is included in the budget. Specification requires that expenditure is allocated to a particular objective; this ensures that it is used for the purposes the budgetary authority intended. There is, however, some possibility for transfers between categories for the effective execution of the budget. The resignation of the Commission in 1999 has demonstrated that the budgetary processes have not always worked as intended. This issue, which is explored later in the chapter, led to dramatic results.

EU budget expenditure

Overall EU budgetary expenditure

The development of budgetary expenditure reflects the development of EU policies. For a long time the budget was dominated by agricultural expenditure. This was because the Common Agricultural policy (CAP) needed to reconcile national agricultural interests and in so doing adopted an expensive and protectionist regime, as detailed by Hatt in Chapter 9. The dominance of agricultural expenditure reflected both the protectionist nature of the CAP and the lack of development of other areas of expenditure. Major areas of public expenditure remained under national control because of the reluctance of national governments to cede control in these sensitive areas. Enlargement increased the heterogeneity of the Community and it was felt necessary to introduce a greater redistributive element into the budget. This was achieved by expanding and concentrating structural fund expenditure. Expenditure on research has increased as a result of concerns over competitiveness. The ending of the Cold War led to increased expenditure on external action as the EU has sought to bring stability to Central and Eastern Europe. Agricultural expenditure under the European Agricultural Guidance and Guarantee Fund (EAGGF) and structural expenditure continue, however, to dominate the budget, as Table 6.1 shows.

The EU budget: a comparison with national government budgets

The EU budget differs from that of national governments in two fundamental ways. First, it is very much smaller, accounting for just over 1 per cent of GNP, and, second, the pattern of expenditure is completely different.

Table 6.1 EU budget expenditure, 1995–7

	1995	1996	1997
General budget (% share of expenditure)			
EAGGF guarantees	51.6	50.8	50.6
Structural funds, of which:	28.8	31.8	32.5
EAGGF guidance	3.8	4.4	4.5
ERDF	12.5	13.8	14.4
ESF	6.8	7.9	7.7
Cohesion Fund	2.6	2.4	3.0
Other	3.1	3.3	2.9
Internal policies	6.0	5.9	6.2
External action	5.5	5.3	5.3
Administration	5.8	5.3	5.2
Compensation to member states	2.3	0.9	0.3
Total general budget (ECU million)	66 901	77 032.2	79 819.1
General budget, % EU GNP	1.06	1.15	1.13

Source: European Commission (1998a).

Table 6.2   Government expenditure by level of government, 1997 (% of nominal GDP)

	Central government	Social security	Central and social security	State and local government	Total general government
Portugal	26.1	13.7	39.8	3.3	43.1
Spain	14.4	19.1	33.5	8.7	42.2
Ireland	20.7	4.6	25.3	9.9	35.1
Italy	24.5	14.4	38.9	11.4	50.2
UK	25.5	6.0	31.5	10.3	41.0
Netherlands	17.5	19.1	36.6	12.2	48.7
France	21.7	24.6	46.2	7.9	54.2
Sweden	27.8	12.3	40.1	22.2	62.3
Germany	25.2	14.1	39.4	3.3	42.7
Non-EU					
Japan	7.5	15.2	22.7	12.6	35.0
Switzerland	8.8	16.6	25.4	23.5	48.8
USA	12.4	8.0	20.4	13.3	33.6

Source: IMF (1999).

Table 6.2 shows government expenditure by level of government as a percentage of GDP, illustrating that, even in countries with very decentralised governments such as Switzerland and the USA, the level of central government expenditure is many times that of the EU budget. Table 6.2 also highlights the considerable differences between government expenditure in different member states.

In most EU states, total general government expenditure amounts to between 40 and 50 per cent of GDP. The highest tier of government accounts for most of that expenditure even in a federal state such as Germany. The largest categories of national government expenditure are social security, health, education, defence and debt interest. There are also major differences between these policies in different countries, reflecting different histories, cultures and preferences. As a consequence, these areas remain firmly under national control and so the EU has a pattern of expenditure totally different from that of national governments.

Common Agricultural Policy guarantee expenditure

Over time, the nature of the CAP has changed from supporting prices to direct subsidies for farmers. This has not, however, reduced the cost of the policy in absolute terms although the share of the CAP in the total budget has indeed fallen as other areas of expenditure have increased more rapidly. CAP guarantee expenditure, however, still remains the largest single item in the budget. The strength of the agricultural lobby and the process of EU decision-making meant that agriculture continued to be a favoured sector, despite the decreasing importance of agriculture in the economy (Grant, 1998).

The CAP provides benefits to the agricultural sector through higher prices for some farm products and direct payments to farmers. The fact that farmers' production patterns are sensitive to CAP prices and subsidies indicates they are very conscious of the CAP. In the past, consumers in most countries were only vaguely aware of the impact of the CAP on food prices but, as direct subsidies have increased in importance, the costs to taxpayers have become more apparent. The costs to consumers and taxpayers of the CAP in higher food prices and higher taxes are considered further in Chapter 9. Agricultural support would not disappear in the absence of the CAP since national governments would, no doubt, support their agricultural industries. The level of support, however, might vary with the power of the agricultural lobby, with the cost of support and with the ability of the national taxpayers to bear this burden. Compared with a similar system of national agricultural support, the CAP results in transfers between countries via the EU budget and through intra-EU trade in food, and these effects are analysed later in this chapter.

Structural policy expenditure

The structural funds, the European Social Fund (ESF), the agricultural guidance fund, the European Regional Development Fund (ERDF) and the Cohesion Fund were developed to try to achieve greater solidarity within the Union. They were justified, therefore, as redistributive policies. It was recognised that there would be political problems unless there was reasonable similarity of living standards across the EU. The EU policy process, in general, and the allocation of expenditure, in particular, are a matter for political bargaining between member states; thus the ESF was included in the Treaty primarily to help the poor southern half of Italy. This use of the structural funds as a side payment to facilitate agreement between member states has continued. The expansion of the structural funds and their concentration on poorer regions in 1988 was part of the bargain to achieve agreement on the Single European Act because Europe's poorer peripheral countries argued that they would be at a competitive disadvantage in a single market. The Cohesion Fund similarly was established by the Treaty on European Union because of similar fears about EMU.

Gradually, the structural funds have been reformed so that expenditure is concentrated on poorer regions and thus on poorer countries. Ireland benefits most from the structural funds, followed closely by Portugal and Greece, as Table 6.3 shows. The benefits of EU structural fund expenditure, however, are not clear to the individual citizen. Although people may benefit from this expenditure when, for example, undergoing training financed by the EU, it may not be apparent who is financing the training. Indeed, structural fund projects are only partially EU-funded,[1] and local or national governments or private institutions – not the EU – will actually provide the training. EU funding may be publicised to indicate the quality of the course, but governments sometimes deliberately underplay the contribution of the EU to create the impression that they are helping the unemployed, those with disabilities and other such needy people. Similarly, ERDF and Cohesion Fund expenditure will provide benefits for citizens in the form of improved infrastructure but, once again, people are often unaware which authority has financed these projects.

EU expenditure on internal and external policies

The impacts of other areas of EU spending on people are even harder to identify. Internal policies include research and technological development expenditure that may benefit the competitiveness of EU industry or impact upon the quality of life in the EU. The relationship between cause and effect is not only difficult to measure, it is also slow to emerge. The other significant areas of expenditure under this heading are education, vocational training, youth and Trans-European Networks (TENs). Education and training is the one area where the EU directly interacts with the people because most of the expenditure in this category finances grants for study in other European countries. Thus, the students directly benefit from Union activity in a very visible way. Unfortunately, such grants are only available to a limited number of people each year although, cumulatively, the numbers involved are quite large. Since most of the students involved in these exchanges are in higher education, these programmes play an important role in shaping elite attitudes for the future. Sadly, this one area of direct contact with EU citizens only absorbs a tiny part of the EU budget, amounting to 0.8 per cent in 1998. By contrast, EU expenditure on TENs which finances cross-border communication networks remains inconspicuous to the people. The development of the TENs is discussed more fully by Cullen in Chapter 8.

External aid is expenditure used to provide help to non-EU countries. There are three groups of countries with which the EU is particularly involved: Central and Eastern Europe (CEE), the Mediterranean and the Middle East, and the African, Caribbean and Pacific countries (ACP). The first two groups represent the EU's geographical neighbours and the third group are less-developed former colonies. The largest component of external aid expenditure is concentrated on Central and Eastern Europe because, with the collapse of communism, this area represents a zone of potential instability within Europe. Large EU programmes in these countries facilitate their transition to a market economy so that they can accede to EU membership. Russia and the other successor states of the USSR have not been offered EU membership, although a closer political and economic relationship is being sought and the provision of economic aid is an important part of this process.[2]

These expenditures benefit the CEE countries and their citizens directly and the EU citizens indirectly by increasing stability and security in Europe. The benefits to EU nations and citizens, however, are somewhat intangible and cannot be measured. There is little evidence that enlargement – let alone aid to CEE – is popular with EU citizens. Only 42 per cent of the people in EU15 currently support enlargement whilst 49 per cent fear that the admission of new members will prove expensive to current member countries (European Commission, 1999c). Aid to the Mediterranean and the Middle East is also designed to increase the stability of this volatile region which lies so close to the EU. Economic development in both these areas would reduce the pressure for migration into the EU, an issue which is explored by Korovilas in Chapter 11. Aid to the ACP is less directly self-interested, reflecting obligations to former colonies. Although there is some public support for such aid, the EU's role is not well-understood, nor is it differentiated from national government aid programmes. The EU's humanitarian aid forms part of a poorly coordinated international scenario and people often confuse EU initiatives with those of other agencies.

Expenditure on administration

The most obvious, most contentious and least understood element of EU expenditure is that on administration. Constant references in the British press to the Brussels bureaucracy and their 'gravy train' lifestyle and pictures of enormous edifices in Brussels and Strasbourg suggest a vast and expensive bureaucracy. Thus, paying for officials, meetings and buildings was the commonest category selected by the public as the area on which most of the EU budget is spent (European Commission, 1999c).[3] This is a very distorted picture since the number of people employed by the European institutions is relatively small, amounting to 31 398 in 1998 (European Commission, 1999a, p48), a modest figure in comparison with national and local governments. For example, the Department of Environment, Transport and the Regions (DETR) had 22 198 employees for its administrative and legal role for only one nation (DETR, 1999) whilst Birmingham City Council had over 50 000 employees just to service the needs of one city (Birmingham City Council, 1999). Comparatively speaking, the Brussels bureaucracy is modest and the idea of the Commission as a vast and unwieldy bureaucracy is false. The salaries of these Brussels officials are, however, high and provide a focus for media attention and public discontent.

The small size of the Commission reflects the limited policies for which the EU is responsible and the way in which these policies are operated. Policy areas such as health, with large numbers of employees, remain within the competence of national governments who are also responsible for implementing many EU measures. For example, national officials carry out support buying, supervise storage and disposal of surpluses and monitor the payment of subsidies for the CAP. Contrary to public perception, administration has remained a small and stable proportion of total expenditure.

With the resignation of the Commission in 1999, many citizens have come to associate the EU with corruption. The problems of corruption in the EU arise because of three interrelated aspects of the EU and its administration. First, due to the multinational character of the Commission, different countries have different ideas about acceptable behaviour; for example, the employment of relatives and friends by government officials is normal in some countries, but viewed as corrupt in others. Once some Commissioners' cabinets became little more than personal fiefdoms and these practices attracted media attention, they could no longer be overlooked.

Second, the small size of the Commission has made it difficult to monitor expenditure and thus there have been difficulties with the employment of contract workers and with the supervision of EU programmes. Third, the primary responsibility for monitoring most programmes is by the member state in which the expenditure is undertaken. The Commission has an ambiguous managerial and supervisory role but, generally, no powers to carry out investigations on the ground.

EU expenditure overall

With most EU budget expenditure on CAP guarantee and Structural Operations, it is the distribution of these expenditures that determines EU expenditure per capita in the member states, as Table 6.3 shows. For example, in Ireland, Greece, Denmark and France, where agriculture is important, CAP guarantee expenditure per capita is well above the average. However, it is not only overall agricultural output that is important but also its composition. In the Netherlands, for example, agriculture is an important industry, but CAP guarantee expenditure is only average for the EU because Dutch agriculture specialises in areas which attract only limited support. As one would expect with Structural Operations, the poorest member states – Ireland, Portugal, Greece and Spain – receive high levels of expenditure. Structural expenditure, however, does not however fall smoothly as income increases. Although operational expenditure – that is, the sum of CAP guarantee and Structural Operations plus expenditure on other internal

Table 6.3   EU expenditure per capita 1996–7 (ECU per capita)

Country	CAP guarantee	Structural operations	Operational	Admin.	Total (Operational + Admin.)*	GNP per head, % EU average
Portugal	65.3	298.0	375.0	1.1	376.1	46.9
Greece	260.9	231.8	505.5	1.1	506.6	52.5
Spain	109.1	161.4	276.0	0.6	276.7	63.6
Ireland	507.4	329.4	861.0	3.3	864.3	76.5
Italy	80.4	51.6	140.3	1.5	141.8	91.8
UK	66.2	33.1	110.1	1.3	111.4	93.8
Finland	117.5	52.2	206.6	2.7	209.3	104.3
Netherlands	104.8	22.0	145.9	2.6	148.4	109.9
France	158.4	37.8	205.8	3.1	208.9	112.1
Belgium	103.9	39.1	192.0	207.8	399.8	115.1
Sweden	76.21	20.4	137.6	1.7	139.3	116.3
Austria	127.0	39.3	185.2	1.4	186.7	121.4
Germany	71.4	43.1	122.1	1.6	123.7	121.8
Denmark	243.5	25.9	293.6	6.0	299.6	138.1
Luxembourg	50.6	41.9	285.8	1894.9	2180.7	189.3
EU average	105.6	67.5	185.3	9.5	194.8	100.0

Note: * Figures in the total column have been rounded.
Source: European Commission (1998a) Annex 8, Tables 1a–1f.

policies – is highest in the four poorest member states, administrative expenditure is heavily concentrated in Belgium and Luxembourg. Whether the people in these countries benefit is another matter. The EU expenditure undoubtedly creates jobs, a considerable advantage to people in Belgium and Luxembourg, but this possibly comes at the expense of social harmony.

The overall outcome is that the poorest member states receive the highest level of operational expenditure per capita but the distribution of expenditure between other member states bears no relation to income, with the two richest states – Luxembourg and Denmark – receiving particularly high levels of expenditure, as Table 6.3 shows. In most countries, the levels of expenditure are comparatively low and thinly spread and, consequently, have little impact on public perceptions of the EU. In some countries, however, the benefits of EU expenditure do seem to become apparent to the people. Ireland and Luxembourg, for example, the countries where the EU expenditure per capita is highest, are also the countries where the proportion of the population believing that membership of the EU is a good thing is highest (European Commission, 1999c). Support for the EU is not just related to EU expenditure, however, because the Netherlands and Italy also have high levels of support despite their below-average level of EU expenditure.[4]

EU budget revenue

Requirements of 'good' tax structures

Tax systems should be fair, efficient and transparent. Fairness can only be evaluated on the basis of consistent principles to decide the tax liability. There are two dimensions to fairness, or equity – horizontal equity and vertical equity. Horizontal equity, identical treatment of people in equivalent positions, implies that those with the same level of income and similar circumstances should pay the same amount of tax. Vertical equity requires the consistent treatment of people in different positions. In general, fairness implies a direct taxation system that is progressive whilst indirect taxes are lower on essentials than on luxuries. In the case of the EU, these concepts of equity can be applied to member states or to the citizens of those member states.

Efficiency requires that the tax system should minimise harmful distortions in market behaviour and, where possible, correct these distortions. Low collection and compliance costs are important aspects of tax efficiency. Transparency requires that the tax system should be simple to understand so that taxpayers are aware of their tax liability and how this is determined. Since taxes are the price of public expenditure, the taxpayer should be aware of the amount paid so that a comparison can be made with services provided and, in this way, democratic account-ability can be established. So how do EU revenue sources measure up to these principles?

Sources of EU budget revenue

The EU is financed by four main sources of revenue:

- the Common Customs Tariff (CCT)
- levies on agricultural imports and sugar production
- Value Added Tax (VAT)
- the GNP-based fourth resource

The total revenue raised by these resources is set at a maximum of 1.27 per cent of EU GNP. The revenue collected from the CCT and taxes on agricultural imports by an individual member state is not nec-essarily a good measure of the cost of the tax to the citizens of that member state. This is because of what is known as the Rotterdam problem. Many German imports enter the EU initially through the port of Rotterdam. Thus, tariffs and other duties are collected in the Netherlands but the cost of these taxes is borne by German people. This problem will, however, diminish because traditional own resources (TOR) now account for less than 25 per cent of EU revenue and will represent an even lower share in the future.

Agricultural and sugar levies are withering away with reductions in agricultural imports and with the limits placed on agricultural

Table 6.4   Sources of EU revenue, 1996–7 average

	Percentage of total revenue	ECU million, 1997 prices
Agricultural levies	1.2	913.6
Sugar and isoglucose levies	1.7	1246.1
Customs duties	19.0	13 858.6
Cost of collecting own resources	–2.2	–1601.8
VAT resources	51.5	37 558.6
GNP resources	28.7	21 121.5
Total	100.0	73 096.6

Source: Court of Auditors (1998).

protection by the General Agreement on Tariffs and Trade (GATT) and its successor, the World Trade Organisation (WTO). Similarly, customs duties have become less important as tariffs are reduced with successive GATT/WTO rounds, as more countries join the EU and as free trade agreements are extended to even more countries. The decision to increase the share of traditional own resources (TOR) retained by national governments will further reduce their importance (European Council, 1999). The remaining two resources – VAT and GNP contributions – no longer bear any relationship to particular taxes and have simply become methods of calculating the national contributions. The VAT contribution was originally supposed to be an actual tax, calculated as up to 1 per cent of the harmonised base, but it was always based on an 'artificial' calculation (Begg and Grimwade, 1998). As a tax on consumption, VAT tends to bear most heavily on poorer countries. To address this issue, the VAT contribution has been capped for member states whose per capita GDP is less than 90 per cent of the average.

Furthermore, indirect taxes and the high CAP food prices penalise people with lower incomes. The GNP resource is simply based on a country's GNP and is worked out by reference to a formula. With diminishing revenue from other resources, the GNP resource will become more important in the future.

Care is needed in assessing the equity of these contributions. The TOR contributions are not affected by income, with the Dutch and Belgium contributions being particularly high. The VAT contribution shows a closer, but far from perfect, relationship between income levels and contributions.[5] The GNP resource alone does show a clear relationship between a country's contribution and its GNP per capita. As a result, the predominance of the VAT and GNP contributions within the budget produces an outcome in which contributions vary positively with GNP per head, as both Table 6.5 and Figure 6.2 indicate.

The financing of the EU is decided by deals between governments at the highest level. This intergovernmental structure is under continuous pressure both from the Commission and the proponents of a more federal institutional balance. For most people, however, the taxes to finance the EU are largely hidden in increased prices for imports whilst the VAT and GNP contributions are simply subventions from general taxation. Thus, in relation to the criteria for good taxes, the EU budget is reasonably efficient but it is not very equitable, nor is it transparent.

Table 6.5   Contributions to the EU budget, 1996–7 (ECU per capita)

Country	Traditional own resources	VAT resource	GNP resource	Total*	GNP per head, % EU average
Portugal	14.9	55.4	28.3	**98.6**	46.9
Greece	15.1	58.2	36.7	**110.0**	52.5
Spain	16.1	69.0	42.2	**127.3**	63.6
Ireland	59.8	85.2	44.7	**189.7**	76.5
Italy	19.1	78.2	58.2	**155.5**	91.8
UK	49.3	42.0	55.9	**147.2**	93.8
Finland	29.2	99.9	70.3	**199.4**	104.3
Netherlands	108.3	118.9	73.7	**300.9**	109.9
France	26.7	120.8	73.6	**221.1**	112.1
Belgium	101.1	103.2	79.9	**284.2**	115.1
Sweden	42.3	123.1	77.9	**243.3**	116.3
Austria	32.4	135.7	81.1	**249.2**	121.4
Germany	42.7	135.7	80.2	**258.6**	121.8
Denmark	53.1	131.7	90.6	**275.4**	138.1
Luxembourg	48.6	226.0	125.3	**399.9**	189.3
Average	37.5	95.6	64.8	**197.9**	100.0

Note: * Figures in the total column have been rounded.
Source: European Commission (1998a) Annex 8, own calculations.

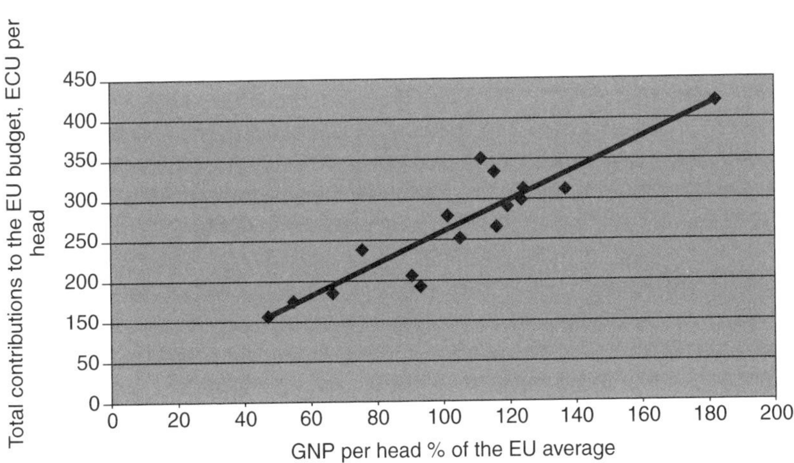

Figure 6.2   Contributions to EU and GNP per head
Source: European Commission (1998a) Annex 8, own calculations.

The overall impact of the EU budget

It is not easy to measure the overall impact of the EU budget on people. This is for the following reasons. First, should we assume that national governments would carry out policies similar to the CAP and structural policies even in the absence of EU membership? Or to put it another way, would the country's citizens choose to finance this expenditure in the absence of EU funding? The impact of the EU budget depends upon the answers to these contentious questions. Subtracting national contributions to the budget from EU expenditure in a member state will provide a measure of the net budgetary contributions of the citizens on a country-by-country basis.

The citizens in the states receiving cohesion funds are all substantial net beneficiaries of the budget although, within this group, there are substantial variations since Ireland and Greece receive exceptionally high net benefits, as Table 6.6 demonstrates. All the other member states, except for Denmark and Finland, are net contributors, although the level of contributions varies substantially. Belgium and Luxembourg's net contributions would be partially offset from the benefits from administrative expenditure. There is, however, a very

Table 6.6   Direct costs and benefits from the EU budget (ECU per capita)

Country	Net budgetary contribution (–)/Receipt (+)	Food cost (–)/ benefit (+)	Direct cost (–)/ benefit (+)	GNP per head, % EU average
Portugal	+276.4	–9.8	**+266.6**	46.9
Greece	+395.5	–11.3	**+384.2**	52.5
Spain	+148.6	–7.2	**+141.4**	63.6
Ireland	+671.2	+62.3	**+733.5**	76.5
Italy	–15.1	–5.4	**–20.5**	91.8
UK	–37.0	–5.2	**–42.2**	93.8
Finland	+7.3	+2.5	**+9.8**	104.3
Netherlands	–155.0	+15.7	**–139.3**	109.9
France	–15.3	+6.9	**–8.4**	112.1
Belgium	–92.2	+6.0	**–86.2**	115.1
Sweden	–105.7	+0.7	**–105.0**	116.3
Austria	–64.0	+1.7	**–62.3**	121.4
Germany	–136.5	+0.5	**–136.0**	121.8
Denmark	+18.1	+21.5	**+39.6**	138.1
Luxembourg	–114.1	+6.0	**–108.1**	189.3
Average	–12.6	0.0	**–12.6**	100.0

Source: Own calculations.

imperfect relationship between per capita net contributions and GNP per head.

Net contributions are, however, only part of the story. In the case of agriculture the CAP raises the internal EU price of food products so that countries which are net internal exporters benefit whilst the net internal importers lose. These costs and benefits were estimated for the commodities for which substantial price gaps were present – namely sugar, beef and dairy products. A crude measure of the food cost–benefit ratio was estimated on the basis of figures for internal trade in these products. These figures, which are presented in Table 6.6, are much lower than earlier estimates (Ardy, 1988) but, given the reform of the CAP and the high level of world prices at the end of the twentieth century, this may not be unreasonable. The cost–benefit for food is negligible for most countries, with the exception of Ireland, Denmark and the Netherlands, which derive significant additional benefits from the intra-EU trade.

In summary, there is a tendency for poorer countries to have net benefits and for richer countries to have net costs in the EU but, beyond this general conclusion, there is no very close relationship between the level of a member state's GNP per head and its direct benefits or costs from the EU. Since there is quite a close relationship between contributions and GNP per capita, the unevenly distributed benefits of EU expenditure are mainly responsible for the uneven impact of the budget.

Conclusion

On the criteria for evaluating tax and expenditure systems, the EU budget scores poorly. The level of direct benefits is only roughly related to the relative GNP of the citizens of the member states. The relationship between revenue and GNP per head is better, but still far from perfect. In defence of the budget, the Commission argues that non-budgetary benefits should be taken into account:

> Budgetary flows do not capture all the benefits from membership in the EU. EU membership, which gives rise to financial and non-financial advantages as well as obligations, has a non-budgetary dimension the importance of which dwarfs the budgetary one. For example, the benefits from the pursuit of common objectives, such as trade liberalisation and European economic integration, cannot be evaluated in terms of budgetary flows alone. (European Commission, 1998a, Annex 3)

Whilst this may be true, it is irrelevant to the fundamental requirement of any government budgetary arrangement – namely that it should be fair. With member states unwilling to increase the expenditure limits, the only way to achieve fair contributions is by basing them on national GNP per head. Since most of the budget is now spent on policies whose benefits can be directly traced to individual countries, fairness also extends to expenditure and to the net contributions of member states. If budget expenditure and revenue are not perceived to be fairly distributed among the member states, the budget will continue to be a matter of contention among national governments. With contributions and benefits largely consisting of additions to and subtractions from national budgets, an equitable distribution of expenditure and revenue among member states is also essential if the budget is to be fair to people within the EU. Although the reduction in VAT contributions and the increase in GNP contributions is a step in the right direction, the other changes introduced by the Berlin Agreement have merely increased the complexity and arbitrariness of budgetary arrangements, storing up problems for the future. The EU, however, seems unwilling to grasp this nettle and settle this issue of budget equity. Consequently, the people of Europe are, at present, poorly served by the EU budget. As the people become better informed and begin to understand the nature of the EU budget, there will surely be pressure for change.

Notes

1. Usually member states pay for 50 per cent of the cost of the project but funding can be higher, for example, for the Cohesion Fund and for particular programmes.
2. EU policy towards the former Yugoslavia is in a state of flux, Slovenia is negotiating for membership, Croatia could potentially join the accession process but at the moment is barred by its rather undemocratic political system, and policy towards other states is evolving as relations change after the Kosovo war.
3. Admittedly only 26 per cent selected this category compared with 31 per cent 'don't know'.
4. Indeed, despite strong public support for EU membership the Netherlands objected very strongly to the high level of its net contributions to the budget in the 1999 negotiations on budget reform.
5. The UK contribution is low because its rebate is given in the form of reduced VAT contributions.

References

Ardy, B. (1988) 'The National Incidence of the European Community Budget', *Journal of Common Market Studies*, vol. XXVI, no. 4 (June): pp. 403–29

Begg, I. and Grimwade, N. (1998) *Paying for Europe* (Sheffield Academic Press, Sheffield)

Birmingham City Council (1999) Number of Birmingham CC Employees – December 1998, http://birmingham.gov.uk/epislive/

Court of Auditors (1999) Annual Report concerning the financial year 1998, http://www.eca.eu.int

Court of Auditors (1998) 'Annual Report concerning the financial year 1997', *Official Journal of the EC C* 349 vol. 41

DETR (1999) Department of Transport, Environment and the Regions, Annual Report 1999, http://www.detr.gov.uk/annual99/

European Commission (1977) 'The Role of Public Finance in European Integration', Vol. I, *General Report*; Vol. II, Individual and Contributions Working Papers, Economic and Financial Series A13 and B13

European Commission (1993a) 'Stable Money – Sound Finances: Community Public Finance in the Perspective of EMU', *European Economy*, no. 53

European Commission (1993b) 'The Economics of Community Public Finance', *European Economy: Reports and Studies*, no. 5

European Commission (1998a) Financing the European Union: Commission Report of the Operation of the Own Resources System, DG XIX, http://www.europa.eu.int

European Commission (1999a) *The Community Budget: The Facts in Figures* (Luxembourg)

European Commission (1999b) *Eurobarometer*, 51

European Commission (2000) White Paper: Reforming the Commission, 1 March, http://www.europa.eu.int/comm/off/white/reform/index_en.htm

European Council (1999) Presidency Conclusion, Berlin European Council, 24 and 25 March, *Bulletin of the EU*, 3/99, http://europa.eu.int/abc/doc/off/bull/ en/9903/i1002.htm

European Union (1997) *Consolidated Treaties* (Luxembourg)

Grant, W. (1998) *The Common Agricultural Policy* (Macmillan – now Palgrave, London)

International Monetary Fund (1999) *Government Financial Statistics Yearbook* (IMF, Washington DC)

7
Protecting Consumers? Regulation of Financial Markets in Europe

Martin Sullivan

Introduction

The creation of a single market for retail financial services products in Europe was an important objective of the 1986 Single European Act. Given the range of activities involved and the differences that existed in national financial systems, this was always going to be a difficult objective to achieve. Although a considerable degree of integration had existed for some time in wholesale financial markets, the retail sector was characterised by segmentation along national lines, brought about by differing national histories, institutional structures and customs, and often by regulatory controls on cross-border activities. The result was that competition was restricted and consumer choice limited, with considerable national differentials prevailing in the prices charged for retail financial services such as motor insurance, home loans, consumer credit, foreign exchange drafts and many securities operations.

According to Cecchini (1988), the liberalisation and integration of Europe's financial services markets would increase competition and lead to a fall in price of retail financial products. The largest reductions would occur in Belgium, France, Italy and Spain. There would thus be a general boost to the whole economy arising from a more dynamic and efficient financial services sector. Although Cecchini's estimates can be criticised as overoptimistic (Llewelyn, 1992), it is generally agreed that real benefits would accrue to the peoples of Europe as a result of financial market liberalisation. However, their gains as customers might be partially offset by local job losses as indigenous firms lose out to foreign competition.

The provision of financial services had always been a highly regulated activity in the member countries of the European Union.

Although considerable variation existed in the precise nature and level of regulation, all member states imposed stringent controls on financial operations across their borders. These controls were invariably justified on the grounds of consumer protection and economic security. In a single market for retail financial services, however, banks, insurance companies and other financial institutions would be free to establish branches and provide services throughout the region, and consumers would be able to borrow, invest and obtain insurance or other financial products in any member state (Henderson, 1993). The Single Financial Market Programme required that all regulatory obstacles to the cross-border provision of financial services be removed. These regulatory barriers included exchange controls, restrictions on foreign participation in domestic stock markets, limits on foreign stakeholdings in domestic financial services companies and disparities between member countries in the licensing arrangements for particular financial activities.

Whilst Chapter 4 explored the opportunities for the whole business sector, this chapter will focus upon the impact of the creation of the Single Market on those firms providing financial services. A brief discussion of the role and operation of the financial sector will be followed by a review of the key theoretical issues relating to regulation. Europe's single licence approach to financial market liberalisation will then be explained. A critique of the single licence approach is provided in which it is suggested that, although a single product licence makes sense in a relatively fragmented market for financial services products and was crucial in getting the integration process under way, it is not sustainable in the long run. Drawing on some theoretical literature, it is shown that, in a highly integrated European market for financial products, the single licence approach could actually expose investors to increased risk of losses resulting from poor regulation. The chapter concludes with the suggestion that further regulatory reform in Europe is, therefore, both necessary and desirable, and considers the case for a single regulatory authority for the European financial services market.

The financial sector

Inevitably in a modern economy there are savers and spenders; those with a surplus to lend and those who wish to borrow. Much of the financial services sector occupies itself with matching up these two groups. Capitalism functions by transferring funds from savers to investors and mass consumption capitalism implies retail financial services, as well as institutions dealing with the corporate sector. So long as these retail services remain local, it is likely that interest rates and transaction costs will vary from place to place. A single market will change these parameters.

The term 'financial services' encompasses a wide variety of specialised activities. These can be broadly classified as banking, insurance, the provision of pensions, stockbroking, foreign exchange transactions, investment services and money market operations. Moreover, the distinction can be made between personal financial services, where those providing and acquiring funds are private individuals, and corporate financial services, where the providers and acquirers of funds are companies. A further distinction can be drawn between retail financial services, involving the sale and purchase of comparatively low-value products such as mortgages, motor insurance and overdrafts, and wholesale financial services, where very large sums, typically in excess of £500 000, are supplied and acquired. These distinctions should not be regarded too rigidly, however, as there is often considerable blurring of the boundaries between the various segments of the financial services sector. Thus, small amounts of money provided by thousands of individual savers, investors and pension fund contributors are collected in the personal-retail segments of the financial services sector and are aggregated into very large sums which are subsequently acquired by commercial companies or public sector organisations through the corporate-wholesale segments.

The principal actors in all segments of this sector are the financial intermediaries, who stand between those supplying and those acquiring funds. These include, for example, banks, insurance companies, building societies, investment management firms, stockbrokers, foreign exchange dealers, pension funds and venture capital firms. While some intermediaries, such as venture capital organisations, provide a very specialised service, others, such as the high street banks, offer their customers a diversified range of financial services. Financial intermediaries earn their income either from fees and commissions charged for the services they provide, or by paying lenders a rate of return which is lower than the rate they charge to borrowers. While some financial intermediaries are mutual organisations, existing for the benefit of their customers, others are companies, seeking to earn profits for their shareholders.

In order to channel funds from those with a surplus to those with a deficit, intermediaries engage in transactions in interconnected financial markets, such as stock markets, bond markets, markets for foreign exchange and wholesale money markets. In addition, contracts between lenders and borrowers can often be established directly in the financial markets, without the need to involve an intermediary. In this case, the markets themselves are performing the role of financial intermediation, as Panah discussed in Chapter 4.

The efficient operation of the financial sector is central to a capitalist economy. Mass consumption of durable goods and the expansion of consumer credit have become important elements in the 'people's capitalism' which is discussed by Bradley in Chapter 3. Financial services nowadays complement other industries. For example, the availability of mortgages affects house building and motor insurance influences car design and hence production. Thus anything that affects financial services can have important consequences for output and employment in other sectors.

Financial markets involve the risk of loss. When people deposit their savings with banks, purchase life assurance, or contribute to pension plans and mutual investment funds, they run the risk of losses arising from the actions of fraudulent, negligent or incompetent firms and industry professionals. Consequently, regulation to protect savers' and investors' funds is an important feature of the financial services sector. Indeed, it is widely believed that, in the absence of such regulation, many consumers would lack the confidence to participate in financial services markets. The scandal surrounding Robert Maxwell's diversion of £400 million from his company pension schemes illustrates the problems that can arise for consumers when regulation is either inadequate or non-existent.

As the following section shows, however, consumer protection is only one of a number of objectives pursued by financial services regulators. Moreover, as the subsequent discussion of Europe's single licence approach to regulation makes clear, the cost of achieving other regulatory objectives may be a significant weakening of consumer protection.

Regulating financial services

Whilst honesty and trust are basic requirements for system integrity, a well-designed regulatory structure is needed to reinforce the moral framework within which the financial system operates. The term 'regulation' refers to the making and enforcement of rules which influence behaviour. These rules can be either negative or positive. Negative regulation involves the prohibition of activities which are thought to be undesirable. A good example of this is the 1934 Glass–Steagall Act, which prohibits American commercial banks from undertaking investment banking activities. The aim of positive regulation, on the other hand, is to compel economic agents to undertake desirable activities. An example of this is the requirement, in the EU, for banks to insure their customers' deposits against bankruptcy. Although regulation is a feature of all business activities, financial services providers are regulated more heavily than most.

The rationale for regulation

The theoretical case for regulation takes a number of forms. First, consumers need to be protected from exploitation by monopolistic suppliers. Although financial services markets are more competitive than other sectors of the economy – being typically characterised by large numbers of firms – cartels and other forms of collusive behaviour can emerge, against the interests of consumers. Moreover, as Goodhart *et al.* (1998) point out, even where competition amongst firms is vigorous, many of the supporting systems and markets are effective monopolies. The payments and clearing system provides a good example: access is controlled, thereby generating monopoly rents. Where monopoly power can be abused, regulation can be justified in the interests of both consumer protection and allocative efficiency.

Regulation can also be justified where the relationship that exists between the buyers and sellers of financial services is one of unequal information. Whilst information asymmetries are unlikely to be a problem for purchasers of wholesale and corporate financial services products, this is not the case for retail consumers. In the UK, house buyers are confronted by a bewildering array of mortgage options about which they know very little. For example, the complexity of the products, and the high level of technical sophistication required to evaluate them properly, means that the suppliers of retail financial services are almost always better informed than their customers. Likewise, consumers will rarely be able to test for themselves the soundness of the firms from which they buy insurance, pensions and the like. Similarly, it is difficult to assess the competence of a particular firm's management. Furthermore, as Steil (1994) notes, many retail financial products, such as life insurance, endowment policies and personal pension plans, are actually trust goods, since the long-term nature of these products means that their true value to the consumer cannot accurately be determined in advance of purchase.

Asymmetric information means that consumers can suffer. Thus, as Howells and Bain (1998) observe, the principle of *caveat emptor* cannot easily be applied in retail financial services markets. Regulation is required to ensure that only honest, prudent and competent practitioners and firms are able to supply these products. Failure to provide adequate safeguards for consumers would discourage risk-averse individuals from participating in financial services markets. The performance of other sectors of the economy, such as manufacturing and non-financial services, would, in consequence, be undermined, since a major function of the financial sector is the provision of funds for investment in the non-financial economy.

These market failures in the financial sector may also justify regulation. Market failures may also occur when the prices charged by suppliers of financial products and the returns obtained by buyers do not reflect the true costs and benefits to each party. As Franks and Mayer (1990) show, if dishonesty is thought to be widespread amongst financial firms, and if consumers are unable to identify honest firms, depositors and investors may require excessively high returns even from these firms.

Regulation is also desirable where systemic risk is present. This is where, because of the phenomenon of contagion, the collapse of one financial institution is likely to bring about the collapse of other, similar institutions. Banks collect short-term deposits, withdrawable on demand, and convert them into longer-term loans, usually repayable over a number of years. Short-term deposits and-long term loans make these institutions particularly susceptible to systemic collapse. If the depositors of a particular bank believe, rightly or wrongly, that it is about to become insolvent, they will panic and rush en masse to withdraw their funds while there is still time. Since banks only hold a small fraction of their depositors' funds as cash, such a run would bring about the immediate bankruptcy of the institution. The failure of one bank is likely to arouse concern in depositors with other banks. Consequently other perfectly sound institutions can experience runs which cause them to fail too. Thus regulations setting out minimum solvency ratios and/or requiring banks to insure their depositors' funds can play an important role in maintaining the stability of the financial system.

In addition, a number of other regulatory objectives exist. These include competition, the direction of financial flows and macro-monetary control (Gowland, 1991). The regulatory regimes throughout the European Union largely reflect the difference in emphasis given to these objectives. In France, for example, where the direction of credit has long been an important feature of economic management, regulation has been used to ensure that certain industries which are thought to be of national importance are able to obtain funds at preferential rates of interest. In Germany, where the majority of financial services products have traditionally been supplied through a highly developed system of private banks, regulation has focused on ensuring the stability of the banking system. Competitiveness, both domestic and international, is the overriding objective of regulation in the UK, although credit ceilings and exchange controls have, in the past, been employed in the pursuit of macro-monetary objectives.

Methods of regulation

As Davis and Lewis (1992) observe, there are two approaches to regulation, focusing upon structure or upon conduct. Structural regulation, which, until the mid-1980s, was the preferred approach throughout Europe, involves the implementation of rules which limit market entry to a limited number of licensed individuals and firms. Licences are only granted to those who can persuade the authorities of their fitness to undertake specified activities such as accepting deposits, managing clients' funds and dispensing financial advice. The structural approach, therefore, seeks to achieve the regulator's objectives by screening out undercapitalised and poorly managed firms or excluding inadequately qualified individuals.

A weakness of structural regulation is that, once licensed, firms have little incentive to maintain high standards, especially where it is costly to do so. Although regulators can revoke miscreants' licences, the need to do so will only emerge after problems have arisen. Losses to consumers will already have occurred. Moreover, the limited number of licences available restricts competition, with a concomitant loss of efficiency and dynamism. It also permits a few privileged firms to earn monopoly profits. Indeed, the potential for licensing to undermine competition and permit some firms to earn monopoly profits lies at the core of the Posner–Stigler critique of regulation (see, for example, Stigler, 1971).

The regulation of conduct – also called prudential regulation – on the other hand, does not place limits on market entry. It should, therefore, facilitate competition and ought to be more effective at preventing financial crises and scandals. Prudential regulation simply requires firms to comply with rules of conduct specified by the regulators. These might include an obligation on deposit-taking institutions to insure their depositors' funds, the requirement for investment management firms to keep their clients' moneys separate from those of the firms themselves and statutory disclosure of commissions by those selling pensions and life insurance.

Structural and prudential regulation are not mutually exclusive, with regulatory regimes throughout Europe actually employing a combination of both types. However, the deregulation of Europe's national financial markets, which began in the second half of the 1980s, has placed greater emphasis on prudential regulation. Indeed, the terms 'deregulation' and 'liberalisation' are somewhat misleading since, as Davis (1995) points out, they really imply a shift in the locus of regulation from structural to prudential rules rather than a scrapping of regulations altogether.

The costs of regulation

When framing regulations, regulators face a trade-off between the benefits of regulation and its associated costs. Regulation gives rise to resource costs because regulators will absorb labour and capital which could be utilised elsewhere in the economy (Foley, 1991). The regulated firms will also incur compliance costs. These arise from the need to devote staff time, office space and other resources to the business of monitoring internal procedures, producing the required documentation and reporting to the regulator. In addition, regulation is likely to generate opportunity costs where, for example, capital requirements oblige firms to hold liquid funds that could otherwise be profitably employed elsewhere. These costs fall particularly heavily on smaller firms.

Regulation can also give rise to economic inefficiency and moral hazard. Inefficiencies can arise where, for example, quantitative restrictions on bank lending result in competition amongst borrowers for the available funds, pushing up interest rates. Moral hazard relates to the potential for regulation to cause consumers and suppliers of financial services to act recklessly because they know that any negative consequences arising from their actions will be borne partially or wholly by someone else. This is a well-recognised problem of deposit insurance schemes. Where depositors' funds are insured, they have no incentive to monitor the lending policies of banks. Likewise, managers may be tempted to take excessive risks with their customers' money. Moral hazard is widely believed to have played a significant role in the collapse of numerous US savings and loans institutions in the late 1980s (see, for example, Hall, 1991).

Creating a single market for financial services

In order to create a single market in retail financial services throughout the EU, action was required in two separate but related areas. First, there had to be complete deregulation of cross-border capital flows. Only then would consumers in any member state be able to make deposits or invest funds with financial firms elsewhere in the Union. The 1988 Capital Movements Directive (CMD), therefore, required member states to abolish all restrictions on the free movement of capital across their borders. While eight members were required to comply with the provisions of the directive by 1990, the Republic of Ireland and Spain were given until 1992. Greece and Portugal, on the other hand, were given the option of deferring full compliance until 1995. This was not the end of capital controls, however. The CMD permits the re-imposition of capital controls, in exceptional circumstances, for periods of up to six months. As Pelkmans (1997) shows, Spain re-introduced capital controls between 23 September and 5 October 1992, during the exchange rate crisis of that autumn.

The second area of action concerned the liberalisation of domestic financial services markets. Measures had to be implemented to remove the plethora of regulatory obstacles to the direct provision of retail financial products across national borders. The approach adopted involved the creation of a single licence, or passport, for financial products based on the principles of home-country authorisation and mutual recognition. These principles were first established in respect of banking services, with the adoption, in 1989, of the Second Banking Coordination Directive. They were subsequently extended to other financial services activities, such as equities dealing, insurance and investment services (see, for example, Henderson, 1993). The Second Banking Directive made it possible for banks authorised in their home-country – the country in which their head office is located – to establish branches and offer banking services in other member states of the Union, without the need for separate authorisation by the host-country regulator. All that was required of non-domestic banks was that they comply with the consumer protection rules applied to domestic banks in host countries.

The single licence approach simultaneously achieves the objective of liberalising cross-border trade in retail financial services, whilst preserving an independent role for national regulatory authorities. The mutual recognition element in the single licence, however, requires coordination of certain essential rules throughout the European Union.

Thus, the Solvency Ratios Directive laid down minimum capital-asset ratios for banking institutions in the Union, and the Capital Adequacy Directive specified minimum capital requirements for other types of financial firm. The regulatory authorities in host countries could therefore be confident that banks and other financial firms outside their jurisdiction were conforming to agreed prudential standards. The freedom of action enjoyed by national regulators was, as a result, constrained by the requirement to incorporate these minimum standards into their national regulatory regimes. This was, of course, consistent with the European preference for subsidiarity – the principle whereby whatever can be decided at a national or subsidiary level should be decided there, with supranational regulation being applied only where it is absolutely necessary.

Although the European Commission sought to impose harmonisation only in areas essential to the effective operation of an integrated market in retail financial services, there was an expectation that competitive pressures would, over time, result in closer coordination of national rules. Competitive pressures arise because the regulatory compliance costs borne by firms are positively correlated to the stringency of the regulatory regime under which they operate. Since firms would be free to establish their headquarters anywhere in the Union, banks and other financial institutions would have an incentive to migrate from regions where regulation is particularly stringent to other regions where it is relatively lax – a practice known as regulatory arbitrage. A process of competition in laxity, was, therefore, expected to bring about uniformity in regulatory rules throughout the EU, as the regulatory authorities in different regions and states sought either to attract new firms into their jurisdictions or to retain their existing firms.

A flawed approach

The single licence approach raises a number of important regulatory issues. The first of these arises from the definition of home and host countries. It only makes sense to treat the country in which a firm has its headquarters as its home country as long as cross-border trade in financial services is relatively underdeveloped. Under these circumstances, the majority of a firm's business will be transacted within its domestic economy. The regulatory authorities in individual member states will, therefore, have the greatest interest in the soundness of their home-based firms, since any losses arising from inadequate regulation will be largely confined to the domestic economy. Yet the purpose of financial liberalisation is to provide the opportunity for the growth of cross-border trade, such that the entire EU replaces the nation as the domestic market.

In a fully developed European market for retail financial services, cross-border trade will be the norm rather than the exception. As O'Brien (1992) shows, in this case some financial firms in small countries could transact the majority of their business in other larger countries. An Irish bank might, for example, attract a larger volume of funds from depositors in France or the UK than from residents of the Irish Republic. It would therefore be more appropriate to treat the larger country as the firm's home base, since, if the bank failed, that is where the losses would be concentrated. In fact, some firms in large countries might also be expected to have the majority of their customers outside the country in which their headquarters is located. The firm might, for example, have a small national market, with a large clientele dispersed widely throughout Europe, with no single country providing the majority of its business. This situation would most likely arise in the case of firms supplying a specialised, niche product. Since any losses sustained by these firms would be felt throughout the region, a home-country definition which relies on the location of a firm's head office, or the majority of its business, would be entirely meaningless.

Not only would the home–host distinction make no sense, in a fully integrated European financial services market it could actually result in greater risk for consumers because national regulators will have an incentive to engage in competition in laxity. This is particularly likely where regulatory capture is present and lower rather than higher standards are favoured. Regulatory capture occurs when the interests of regulators become closely aligned with those of the firms they regulate. In an integrated financial services market, national regulators would be aware that the bulk of any losses arising from low standards would fall on consumers elsewhere in Europe, while the cost savings would accrue to their domestic firms (McGowan and Seabright, 1995). Consequently, the temptation to stick to agreed minimum standards might be too much for regulators to resist, even though tighter controls would be desirable for consumers in other countries. Reluctance to go beyond the bare regulatory minimum would be strongest in those countries like Luxembourg and the UK where the financial services industry accounts for a significant proportion of domestic income and employment.

The single licence approach also has implications for the future stability of Europe's financial system. In the absence of large-scale cross-border trade in financial services, the consequences of a systemic collapse in any particular member state are likely to be confined to that country. It makes sense then for national authorities to be responsible for the solvency of their domestic firms and, hence, for the stability of their financial systems. On the other hand, in a fully developed European market, where cross-border trade is the norm and where there is widespread ownership of firms in one country by firms in other countries, the failure of one financial institution may infect similar institutions elsewhere in the EU. Yet national regulators will be reluctant to adopt high prudential standards or to act swiftly and decisively, since the costs of ensuring systemic stability will be borne locally, while the benefits will be diffused across the region. The inequitable distribution of the costs and benefits of regulation and enforcement is a particularly pervasive issue within the EU and has already made itself apparent within the farming and fishing sectors.

Finally, the division of responsibilities between home and host authorities makes it difficult to ensure equality of treatment for consumers. In general, home-country regulators are responsible for the solvency of firms and the stability of the financial system. The regulators in host countries, on the other hand, have responsibility for the conduct of business and consumer protection. Whilst minimum standards have been agreed with regard to investor protection (see, for example, Howells and Bain, 1998), individual states are free to offer levels of protection and compensation above the specified minimum. Thus, although the EU directive on deposit insurance set out minimum levels of protection for retail depositors, in the mid-1990s, the Italian deposit insurance scheme covered losses up to a maximum equal to approximately thirty times those covered by the equivalent UK scheme (Green, 1995).

A single European regulator?

The likelihood that the current single licence arrangements will prove inadequate, in a fully integrated European financial services market, suggests the need for further regulatory reform. If future crises are likely to arise, or be exacerbated, as a result of the existing home–host distinction and the division of responsibilities, a single, unified, regulatory authority for Europe might be preferable. Not only would a move to a single pan-European regulatory regime be problematic, because the single licence is now enshrined in EU law, it would only be worthwhile if it could be shown that centralisation of regulation would be superior to the current arrangements. This point is debatable because the centralisation of regulation could well result in the rules reflecting political interests and bargaining strength rather than the economic imperatives of the industry. Examples of this process in the context of the EU budget and the Common Agricultural Policy are discussed in Chapters 6 and 9.

Gatsios and Seabright (1989) suggest that when one member state is affected by the regulatory decisions taken by another, a cooperative approach to regulation will benefit all member states. Moreover, cooperative regulation does not imply a transfer of powers from nation states to a supranational regulatory authority. It simply involves the uniform application of a common set of rules throughout the region. In practice, however, because of problems of coordination and credibility, cooperation amongst Europe's different national regulators may be very difficult to achieve (McGowan and Seabright, 1995). For example, where there is more than one optimal set of regulations, each of which differs only in its distribution of costs and benefits among the participating countries, lengthy disputes will arise. Problems of credibility can arise because national authorities will have an incentive to breach any cooperative agreement, where doing so would result in competitive advantage for their local firms. Because of the problems of coordination and credibility then, centralisation may prove to be the best way to obtain the benefits of cooperative regulation.

Centralisation of European financial services regulation in a single, supranational, authority ought to lead to improved regulatory standards. This is because the minimum standards set under the existing arrangements are the outcome of a protracted process of negotiation and compromise. Considerable scope exists therefore for lobbying by producer groups and for misrepresentation of the costs of regulation by national governments, in order to benefit their domestic firms. Though a single regulatory authority would still be vulnerable to lobbying by producers, in setting standards, it would be free from the domestic political pressures faced by national regulators. The duty of the regulator would be to the Union rather than to any particular member state. The experience of the CAP, however, casts some doubt upon this aspiration, as Hatt discusses in Chapter 9. The single regulator would also need to set regulations which achieved its domestic objectives, but which did not simultaneously place European firms at a competitive disadvantage in global financial services markets.

A single European regulatory regime offers the opportunity to create better arrangements for monitoring and enforcement. Regulatory systems will be able to detect and rectify problems early enough to prevent them turning into full-blown crises where firms are stringently monitored and rules are enforced. Differences will arise in the extent to which national regulators monitor their firms and enforce compliance. The interval between problems arising and remedial action being taken would therefore depend on where such problems actually arose. A single regulatory regime, on the other hand, will imply a uniform approach to both monitoring and enforcement throughout the entire region.

A satisfactory regulatory regime would have to be designed to ensure equality of treatment for consumers regardless of their geographical location. The responsibility for failure would then lie unambiguously with the single regulatory authority. At the same time, a regulatory regime which embodied both prudential regulation and consumer protection might avoid inequalities of treatment. By unifying the functions divided between home and host countries, the single regime would minimise the differences that could arise in the event of a financial crisis leading to widespread losses throughout the EU.

The introduction of the euro, on 1 January 1999, as Europe's common currency further strengthens the case for centralised financial services regulation. In a multi-currency Europe, differences in national regulatory regimes were, in part, a reflection of differences in domestic monetary policy objectives. With a single monetary policy now in place throughout the common currency area, the case for local regulatory autonomy is substantially weakened. In addition, the trend, during the 1990s, towards economic policy convergence throughout the EU – characterised by wide-spread privatisation and a retreat from interventionism and a preference for resource allocation through competitive markets – has further weakened the case for regulatory sovereignty.

Conclusion

The adoption of the single licence approach to financial regulation, in the late 1980s, was the blueprint for the liberalisation and integration of Europe's national financial services markets. The single financial licence could, however, expose consumers to heightened risk and may even threaten the stability of Europe's financial system. As integration increases, a move to a cooperative approach to regulation, based upon common rules uniformly applied throughout the Union, would seem desirable. Yet such a move is likely to be problematic and difficult to achieve in practice. The centralisation of national powers in a single, pan-European, regulatory authority for financial services might, therefore, be preferable, but might be difficult to negotiate.

The transfer of regulatory powers from lower, national, authorities to a higher, supranational, authority would, as Green (1995) shows, be perfectly consistent with the principle of subsidiarity. Furthermore, centralisation of regulation need not extend to the whole financial services sector. The regulation of firms providing localised financial services such as credit unions, regional or national banks and insurers, could safely be left to national authorities. A pan-European regulator will only be preferable to local regulation where and when regulatory externalities expose consumers in one member state to losses arising from the failure of regulators in another, or where the stability of the entire financial system is threatened. As *The Economist* (1999) reports, the introduction of the euro is already accelerating the process of financial market integration set in motion by the adoption of the single financial licence. Thus the moment when centralisation becomes the most appropriate form of financial services regulation for the EU is likely to arrive sooner rather than later.

References

Cecchini, P. (1988) *The European Challenge 1992: The Benefits of a Single Market* (Gower, Aldershot)

Davis, E. P. (1995) *Debt, Financial Fragility and Systemic Risk* (Oxford University Press, Oxford)

Davis, K. T. and Lewis, M. K. (1992) 'Deregulation and Monetary Policy', in Dowd, K. and Lewis, M. *Current Issues in Financial and Monetary Economics* (Macmillan – now Palgrave, London)

Foley, B. (1991) *Capital Markets* (Macmillan – now Palgrave, London)

Franks, J. and Mayer, C. (1990) 'Capital Requirements and Investor Protection: An International Perspective' *National Westminster Bank Quarterly Review*, August, pp. 69–86

Gatsios, K. and Seabright, P. (1989) 'Regulation in the European Community', *Oxford Review of Economic Policy*, pp. 37–59.

Goodhart, C., Hartmann, P., Llewellyn, D., Rojas-Suarez, L. and Weisbrod, S. (1998) *Financial Regulation* (Routledge, London)

Gowland, D. (1991) *The Regulation of Financial Markets in the 1990s* (Edward Elgar, Aldershot)

Green, D. (1995) 'Banking Supervision in the New Europe', *European Business Journal*, pp. 26–33.

Hall, M. (1991) 'The Savings and Loans Debacle: A Regulatory Nightmare'. *National Westminster Bank Quarterly Review*, November, pp. 2–13

Henderson, R. (1993) *European Finance* (McGraw-Hill, Maidenhead)

Howells, P. and Bain, K. (1998) *The Economics of Money, Banking and Finance: A European Text* (Addison Wesley Longman, Harlow)

Llewellyn, D. (1992) 'Banking and Financial Services', in Swann, D. (ed.), *The Single European Market and Beyond* (Routledge, London)

McGowan, F. and Seabright, P. (1995) 'Regulation in the European Community and its Impact on the UK' in Bishop, M., Kay, J. and Mayer, C. (eds), *The Regulatory Challenge* (Oxford University Press, Oxford)

O'Brien, R. (1992) *Global Financial Integration: The End of Geography* (Royal Institute of International Affairs, London)

Pelkmans, J. (1997) *European Integration* (Addison Wesley Longman, Harlow)

Steil, B. (1994) *International Financial Market Regulation* (Wiley, Chichester)

Stigler, G. J. (1971) 'The Theory of Economic Regulation', Bell *Journal of Economics and Management Science*, Spring, pp. 3–21.

The Economist (1999) 'Much Indebted to EU: European Capital Markets', 18 September.

8
Moving People and Goods

Peter Cullen

The importance of free movement to the European Union

> The transport sector makes a vital contribution to the European
> Community's frontier-free single market. Without efficient trans-
> port networks, two of the European Community's basic principles –
> the free movement of goods and people – would not function.
> (European Commission, 1993)

As the quotation states, free movement of people and goods is a fundamental principle of economic integration and the establishment of a
common market; as such it appears in Article 3[c] of the Treaty of
Rome.[1] Further, Article 3[e] calls for 'the adoption of a common policy
in the sphere of transport'. This principle has been implicit in the discussion in many other chapters of this book.

Efficiency and reliability in all sectors of economic life are worthwhile objectives in themselves, leading, as economists never tire of
stating, to the desirable allocation of resources and the maximisation
of individual and aggregate utilities. Transport, however, is unusual in
that it impinges on all economic activities and plays a vital part in
determining the competitiveness of individual firms, regions and
economies. Generally speaking, the larger the geographical area and
the more diverse an economy, the greater the impact transport will
have on overall efficiency. To achieve economic efficiency, raw materials and labour must be mobile whilst products and consumers must be
able to reach markets.

Transport provision and economic development are closely related:
in the UK development of canal, and later rail, networks delivered the
factors of production for, and products of, the Industrial Revolution.

Advanced economies need comprehensive and efficient transport networks to produce and sustain growth. A single market as large and disparate as the European Union (EU) requires a comprehensive transport system and puts great demands on it. This chapter therefore considers the principles and policies necessary for a transport structure that will enable the free movement of people and goods. The economics of transport, its importance to the people of Europe, and the role of the European Union in formulating policy are all considered and the specific case of air transport is investigated in some detail.

Free movement – what it means

An important distinction must be made between the right to free movement and implementation of this principle in 'a space without internal frontiers'. In many parts of the world, the right to free movement can be, and is, achieved while maintaining immigration and customs controls. Documentation such as visas and import or export licences must be produced at borders but, as long as these are in order, transit is not denied. Control and monitoring coexist with rights of passage.

A 'space without internal frontiers' implies that border checks do not exist and that crossing borders is as simple as moving within them. Within the EU, each citizen possesses rights of entry to other member states for residence, economic purposes – work, cross-border consumption, tourism – or any other reason. Goods and services flow freely without additional bureaucracy or other costly measures. In effect, borders become nothing more than lines on a map; traditional customs and immigration posts simply do not exist.

Creating a structure that permitted free movement of goods, services and capital was the focus of the 1992 Single Market programme. The ability of goods to cross borders without hindrance was identified by the Cecchini Report as one of the major benefits to be derived from a single market since bureaucratic procedures such as VAT adjustments were causing major problems. In the vast majority of cases, goods and people have crossed borders unimpeded since 1 January 1993.

The free movement of people has proved far more contentious due to the attendant threats of security breaches and illegal immigration, issues which Korovilas explores in Chapter 11. The ability to control population movement and borders is one of the key factors defining the nation state and competencies over rights of entry and residence are traditionally one of the primary powers of government. The 1985

Schengen Agreement introduced the concept of free movement through the removal of immigration controls at internal borders.[2] The Agreement was regularised with the signing of the Treaty of Amsterdam in 1997 although certain states were allowed to derogate. As part of the *acquis communautaire,* new members will be expected to accept Schengen. Continuing concerns over illegal migration, cross-border criminal activities and the lack of common immigration and asylum rules mean that, in many cases, border controls have been replaced by spot checks away from borders. Weak points on the borders between member states and non-members[3] mean that the ideal of a common external border, but with complete freedom for all within it, is still some way off.[4]

Those states that have historically exercised strict control over borders appear most disinclined to give up this right. The UK and Republic of Ireland are both reluctant to adopt Schengen regulations, although, interestingly, one does not need a passport to travel between the two countries. States such as Germany, Greece and Finland, with long land borders which are difficult to monitor and control, generally require citizens to carry identification at all times and, for them, the removal of border controls is more acceptable. Island states, and other countries with relatively few points of entry and clearly defined borders, exhibit an insular psychology. In other parts of Europe, where borders have changed over time and where ethnicity does not conform to current political geography, the situation is different.

Providing for free movement: economic principles relating to transport

Establishing the right and ability to move is only part of the story. A properly functioning market of the EU's magnitude and complexity requires an effective, efficient and sustainable multimodal transport system if is to maximise competition and regional advantages. From the earliest days European integrationists recognised the importance of the transport sector, not just for itself, but also as a catalyst to the achievement of other fundamental objectives.

Transport is a crucial sector of any economy as it not only creates a valuable product itself, but the system's efficiency and reliability have ramifications for all other activities.[5] It is through transport that raw materials and goods are gathered together and distributed, labour markets function, and people can travel for business and leisure pur-

poses. The economic underdevelopment of some regions can be attributed to poor transport links with suppliers and markets. There are
numerous examples where a new road, railway or airport has stimulated a region's economy: for example, Lille has benefited from being
located on an *autoroute* junction and *Train à Grande Vitesse* (TGV) *Nord*
rail links that give access to the Channel Tunnel, Paris, Belgium and
beyond.

Transport sectors require two complementary components: infrastructure and service providers. Infrastructure includes termini for
starting and finishing journeys, such as railway stations and ports,
some form of route, such as roads and rail track, and flow management
systems – traffic signals or air traffic control. Service providers operate
the vehicles that use the infrastructure and these can be individuals,
private sector companies, or public sector operators.

In Western Europe, the provision of transport is a complex interaction between the public and private sectors. Infrastructure has usually
been provided by the state from public funds, either free at the point
of use or through cost-related charges to users. In the latter case, they
increasingly include a charge to cover marginal social cost. The shift to
neo-liberal economics and market solutions to resource management
problems has involved the private sector in the supply of infrastructure. Britain has led the way in this respect as in, for example, the privatisation of the British Airports Authority and the increasing use of
public–private partnerships (PPPs). Such initiatives are gaining the
approval of the Commission, with the qualification that 'the private
sector must take account of the "public good" aspect inherent in the
networks. At the same time, the public sector has to understand how
important it is proportionately to relinquish control of large infrastructure projects to the private sector. This requires a fundamental shift in
attitudes' (European Commission, 1999b).

Public sector service providers are common in the railway and local
road passenger transport sectors; they price for full cost recovery, or are
subsidised to a greater or lesser degree. Private operators dominate
road, inland waterway, sea transport and, to an increasing extent,
other modes of transport, such as air and rail. Where private operators
use public infrastructure, payment can be through direct charges,
specific taxes, or general taxation. Transport is a major revenue earner
for governments, with users normally subsidising other areas of public
expenditure. In most EU states hypothecation, that is, allocating
specific transport tax revenues to related infrastructure and service
expenditure, is a new and little-used procedure. However, it has the

attraction of allowing taxpayers to see their payments being used to their immediate benefit and may become more common.

Pricing transport services is problematic. The marginal cost is often extremely low compared to the average total cost including overheads. Carrying an extra passenger on a scheduled service costs very little but setting prices at marginal cost will involve an accounting loss for the enterprise. Efficiency maximisation or lowest average cost occurs when every seat is filled, but setting the price to achieve this may generate insufficient revenue to cover total costs. Thus many transport operators have developed complex price discrimination structures to minimise consumer surplus and maximise revenue. 'Business' users, or more accurately anyone who wishes to travel at peak time or to have the flexibility of travelling when they choose, can pay four or five times as much on the same train or aircraft as those who can specify services, meet certain criteria, book well in advance, or wait for a spare seat to be available.

Public transport services may have the additional complication that they are natural monopolies or oligopolies. There is simply not enough traffic to ensure real competition on low-density bus or rail routes. Operators and regulators must determine whether the social benefits of such a service deserve non-commercial pricing and/or public subsidy. Free marketeers criticise this practice as it removes efficiency and profit-maximising incentives. Two fundamental questions confront policy-makers:

- Where a route can sustain only one operator, should it be regulated private sector or cost-priced public sector? If a surplus is possible, should it be used to cross-subsidise other services?
- If there are gains to the network as a whole or if there are wider economic and social benefits, should a public subsidy be granted to a route which is not viable at market prices?

Transport policy-makers also have to contend with considerable externalities. Balancing the economic and social benefits of infrastructure investments against costs borne by travellers, non-travellers and society at large has resulted in complex modelling and costing techniques. The conundrum is that people want better transport at minimum personal cost and do not perceive themselves as part of the wider problem. The classic case is road congestion where 'all this traffic' imposes costs on users through delay and wasted time. Their vehicle, of course, is part of the problem and they are both victim and perpetrator of the congestion.

The traditional approach of transport planners has been reactive; that is, adjusting supply to demand through a 'predict and provide' policy (Potter, 1997). Experience suggests that the weakness of this approach is that predictions significantly underestimate future demand. One reason is that transport exemplifies Say's law – that supply creates its own demand. Building more transport facilities will therefore simply lead to greater use, constrained only by rising congestion costs. Various studies (Button, 1993) place income elasticities for transport services well over one. Empirical evidence suggests that as cheaper and more efficient transport becomes available, and national income rises, infrastructure struggles to cope with demand – for example, the M25 around London, various major airports and the 'old' Severn crossing near Bristol.

Ultimately, it is an interplay of economic, political, social and publicity factors that determines decisions on infrastructure. For example, UK authorities spent years debating the route of a high-speed rail link between London and the Channel Tunnel. Each proposal attracted delaying tactics from 'not in my backyard' pressure groups with considerable influence. Ironically, in France councillors lobbied the government to site a station in their towns and make them part of the TGV network. Bringing improved transport links to a region is a means of gaining political advantage – a point familiar to local, regional, national and European politicians. As in so many cases cited in this book, some people gain from these networks whilst others lose.

The transport sector comprises a highly complex network of routes and intermodal connections but any chain is only as strong as the weakest link. The provision of services may be adequate over 90 per cent of an area, but bottlenecks and pressure points can severely reduce the effectiveness of the whole network. In Europe, such problems arise at natural barriers, for example the Alps and Irish Sea, or because of an underprovision of infrastructure, as in the cases of the Paris *périphérique* and the road links between Western and Central Europe. Changing the mode of transport increases journey time and hence costs, so intermodal junctions, such as ferry terminals and airports, are also often weak points in the network.

Provision of transport has evolved into one of the most regulated and complex sectors of the West European economy. It involves government at all levels, private firms from the very small to global players, and individuals in all aspects of their lives. The ability to move goods and people around is one of the big political and economic issues confronting Europe in the early twenty-first century.

The European Union and transport policy

Unlike the infamous CAP discussed in Chapter 9, the Comman Transport Policy (CTP) has involved the development of a non-discriminatory environment and supranational regulation. Article 75 requires common policies for cross-border transport, but Articles 77–80 allow for national subsidies to internal transport services in order to aid regional development, or to meet public service needs.

As most transport services are national, regional or subregional, they display considerable diversity. As a result, countries can learn from each other's experiences. In keeping with the principle of subsidiarity, the Commission has little regulatory power over governments and local authorities that subsidise internal networks from local taxes. There are no implications for other member states or trade, except possibly to reduce costs marginally for indigenous producers. Where routes cross borders, or operators from different member states compete directly, however, common regulation is needed. By the late 1970s, the only real progress had been in developing common regulations for road-hauliers and limits on rail subsidies. Progress was so slow that in 1985 the European Court of Justice ruled that the Council of Ministers had failed to fulfil its requirements under the Treaty of Rome. This, plus the 1992 programme, speeded up the development of a CTP. Articles 129b–129d of the Treaty on European Union (1992) committed the EU to the development of trans-European networks (TENs) to ensure the effectiveness of economic integration. Subsequently, the CTP 'shifted its emphasis towards pro-active policies' (El-Agraa, 1998).

By 1978, the Commission recognised the need to coordinate infrastructure programmes in order to improve the efficiency of the Community's transport network and eliminate bottlenecks that inhibited the free movement of goods and people. Specific problem areas were identified and projects to improve matters were eligible for co-funding from the European Investment Bank (EIB) and European Regional Development Fund (ERDF). The accession of peripheral members Greece, Spain and Portugal in the 1980s gave a new dimension to the transport question. In 1986, the Medium Term Transport Infrastructure plan was adopted with EU involvement in four areas:

- Land–sea corridors
- Links to peripheral regions
- A high-speed rail network
- Reducing transit traffic costs

In 1990 the Council agreed an Action Plan that called for trans-European networks in telecommunications, energy and transport. The maximum Community involvement in financing was set at 25 per cent of project costs, and 50 per cent of a feasibility study. The advent of the Single Market made it 'more vital than ever to turn a patchwork of transport infrastructure into truly Trans-European Networks' (European Commission, 1999). Despite the increasing influence and importance of EU grants and loans in providing transport infrastructure, grants still account for less than 10 per cent of total budget disbursements.

In addition, TENs 'provide an extra dimension to the European single market' (European Commission, 1994b). The aim is to revitalise the community, decentralise economic activity and benefit small and medium-sized enterprises (SMEs). Enhancing cross-border and internal networks will permit firms and individuals access to the wider transport network. Links with other European Economic Area states, Central and Eastern European economies, and North Africa are also covered by the plan. TENs are perceived as an essential element in the cohesion process, encouraging the rejuvenation of disadvantaged regional economies by promoting growth, employment and competitiveness.

The Union's role is to act as a catalyst to the creation of networks through:

- Coordinating national plans
- Promoting cooperation between operators, users, researchers and industry
- Creating common standards to allow integration
- Developing policies to improve the internal market
- Encouraging private investors through advice, data and financial help

Upgrading and completing infrastructure for TENs is a very expensive business, estimated at 400–500 billion euros by 2010, and while most will come from public and private sources within member states, the Union believes that it should provide up to 20 billion euros per year from its budget and through European Investment Bank (EIB) loans. Examples of supported infrastructure projects include high-speed rail lines, such as Madrid to Perpignan and the Channel Tunnel links, road upgrading, for example, Nuremburg to Prague and Holyhead to Harwich, inland waterways, cross-community projects and the development of the 'Galileo' satellite global positioning system.

The Common Transport Policy is being redefined to recognise the social and environmental impacts of transport, as well as its economic importance (European Commission, 1999). Completing the Union-wide Trans-European Transport Network (TEN-T) remains central, but there is an explicit desire to make the system intermodal, efficient and sustainable. The issue of pricing is addressed through demands that fares are fair, transparent and reflect marginal social costs. The Commission has powers to regulate on behalf of consumers where market power is asymmetric and a system of benchmarking for urban public transport is to be introduced. Future and existing transport systems must take account of their environmental impact and meet the EU's responsibilities under global treaties on carbon dioxide emissions and aircraft noise. This, however, does not take account of hidden costs falling directly on people. Although improvements in transport are broadly beneficial, this is not always the case. The asylum-seeking illegal migrant makes use of improved transport networks but incurs tremendous risks. Cheap animal transport has brought down food prices but has also facilitated the spread of disease as the foot and mouth outbreak demonstrated in the spring of 2001.

The traditional concerns of safety and social protection for transport workers are also addressed. The EU has been active in this area for many years as is illustrated by the introduction of tachographs – the infamous 'spy in the cab'. National authorities, however, still differ considerably in their enforcement of national and EU regulations relating to heavy road vehicles and their drivers. Simultaneously, standards of safety and social protection are being eroded by the increasing level of privatisation and market forces in transport which put pressures on staff to perform. Workers are subject to unsocial working practices and obliged to maintain the schedule. The fear is that this may compromise safety. It is no coincidence that all developed countries regulate transport workers through licensing, setting maximum working hours and rest periods. Competition, a common regulatory policy and an enforcement framework are vital to a CTP. In many sectors throughout the EU, the fear is that the 'race to the bottom' will impose costs on people, as workers. This is all too apparent in the transport sector.

The European Union and the deregulation of air transport

Air transport is the most international mode within the EU. States, however, retain considerable jurisdiction over airspace, airports and air traffic control. In the postwar period, air transport developed a standard model of planned duopoly on most high-density European routes. Two airlines, generally state-owned, agreed to share capacity and set equivalent prices and standards. Low-density routes often had only one carrier.[6] For the consumer this restricted choice but there was the advantage that tickets were usually interchangeable between carriers. Any price dynamism within the scheduled market had to be agreed by all parties. A separate market existed for cheaper charter flights, usually operated by specialist airlines, but, in order to qualify, travellers had to meet strict conditions such as membership of a club, a long minimum stay, or buying accommodation with their flight ticket.

By the late 1970s, airline deregulation was under way in the United States, and the Commission published recommendations proposing a similar strategy, though not as radical or rapid (European Commission, 1979, 1984). The aim was to dismantle the plethora of bilateral agreements governing air transport and replace them with flexible common rules that encouraged dynamism and competition. Scheduled airlines and governments were generally opposed to these recommendations. The UK was the major exception because it had followed neo-liberal free market ideology, had deregulated internal air transport and privatised its major carrier, British Airways, by the mid-1980s.

In 1985, the Court ruled on the *Nouvelles Frontières* case, stating that air ticket prices could be discounted by travel agents. This precedent applied the competition articles of the Treaty of Rome to air transport, and the Commission consequently demanded that member states accept its reform package (McGowan and Seabright, 1989). The difficulty in deregulating air transport was the accumulation of comprehensive regulations, and its dependence on a number of complementary services in the control of national governments, notably airports and air traffic control. Consequently European reform and change has been a slow evolutionary process. In this respect it differs markedly from America's revolutionary 1979 Airline Deregulation Act (ADA). In America, airline deregulation was swift and radical, resulting in rapid, far-reaching transformation: many new low-cost airlines emerged. Some succeeded, for example Southwest Airlines, others failed, such as People Express. Some well-established major carriers, including Pan American, ceased trading, while others, for example Delta, restructured and undertook merger activity. The result was that, after ten years, concentration levels had actually increased. Whether the ADA brought long-term benefits to the US airline business or only delivered temporary instability is disputed, but it certainly changed the way that air transport is organised in America. Most consumers undoubtedly benefit from lower fares and/or more frequent services, but some marginal routes have lost carriers and traditionally powerful airline staff face changed – some would argue worse – working conditions.

The Commission believes that the phased approach of European deregulation had advantages over the 'big bang' of the USA as it avoided the boom–bust of the early 1980s American market. This is despite the fact that the slower pace of deregulation, and state ownership of many major carriers, allowed established airlines to rethink strategies, prepare for each tranche of reform and take defensive action through links with powerful allies. Research shows that fares have fallen on high-density routes, usually as a result of breaking up established duopolistic structures, though it is also recognised that standard and business class fares have remained disappointingly sticky (European Commission, 1996, 1999b).

Various actions were instigated in an attempt to create a more competitive environment. For example, in 1987 the merger between British Airways and British Caledonian was only approved subject to conditions, and SABENA was fined for denying other airlines access to its computer reservations system. In the ruling on the 1989 *Ahmed Saeed* case, the Court of Justice confirmed that competition rules applied to air transport and this encouraged smaller carriers to challenge the established airlines and regulators. Subsequent packages of reform[7] both deregulated the airline industry still further and transferred some regulatory controls from states to the Union.

The Commission has taken responsibility for determining whether airline alliances, mergers and takeovers are in the public interest. There is no clear stance, except that alliances both with other EU carriers and non-EU airlines, are usually allowed, the rationale being that if Union airlines are barred from the globalisation process, the long-term effects will be damaging to European industry and employment. Many complex relationships now exist such as the Star Alliance that includes Lufthansa, SAS, Thai International, VARIG, Air Canada, United and British Midland International at the last count.

The approach to takeovers has been flexible. They met mixed fortunes, sometimes disallowed (British Airways–SABENA), sometimes permitted with conditions (British Airways–British Caledonian), sometimes condoned (KLM–Martinair). Airline ownership in Europe ranges from state-owned (Olympic and Aer Lingus) through partial shareholdings (Air France, SABENA) to public companies (British Airways and Lufthansa).[8] Commission decisions often bring it into conflict with member state governments; the issue of subsidies has caused particular difficulties in a sector where private sector commercial companies compete directly with nationalised industries.[9]

Full deregulation in 1997 delivered open skies and European cabotage – the ability of any EU airline to transact business in any member state. New 'low cost' airlines emerged, breaking the price discrimination approach favoured by established carriers. Ryanair and easyJet entered the market early and posed a threat to incumbents, so much so that British Airways tried to buy out easyJet in its infancy. Whilst these enterprising carriers clearly bring consumer benefits – prices, for example, are often only 25 per cent of standard fares – they are accompanied by lower quality, though most prefer the term 'no frills'. They usually use smaller, less well-established, or remote, airports such as London Stansted or Berlin Schönefeld to reduce handling costs and avoid congestion at major airports. Food is an extra, rather than included in the price. Some of the low-cost carriers have failed, for example Debonair and Air Europe; some have been taken over by established carriers, for example, EuroBelgian became Virgin Express. So far low-cost airlines have constituted a dynamic force for change within the industry. The perceived threat is such that some established carriers have started their own low-cost subsidiaries, for example BA-Go, KLM-Buzz. People, as consumers, have benefited.

Air transport is more 'European' that at any time in the past. Deregulation has succeeded in bringing competition to much of the market, conferring considerable benefits on many consumers. Whether this is a permanent change in the environment, or whether business pressures will force an ever more concentrated European, or global, air transport market is disputed. If the former is the objective, then in order to maintain competition, future policy may have to be reregulatory rather than deregulatory.

The demand for transport

There is strong empirical evidence that the demand for all transport is income-elastic. This is especially true in the case of personal transport and longer distances which, in Europe, implies cross-border, leisure travel. Higher incomes and increased leisure time mean people want to travel more frequently, further, and with greater personal freedom. Car manufacturers and airlines have been the main beneficiaries of this trend, with roll-on roll-off ferries gaining to a lesser degree. On the

Table 8.1   Transport of goods by different modes, 1987–98 (billions of tonnes per km)

Goods transported by:	1987	1990	1992	1994	1996	1998
Road	784	931	1,027	1,095	1,148	1,255
Rail	208	215	219	218	220	240
Inland waterway	na	na	105	111	111	121

Note: The unification of Germany in 1991 accounts for some of the 1990–2 increase.
Source: European Commission, 1998 and 2001.

other hand public transport – rail and buses – have taken a declining share of the market.

Rising real incomes produce more demand for goods and services which in turn puts pressure on the distribution network. Fiercer competition between firms requires efficiency gains that are often achieved by centralising production and relying on better distribution. Just-in-time production and Internet shopping, which are referred to by Panah in Chapter 6, depend entirely on fast, efficient distribution networks. As economic activity becomes less localised, transport networks are required to work harder, as Table 8.1 demonstrates.

Across Europe the late 1980s was a period of rapid economic growth, followed, in the early 1990s, by one of the most severe postwar recessions. Despite the cyclical nature of activity, the overall upward trend is clear from Table 8.1. Roads in particular took the burden of a generally increased demand, recording a 60 per cent increase in tonne-km between 1987 and 1998.

Within member states the pressures of increased demand were even more apparent: for example, between 1987 and 1996, goods transported by road increased by 70.2 per cent in Belgium, 49.8 per cent in Spain, and around 40 per cent in the UK, France and Sweden. This issue confronts the whole Union, and affects all regions; infrastructure provision and quality must increase to cope with the demands placed upon it.

Rail is losing its share of freight traffic – down from 32 per cent in the early 1970s to 14 per cent by the mid-1990s. Some states, like Portugal, have seen increases in absolute terms whilst others, like Greece, have seen big declines. Everywhere in the EU, however, rail transport is losing out to road transport. Passenger transport has experienced similar trends.

Table 8.2 shows that the number of passenger kilometres travelled by road increased by 32.9 per cent and by rail by 20.6 per cent. It is noteworthy that during one decade, the motorways increased in mileage by

Table 8.2   EU15 passenger transport data, 1987–98 (billions of passenger km)

Transport by:	1987	1990	1992	1994	1996	1998
Road	2,840	3,166	3,455	3,534	3,673	3,776
Rail	240	257	275	269	280	290

Note: The unification of Germany in 1991 accounts for some of the 1990–2 increase.
Source: European Commission, 1998 and 2001.

nearly one-third while the length of rail track fell slightly. There is a clear correlation between GDP per capita and car ownership. In 1998, Luxembourg had 572 cars per 1000 population, Germany 508, France 456 down to Ireland 309 and Greece 254. Nonetheless there is evidence that countries with effective public transport alternatives can reduce car dependence. In the Netherlands where income per capita is high and public transport networks are good, car ownership is less than that in Spain – 376 per 1000 in the Netherlands and 408 in Spain – a country with a far lower GDP per head. With all applicant members having GDP per capita figures well below the EU15 average, increases in private car ownership are likely to bring serious implications for infrastructure and the environment. This is one of the less obvious issues the EU has to face as enlargement looms.

Governments in Europe have responded to these trends in different ways. There are differences in the level of taxes on fuel and in subsidies to public transport. Britain has the highest fuel taxes and the lowest subsidies whilst Luxembourg has one of the lowest fuel prices and generously subsidised public transport. Britain has also gone further than other European states in promoting the private ownership of public transport: bus services were deregulated and air transport privatised in the mid-1980s; rail transport followed in the 1990s. The British experience appears to be that without a regulated, integrated alternative, the private car has few substitutes on journeys of less than about 300 kilometres, particularly between points remote from public transport intersections such as bus and railway stations. The private car is quicker, more convenient and, once owned and considering marginal costs only, cheaper, particularly if two or more people are travelling. There is little evidence that demand has peaked even under present pricing regimes.

People and transport

People in Europe are certainly enthusiastic about freedom of movement. Eurobarometer in 1993 discovered that 70 per cent of polled citizens agreed with the proposition that Europe cannot be united unless free movement of people exists. The Luxembourgeois and the Dutch provided the largest affirmation, with the British, the Greeks and the Danish being relatively sceptical (European Commission, 1994a).

The importance of transport to the people of the European Union is indisputable. In addition to the economic benefits of free movement and enthusiasm for travel outlined above, six million people work in the transport sector, with a further eight million in equipment production and support industries. This represents 10 per cent of all employment. About 14 per cent of household income is spent on transport. It is anticipated that long-term demand growth of 2 per cent per annum will continue, with some sectors experiencing considerably more – for example, Since the 1980s, international traffic has risen by an average 2.4 per cent annually. People like to travel, and greater prosperity encourages them to do so. Consumption patterns in goods are putting heavier demands on transport networks.

The problem is that increased and more independent travel is resource-intensive, using private cars rather than public transport being the most obvious example. Freedom brings negative consequences – and not just to travellers. It is estimated that transport's external costs amount to 4 per cent of GDP – ironically almost exactly the same as the value added by the sector if expenditure on new vehicles and infrastructure is excluded. About 45 000 EU citizens die in transport-related accidents each year, and 1.7 million are injured sufficiently to require hospital treatment – over 97 per cent of casualties arise on the roads. Transport also accounts for about a quarter of carbon dioxide emissions, and almost two-thirds of nitrogen oxide emissions.

Conclusion

Free movement and the ability to move goods and people efficiently, safely and reliably are fundamental to the ambitions of the European Union. Like freedom of speech and democracy, they are principles with which it is hard to disagree. However, what the Single Market requires is not always what individuals, regions or states desire. Maximising the benefits while minimising the costs to those who bear the burden of increased freedom and greater mobility must be the prime function of Europe's transport policy.

There is no reason why a truly-frontier free European Union cannot exist. Indeed, in many respects, it already does. Without secure external borders, a unanimously agreed immigration policy, an enforceable asylum policy and greatly improved cross-border policing and intelligence-gathering, it is difficult to envisage a Union where all are free to travel unhindered without documentation. The discussion of the Schengen Agreement by Korovilas in Chapter 11 explores these issues in greater depth.

The Commission must create and enforce a Common Transport Policy within the constraints of other objectives, such as freedom of movement, global competitiveness, barrier-free trade and meeting environmental targets. Coordinating national policies and cross-border infrastructure development, encouraging competition and developing a level playing field for operators have been the main areas of progress to date. While genuine progress has been made, much remains to be done.

The problems are different throughout the EU. The overcrowded regions of central Western Europe face gridlock; peripheral regions of existing and new members are underdeveloped and need infrastructure to exploit their potential to the full. The objective is to provide people with the freedom and opportunity to travel widely throughout the Union and beyond. If this is to be achieved, then Europe-wide policies, regulation and enforcement regimes are essential. At the same time, subsidiarity must be respected. In this way, regions and local authorities will be able to explore solutions and to learn from each other. Good practice can be disseminated across the EU to the benefit of all.

Notes

1. Article 3[c] also includes the free movement of capital which is outside the scope of this chapter.
2. The Schengen Agreement was initially signed by France, Germany and the Benelux states, and had been adopted by all states except the Republic of Ireland and the United Kingdom at the time of writing. Iceland and Norway have agreed to the principles of the agreement too.
3. The Mediterranean coast of Spain and the border between Greece and its northern neighbours (see Chapter 11) are cited as particular problem areas.
4. In January 2000, Belgium and Luxembourg reintroduced passport controls temporarily (as allowed under the Schengen Agreement) because of concerns over the level of illegal immigration.
5. An Italian study discovered that 30 per cent of the final price of perishable goods and low technology manufactures (textiles) was attributable to logistics and distribution costs.

6. A study by R. Pryke (1991) found that of 750 intra-European air routes surveyed, 71 per cent had one carrier, and 24 per cent two. See D. Banister and K. Button *Transport in a Free Market*.
7. Three packages were introduced in 1987, 1991 and 1993, though the full raft of deregulation (including EU-wide cabotage) did not appear until 1997.
8. The examples are true in early 2000, though several states have full or partial privatisation plans in place.
9. Air France and Iberia were particularly closely scrutinised in the late 1990s, and subsidies allowed only under strict conditions.

References

Banister, D. and Button, K. (1991) *Transport in a Free Market* (Macmillan – now Palgrave, London)

Button, K. (1993) *Transport Economics* (Edward Elgar, London)

El-Agraa, A. M. (1998) *The European Union: History, Institutions, Economics and Policies* 5th edn (Prentice-Hall, London)

European Commission (1979) *Air Transport – A Community Approach*

European Commission (1979) *Bulletin of the European Communities*, Supplement 5/79

European Commission (1984) Civil Aviation Memorandum No. 2: *Progress Towards the Development of a Community Air Transport Policy*, COM(84)72

European Commission (1993) *Transport in the 1990s*

European Commission (1994a) *Freedom of Movement*

European Commission (1994b) *Trans-European Networks*

European Commission (1996) *Impact of the Third Package of Air Transport Liberalisation Measures*, COM(96)514

European Commission (1999a) *Eurostat Yearbook: A Statistical Eye on Europe, 1998/99* Edition 98/99 (Luxembourg)

European Commission (1999b) *Moving Forward: The Achievements of the Common Transport Policy*

European Commission (2001) *Eurostat Yearbook: The Statical Guide to Europe* (Luxembourg)

McGowan, F. and Seabright, P. (1989) 'Deregulating European Airlines', *Economic Policy*, November pp 283–344

Potter, S. (1997) *Vital Travel Statistics* (Landor, London)

9
Supporting Farmers or Consumers?

Sue Hatt

Introduction

Since the 1960s European agriculture has been shaped both by the common policy regime and by technological change. Improved farm machinery, chemical fertilisers, new breeds of animals and biotechnology have resulted in increased yields while the high prices have rewarded those producers who responded to these incentives. These developments have not always been popular with food consumers – nor have they been equally accessible to all those within the agricultural community. Indeed, technological change brings benefits to some but costs to others and the distribution of these gains and losses has been influenced by the policy regime and its interaction with new technologies.

This chapter will trace the interaction between policy and technology in the agricultural sector of the EU and will consider the consequences of this interaction for food producers, consumers and taxpayers. The Common Agricultural Policy (CAP) has, essentially, been a price support mechanism, designed to transfer resources from food consumers and taxpayers to food producers. The impact of the CAP upon these groups of people has depended upon the particular instruments which have been put in place and upon the efficiency with which these measures have operated. This chapter will, first, consider the reasons why the European Community (EC) decided to establish a common policy for the agricultural sector; it will then discuss the policy regime, considering the interaction between the CAP and technological change. Finally, the consequences of the CAP and the distribution of benefits between food consumers, producers and taxpayers will be discussed.

The rationale for the CAP

From the initial discussions leading to the formation of the European Economic Community (EEC) in 1958, the member states wanted to establish a *common* policy for the agricultural sector. The development of at least one common policy regime was a political objective, offering member states a collaborative project to build cohesion within the community. The agricultural sector seemed appropriate for the development of a common policy in that all the initial signatories to the Treaty of Rome had already established national agricultural policies to deal with the economic issues concerning food production and consumption in an advanced industrial economy. In markets for agricultural commodities, supply fluctuates considerably from year to year, depending on the harvest, whilst demand remains constant and is inelastic with respect to price. Market prices for agricultural commodities are thus very unstable. Furthermore, the vulnerability of depending on imported foodstuffs had been highlighted during the Second World War. All six member states perceived the need to provide support for farmers' incomes in this vital, yet declining, industry and these common objectives could, it was argued, be addressed through a community-wide policy. While the issues it was designed to address were primarily economic, the CAP was to provide the 'political glue' to fix the six sovereign nation states together into one community. From its inception therefore, the CAP had both an economic and a political rationale and this dual focus has accounted, in part, for the problems it has encountered.

In 1958, the agricultural sector in the Six was of considerable economic significance. It accounted for the employment of 16 million people, representing 20 per cent of total civilian employment (OECD, 1987). The Treaty of Rome therefore made explicit reference to the development of an agricultural policy, the objectives of which were detailed in Article 39 of the Treaty of Rome (see Box 9.1).

Once the Treaty of Rome was signed, the challenge was to establish a policy regime, acceptable to all member states, without wasting scarce resources in the process. The objectives in Article 39, however, reflected the underlying tension between producers' and consumers' interests. Whilst the second objective states a commitment to maintaining a 'fair standard of living for the agricultural community', the fifth refers to 'reasonable prices' for consumers. Until 1992, farmers' incomes were supported mainly by the prices paid for agricultural commodities and keeping these prices high had inevitable consequences for food con-

---

Box 9.1   Article 39 of the Treaty of Rome

The Common Agricultural Policy shall have as its objectives:

(i)   to increase agricultural productivity by promoting technical progress and by ensuring the rational development of agricultural production and the optimum utilisation of the factors of production, in particular, labour;

(ii) thus to ensure a fair standard of living for the agricultural community, in particular by increasing the individual earnings of persons engaged in agriculture;

(iii) to stabilise markets;

(iv) to assure the availability of supplies;

(v)   to ensure that supplies reach consumers at reasonable prices.

---

sumers. Some people gained whilst others lost from the policy regime which resulted from the political negotiations. The next section will analyse the original price mechanism.

The CAP regime

The CAP operated through a series of administered prices for basic agricultural commodities, such as milk and cereals. These prices – the threshold price and the intervention price – have been set annually through negotiations between the agricultural ministers of the member states. The political procedures established at the Community level led to protracted negotiations and the outcome has often reflected the political 'weight' of participants rather than the market logic. Agricultural exporting countries within the Community, such as France, the Netherlands, Denmark and Ireland, wanted high prices since these would benefit their farmers whilst the common financing of the CAP meant that the bill was paid, not by their own taxpayers, but from the EU budget. Consequently, prices have usually been set at high levels relative to both previous price levels in member states and world market prices. The strength of farmers' interest groups relative to those of consumers and taxpayers has made it extremely difficult to secure fundamental reform. Consequently, these high prices have stimulated production but deterred consumption, resulting in market imbalance.

Within EU markets, this pricing mechanism has enabled European producers to undercut world producers whose produce can only enter the EU market at the threshold price (see Figure 9.1). EU farmers have thus enjoyed protection from external competition through the variable import levy, bringing the price of imported foodstuffs up to the threshold price which has been slightly above the intervention price. The variable import levy fluctuated to reflect the difference between world prices and the EU threshold price. This ensured that EU produce was always available on preferential terms and there was no way in which low-cost world producers could gain a price advantage in the EU market. This situation persisted until the mid-1990s when tariffs replaced the variable import levy so that costs and prices in other parts of the world were reflected in the price at which imported commodities were available in the EU.

Through the CAP, EU farmers have benefited from being able to sell all they can produce at a minimum intervention price. This has provided a guaranteed 'fall-back' position and, with the threshold price acting as a ceiling and the intervention price as a floor, farmers have enjoyed a relatively stable market, offering high prices and enabling them to earn incomes in excess of those which they would have achieved in a free market.

Stimulated by the price incentives, farmers have increased production, ensuring for consumers the security of basic food supplies. However, for consumers, the CAP has imposed penalties as well. Denied access to low-cost imported supplies, they had no option but to purchase food at prices considerably above world market levels. One estimate suggests that in 1996–7 EU consumers were paying 168 ECU per head in higher food prices (Ardy, 1999). These high prices for food

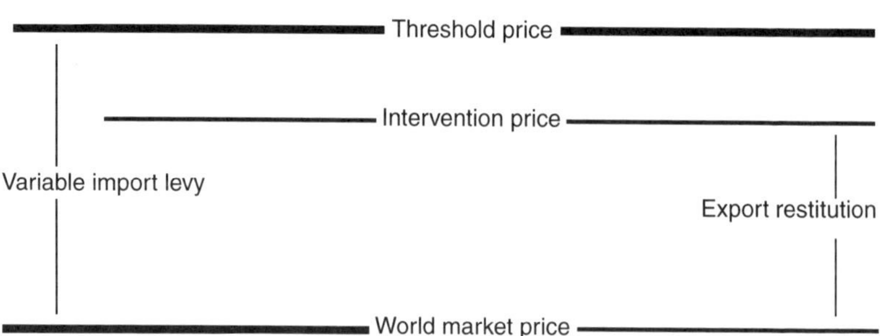

Figure 9.1   The CAP price mechanism

have represented a hidden cost to consumers, lacking the transparency of direct subsidies and distorting consumer demand. Since high prices have encouraged farmers to produce more than they would have done at the market equilibrium price and more than consumers have been willing to consume, the CAP has led to the production of a surplus which has been purchased into 'intervention' by the authorities, resulting in the infamous 'butter mountains' and 'wine lakes'. The cost of intervention buying has been borne by EU taxpayers and has been quite substantial, amounting in 1996–7 to 100 ECU per head (Ardy, 1999). Since many people are both food consumers and taxpayers, they have supported farmers' incomes twice over: first, as consumers, through the increased price paid for agricultural commodities and, second, as taxpayers, through contributions to the EU budget which have been used to purchase and store the surplus produce, to destroy perishable commodities and to subsidise exports to enable them to compete on world markets.

The people and the CAP: France and Italy compared

When the CAP was initially established, France was expected to benefit most from the policy. With over 22 per cent of its workforce employed in agriculture which accounted for 10 per cent of GDP, the French economy was heavily involved in maintaining the strength of its agricultural sector. Accounting for 40 per cent of EC food production in the 1960s (Fearne, 1997), French farmers produced a considerable surplus of grain which, under the CAP, could be exported on preferential terms to the other member states. French farmers stood to gain substantial benefits from this common policy and from the rise in prices which it entailed. Between 1960 and 1966, French agricultural exports increased in value more than threefold (Fearne, 1997) and the modernisation of agricultural production released labour to other sectors of the economy, contributing to a rapid rate of economic growth and raising living standards for all French citizens. People in France certainly received benefits from the CAP, whether or not they were engaged in farming.

Prior to the CAP, France, with a relatively efficient agricultural sector, had lower agricultural prices than the other member states and, ironically, the French government, fearing adverse inflationary effects, resisted high prices. Germany, however, negotiated for high agricultural prices to cover the high costs of their smaller farms in Bavaria and

Table 9.1   France and Italy compared

	France	Italy
Number employed in agriculture (000s) (1958)	4453	6974
Percentage of civilian employment in agriculture (1960)	22.4	32.8
Value added by agriculture as % of GDP (1960)	10.6	12.2

Source: OECD (1987) *Historical Statistics 1960–1985*.

southern Germany. Their success in the political bargaining meant that French farmers, as large producers, received substantial benefits.

Like France, Italy was heavily dependent on farming. As Table 9.1 shows, one worker in every three was employed in its agricultural sector which accounted for a larger percentage of GDP than in France. Italy was also a substantial agricultural producer accounting for 26 per cent of EC food production.

Italy, however, produced very different commodities from France, being self-sufficient in wine, olives, fruit and vegetables but importing cereals and dairy produce. The Italian government wanted a low price for cereals and dairy produce but substantial support for fruit and vegetables. Adopting this contradictory position, the Italian government was unable to secure a favourable outcome from the negotiations and the high prices established for cereals and dairy products were disadvantageous for Italian consumers and taxpayers. Not only did the price of food rise, for Italian citizens the CAP regime had other implications as well. The high prices of cereals and dairy products increased the costs of imports, adding to their weak balance of payments position and restricting the rise in real living standards. At the same time, contributions to the EC budget, based as they were on imports, imposed considerable costs on Italian taxpayers. Italian farmers, meanwhile, gained very little from the CAP as the support for fruit, vegetables and olives was limited. Consequently, Italy, with a lower gross domestic product per capita than France, became a net contributor to the CAP. Ironically, Italian consumers and Italian taxpayers were thus transferring resources to French farmers and citizens and contributing to the rise in French living standards.

The CAP and technology

Since the CAP was established, technological developments have affected agricultural production in many ways. Selective breeding has

Table 9.2   Annual yields, 1978–97

Annual yield	1978 (EU9)	1997 (EU15)
Milk (kg per cow)	4002	5387
Common wheat (100 kg per hectare)	47.4	66.9
Maize (100 kg per hectare)	57.3	84.5

Source: European Commission (1980, 1999).

raised milk yields, new plant strains have increased cereal output, improved herbicides and insecticides have reduced the incidence of pests and disease whilst mechanisation has reduced unit costs. As Table 9.2 shows, cereal and milk yields in the EU have increased considerably since the 1970s.

Whilst global forces and the power of multinational corporations influenced the direction of research and development, the take-up of new technology has been shaped by the policy regime. Unlike the free market where an increase in supply would benefit consumers through a fall in price, the guaranteed CAP prices have meant that producers have faced no penalties for increasing production. The intervention price has been the minimum price for their produce. Increasing output led to higher revenue, often accompanied by lower unit costs. Not surprisingly, by the early 1980s, the European Community was producing more of its major crops than it was consuming.

Under this policy regime, the gains from innovation went overwhelmingly to food producers – and especially to the large farmers who could afford to innovate. In 1991, the European Commission estimated that only 20 per cent of EU farmers received 80 per cent of the payments from *Fonds Européen d'Orientation et de Garantie Agricole* (FEOGA) (European Commission, 1991). Thus, with only a small proportion of FEOGA expenditure directed towards small farmers struggling to survive in adverse conditions, the policy exaggerated, rather than reduced, the inequalities within the agricultural sector. In a market where supply exceeded demand, increasing yields were problematic and, with growing concerns about food safety, consumers have questioned the value of technological innovation.

The MacSharry reforms

Almost as soon as it was established, the CAP was problematic. It was expensive, bureaucratic and difficult to reform. By the late 1980s, it had become a very contentious issue both within the Community and between the EC and its trading partners. As Ardy has shown in Chapter

6, intervention buying was absorbing a large proportion of the Community's budget, leaving little scope for new initiatives. Export restitutions alone were expensive to EU taxpayers and were a source of grievance to other agricultural exporting nations who perceived this practice as amounting to 'unfair trading'. The antagonism of the USA to the European agricultural regime was supported by the members of the Cairns group, delaying the successful conclusion of the Uruguay Round from 1990 until 1994.

This combination of domestic and international pressure resulted, eventually, in a reform package introduced by the Commissioner for Agriculture, Ray MacSharry, and agreed in the Council of Ministers in 1992. The MacSharry reforms included three significant measures: a substantial reduction in price for cereals, milk and beef, a 'compulsory' set-aside scheme for all but the smallest farmers and the introduction of acreage payments to compensate for the lower prices. The original proposal put before the Council was that the compensation payments should be 'modulated' so that they were only available to farms below 50 hectares, leaving the larger farmers, the main beneficiaries of the technological developments and the intervention buying, to fend for themselves in the free market. Strong objection to modulation came from the British government since farms in the UK are larger than those elsewhere in Europe. When the recently reunified Germany supported this objection, the compensation was extended to farms of all sizes and, as a result, the reform CAP cost the EU taxpayer more that the pre-1992 CAP. Not for the first time – nor the last – political bargaining frustrated a 'rational' economic outcome.

Despite these modifications, MacSharry's reforms brought significant changes to the CAP. Substantial price cuts of 29 per cent for cereals, 10 per cent for milk and 8 per cent for beef were agreed. These price reductions were more far-reaching than any previous reform measures and might indicate a belated political willingness to reorientate the EU agriculture towards a market-based regime. The reforms introduced as part of Agenda 2000 have continued to reduce prices.

The people and the CAP

Food for people

From the outset, the CAP had two objectives so far as consumers were concerned; firstly, 'to assure the availability of supplies' and, second, 'to ensure that supplies reached consumers at reasonable prices'. With respect to the first, the CAP has encouraged farmers to increase

Table 9.3   Self-sufficiency ratios, 1995

Crop	Self-sufficiency ratio
Wheat	116
Total cereals	108
Sugar	114
Oilseeds	101
Eggs	102

Source: European Commission (1998).

output and, in 1995, the EU was producing more than sufficient of the major foodstuffs to meet consumers' demand, as Table 9.3 shows. Supplies have been assured and this particular goal has been attained, although the extent to which the policy regime, rather than technology, was responsible for this achievement has remained an open question.

The increased availability of food supplies to consumers has come at a cost, however, in that the prices of agricultural produce within the EC have remained considerably above world market levels. In 1993, it was estimated that butter was costing 62 pence per 250 gram pack in the UK as opposed to only 22 pence on international markets, and similar price differentials were observed for beef, cheese and sugar (Consumers in Europe Group, 1994). It would, however, be simplistic to conclude that the difference between these two price levels represented the cost of the CAP to consumers since the export of the surplus produce has added to supplies on world markets, depressing the price and widening the gap between CAP and EU price levels. Although the reforms to the CAP in the 1990s have reduced the gap between EU and world prices, the costs to consumers remain considerable and depend upon the staple diet within the different EU countries. In 1996–7 these costs were estimated to vary between 131 ECU per head in Greece and 256 ECU per head in Finland (Ardy, 1999).

In most developed countries of the world, however, the agricultural sector has been the recipient of some government support and it would be reasonable to conclude that this would probably have been the case in Western Europe, even had the CAP never been established. Many, though not all, of these alternative policy instruments raise the price of agricultural commodities to the consumer and so, within this context, the cost of the CAP becomes the difference between the CAP price and the alternative which might have prevailed under a different policy regime.

Table 9.4   Food expenditure as a percentage of total expenditure, 1995

EU15	17.5
Germany	14.2
Netherlands	14.1
UK	19.9
Portugal	28.0
Ireland	30.7

Source: European Commission (1999).

Since, in most countries, food expenditure accounted for only a small per centage of total household expenditure in 1995, higher prices might not have placed an unreasonable burden on consumers. Table 9.4 shows the percentage of total household expenditure which was spent on food in 1995.

In the EU15 less than 20 per cent of total expenditure was on food with the proportion falling as low as 14 per cent in the Netherlands. However, since everyone must eat, the demand for food is inelastic with respect to income and so household expenditure on food does not vary proportionately with incomes, leaving poorer consumers spending a large proportion of their incomes on food. Even in countries with high average incomes per head, the low-income groups suffer disproportionately whilst, in Greece and Ireland, countries with relatively low GDP per head, over one-third of consumer expenditure has gone on food. The price increases caused by the CAP have not been equitably distributed between rich and poor; 'reasonable prices' for well-off consumers in the high-income countries of northern Europe have seemed far less reasonable in the context of lower incomes in the Mediterranean countries. Indeed, the burden of the CAP has been regressive with respect to income and the CAP has placed a disproportionate burden on low-income consumers.

Whilst technology has reduced costs, increased output and raised farmers' incomes, the policy regime has prevented these gains from translating into lower food prices. Consumers have become increasingly concerned about the safety and quality of food produced by hi-tech means. Intensive production of poultry and pork has led to the routine use of antibiotics as growth promoters to hasten the animals towards maturity. Although these drugs have been in use since the early 1950s, their use has increased substantially and this had contributed to concerns about the emergence of antibiotic-resistant strains of 'superbug' which could pose a threat to human health. The Consumer Committee of the EC has expressed doubts about the safety

of the routine use of antibiotics as growth promoters and has supported those governments, such as Sweden, which have already banned the use of antibiotics in feedstuffs. Initiatives on food safety still tend to originate with the nation state rather than the EU.

The introduction of genetically modified organisms (GMOs) has also given consumers cause for concern. In 1998, the possibility that GMOs might damage the human immune system was voiced and, by 1999, 20 per cent of consumers reported that they would never knowingly eat, or feed their family, GM foods (Gregoriadis, 1999). Yet, with GMOs used in the manufacture of a wide variety of food products, including soft drinks, rennet, soy sauce, ketchup and mayonnaise, avoidance might be difficult for all but the very well-informed consumer. Although, as individuals, consumers cannot prevent the introduction of GMOs, collectively it is a different matter. Consumer pressure in the UK has resulted in several big supermarket giants banning the use of GMOs in their own-brand products (Finch, 1999). This pressure has been felt by farmers as well as food retailers. Those participating in GMO field trials have also faced direct action from environmental pressure groups seeking to destroy crops. These groups have been concerned about the risks of cross-pollination and the contamination of neighbouring plant species. These risks would seem to be greater within the EU, with its mixed agricultural system, compared to the persistent monoculture of the grain and soya belts in the Mid West of the United States of America.

The bovine spongiform encephalopathy (BSE) scare in the UK has provided another example of consumer anxieties about food safety. Fears that new variant Creutzfeldt–Jakob Disease (CJD) can enter the human food chain from cattle infected with BSE have exemplified the risks to consumers. Rewarding production, subject only to a minimum quality threshold, has meant that safety, health, flavour and variety – all significant from the consumer's perspective – have been easy casualties. In a competitive market regime producers would have some incentive to be responsive to consumers' demands.

On the other hand, it can be argued that the CAP has promoted healthy eating through its pricing structure – albeit unintentionally (Ritson, 1997). The consumption of foods such as beef and dairy products, deemed 'unhealthy' due to their high fat content, has been discouraged by high prices. Fruit, vegetables and olive oil, on the other hand, have attracted lower support prices, encouraging consumption of these relatively 'healthy' products. This outcome, however, was accidental rather than intentional on the part of the policy-makers. The price structure was the result of political negotiations and reflected the relative bargaining strengths of the countries producing these commodities (Ritson, 1997). The strong position of the countries of northwest Europe accounted for the high prices for dairy products while the relatively weak position of the Mediterranean states led to low prices for olives, fruit and vegetables. Producer rather than consumer interests dominated the pricing structure. The CAP has been an *agricultural* policy, not a food policy, and, perhaps for this reason, consumers have lost out.

Taxes: A fair way to pay?

Taxpayers, like consumers, have borne the costs of the CAP amounting, in 1995, to 94 ECU per head (European Commission, 1998). Whilst this represents less than 0.5 per cent of GDP (European Commission, 1998) and might, at first, seem almost insignificant, in total these sums represented a considerable transfer of resources from taxpayers to food producers. The overall cost to the EU budget amounted to 45 billion ECU in 1998 (European Commission, 1998). The efficiency with which the CAP effected this transfer will be considered in this section. The CAP regime has resulted in high price levels and market imbalance, with taxpayers funding the bill for buying

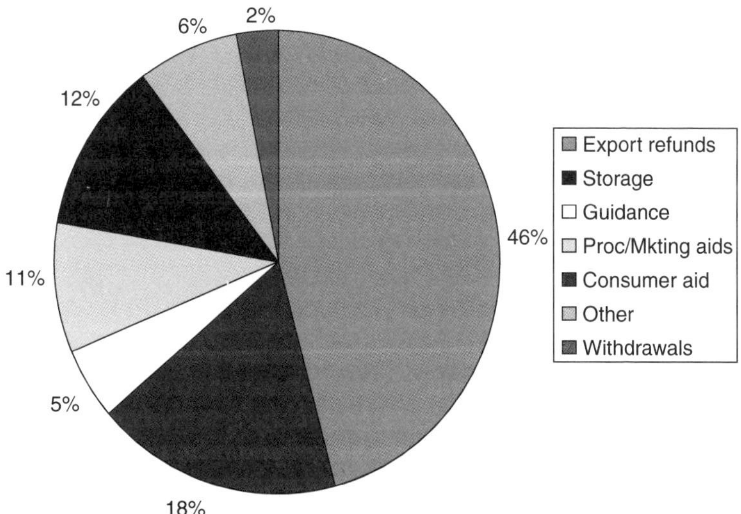

Figure 9.2 FEOGA intervention expenditure, 1997
Source: European Commission (1998).

surplus produce into intervention, for storing the produce, for destroying perishable commodities and for subsidising exports to enable them to compete on world markets.

Although the MacSharry reforms have helped to move the EU towards market balance by reducing intervention prices, even after these measures had taken effect in 1999, there were still over 5 million tonnes of wheat and 46 000 tonnes of butter and skimmed milk powder in storage. In total EU stocks were valued at 1.6 million euros in 1999 (European Commission, 2000). These payments were supplemented by direct payments such as set-aside and acreage payments so that, in 1999, FEOGA was transferring nearly 40 billion ECU of taxpayers' money to farmers.

Surpluses of commodities like wheat and barley could be exported for sale on world markets but, as EU prices have been well above world market prices, such sales could only be secured if the EU taxpayer funded the difference between these two price levels through the export restitution. In 1997, as Figure 9.2 shows, 46 per cent of FEOGA market intervention was allocated to export refunds (European Commission, 1998). Whilst these payments have insulated EU producers from movements in world markets and have supported their incomes, they have had a depressing and destabilising effect on world market prices, impacting adversely on producers elsewhere. Taxpayers might also argue that their money has not been put to good use since these payments have prevented EU farmers from adapting to a market-orientated regime. However, under the Uruguay agreement, the extent to which the EU will be able to use export restitutions from the late 1990s onwards has been curtailed by both volume and value.

The CAP regime has differed between sectors and has involved a multitude of administrative arrangements. Since much of the administration has been done by the national authorities, there is a problem in securing a consistent application of the rules. In addition, the CAP has been complicated still further by fluctuating exchange rates. The rules and regulations that have arisen to administer this complex regime have provided plentiful opportunities for 'playing the system' and for fraud at the taxpayers' expense. Cattle have been smuggled over borders between the Irish Republic and Northern Ireland to be driven back openly, in order to claim subsidy; olive producers have claimed subsidy twice over – once for their olive trees and a second time for the oil; commodities have been moved around unnecessarily to exploit the differences in subsidy regimes whilst set-aside has presented ample opportunities for misappropriation. Fraud represents a dead weight loss

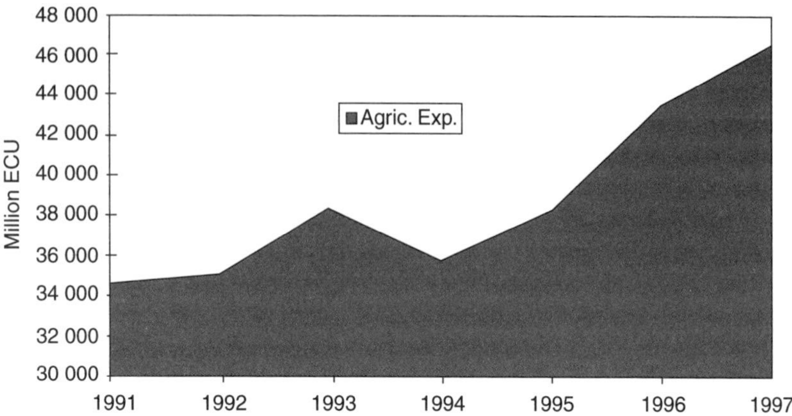

Figure 9.3   Agricultural expenditure, 1991–7
Source: European Commission (1999).

to taxpayers and the complex procedures required to police the system
have added still further to the cost.

Although taxpayers' money has not always been well used, nevertheless, supporting farmers from taxpayers' rather than consumers'
pockets has some advantages, since taxes are transparent and can be
related to 'the ability to pay'. Indeed, by reducing the level of support
prices and introducing acreage payments and set-aside, the MacSharry
reforms have redistributed the costs of the CAP away from the consumer and towards the taxpayer. Although the MacSharry reforms were
intended to reduce the budgetary cost of the CAP, ironically, the total
cost of agricultural support has risen since 1991, as Figure 9.3 shows.

However, despite an increase in the overall cost to the taxpayer, by
1997, agriculture accounted for a slightly lower percentage of the EU
budget. In 1991 total agricultural expenditure had absorbed 64 per cent
of the EU budget; by 1997, agricultural expenditure had fallen to
56 per cent of the budget.

Although MacSharry had not succeeded in reducing the total budget
costs of the CAP, the reforms had redistributed the burden between
taxpayers and consumers. The substantial cuts in the prices of cereals,
milk and beef reduced the price differential between the EU and the
rest of the world and thus benefited the EU consumer, whilst the shift
to acreage payments and set-aside increased the burden on the EU taxpayer. Since taxes are less regressive than food prices, low-income
groups benefited and the reforms have made the CAP somewhat more
equitable.

Farmers and the CAP

Throughout the second half of the twentieth century, one of the greatest assets European farmers has possessed was the fund of goodwill, stemming, in part, from the memories of hunger and rationing during the war years (National Consumer Council, 1988). Transfers from consumers and taxpayers to EU farmers were acceptable because food was perceived as a vital necessity, supplies of which needed to be secured, even at a cost. The CAP has drawn upon this fund of goodwill and has attempted 'to ensure a fair standard of living for the agricultural community', as the Treaty of Rome stated.

In all advanced industrialised countries, the supply of agricultural products has been expanding faster than the demand and, as market prices for agricultural commodities have fallen, the share of total national income going to the agricultural sector has declined. The CAP was established to manage this process of decline since, if left to market forces, farmers would have faced rapidly falling profits, causing them to leave the industry. The CAP was set up to support farmers' incomes in order to maintain a rural way of life, based upon the family farm.

Despite high prices for consumers and high costs to taxpayers, agricultural incomes have not kept pace with those in other sectors of the economy. Furthermore there have been wide variations in the experience of farmers in the different member states. In some countries, such as Denmark and the UK, real net agricultural income has fallen quite markedly whilst in other countries, like Ireland, there have been substantial increases.

Evaluating the impact of the CAP upon food producers involves assessing how farmers would have fared under some alternative regime which might have been in place had the EU never devised the CAP. The comparison with national alternatives suggests that some farmers might indeed have been better off without the CAP, particularly those in countries such as Germany and the UK where average incomes have been relatively high and the number of farmers low. Under these circumstances, national taxpayers would not have found it an undue burden to provide generous support to this small group and yet, under the CAP, real incomes per head from agricultural activity have fallen in Germany and the UK. The situation has been very different in countries with large numbers of farmers, especially when average incomes per capita were low. Irish farmers, in particular, have fared much better under the CAP than they would probably have done under a national regime funded by Irish taxpayers alone.

The CAP has transferred substantial resources to the agricultural sector but these funds have not been equitably distributed amongst different groups within the farming community. The costs and benefits to farmers have differed depending upon the country in which they were located and also upon the size of the farm and the crops they produced. Large farmers – especially those in north-west Europe – have been the main beneficiaries of the CAP regime which has indeed accelerated the increase in farm size. When the CAP was first established in the 1950s, the agricultural sector employed a large number of people – nearly 15 million or 20 per cent of the labour force (Hill, 1984). By 1991, agricultural employment in the twelve member states had fallen to 5.1 per cent of total employment whilst the average size of holdings had risen to 17.5 hectares (European Commission, 1998). Those farmers who have found it hardest to survive have been the smaller farmers who have not produced sufficient quantities of output to qualify for generous support. As their incomes have fallen, these smaller farmers have left the industry and their farms have been amalgamated into larger holdings.

Larger farms have produced a substantial volume of output which they have been able to sell at the guaranteed prices. This has increased their profits, enabling them, in turn, to introduce the new technology, and bringing substantial benefits to the ancillary industries producing agricultural machinery, seeds and fertilisers. Yet these large farmers are best placed to survive in a competitive market. In 1991, most EU support was being received by farmers producing large surpluses of cereals and milk. Many of these producers were located in the comparatively affluent countries of north-west Europe.

By contrast, the small family holdings – especially those in southern Europe – have received considerably less support. Olives, fruit and vegetables have not attracted high prices; dairy farmers, on the other hand, have been well-treated under CAP. They have epitomised the concept of the 'family farm' and have been critically dependent upon the revenue from milk sales. By the early 1980s, 30 per cent of FEOGA support was used to buy surplus milk. The introduction of milk quotas in 1984 was a way of maintaining high prices for milk, whilst containing the costs of support through limiting the quantity of milk which could be sold at the supported price. The effectiveness of the quota system has depended upon the extent to which and the ways in which it has been implemented in each member state. However, the cost of FEOGA support has been curtailed and in some countries the dairy sector has undergone substantial restructuring. For farmers who have gone out of business, the benefits of the CAP seem illusory indeed.

Conclusion

Although the Common Agricultural Policy was established to address the economic difficulties of the agricultural sector, the details of the regime have reflected the political strength of the countries and groups concerned. Consequently, farmers, rather than consumers or taxpayers, have been the main beneficiaries of the policy. Technology has increased output, raising farmers' incomes at taxpayers' expense and exposing food consumers to a degree of risk which they are beginning to find unacceptable.

Even for farmers, the impact of the CAP is complex. Large farmers have undoubtedly gained – especially if they have been located in countries which would have found it difficult to be so generous to farmers without the help of taxpayers in other member states. On the other hand, small farmers in southern Europe, growing crops which have not attracted high levels of price support, have not been so well served by the CAP.

Taxpayers – especially those in the UK and Germany – have contributed the most to the cost of the policy and low-income consumers have found high food prices absorbing a large proportion of their budget. The policy has not been targeted to sustain the incomes of the marginal farmers who have struggled to survive without support. It has not provided an effective redistributive mechanism.

Politically, however, it is a different matter; the CAP was designed to hold the Community together and, indeed, that unity has remained intact. However, as the next round of applicant countries from Central and Eastern Europe seek membership, the CAP could prove a barrier to their admittance since their large agricultural sectors could make the CAP unacceptably expensive. The very policy which, to date, has bound the community together could prevent the EU from enlarging to encompass a wider Europe.

References

Ardy, B. (1999) 'The EU Budget and EU Citizens', unpublished working paper, South Bank University

Consumers in Europe Group (1994) *The Common Agricultural Policy: How to spend £28 billion a year without making anyone happy* (CEG, London)

European Commission (1980) *The Agricultural Situation in the Community, 1979 Report* (Brussels)

European Commission (1991) Reforming the Common Agricultural Policy ISEC/B8/91

European Commission (1998) *The Agricultural Situation in the European Union, 1997 Report* (Brussels)

European Commission (1999) *The Agricultural Situation in the European Union 1998 Report* (Brussels)

European Commission (2000) T*he 29th Report on the Agricultural Guarantee and Guidance Fund* (Brussels)

Fearne, A. (1997) 'The History and Development of the CAP 1945–1990', in Ritson, C. and Harvey, D. (eds), *The Common Agricultural Policy*, 2nd ed (CAB International, Wallingford)

Finch, J. (1999) 'Test Fields of Conflict', *The Guardian*, 5 August

Gregoriadis, L. (1999) 'GM Foods Overtake BSE as Top Safety Concern', *The Guardian*, 4 September

Hill, B. (1984) *The Common Agricultural Policy: Past, Present and Future* (Methuen, London)

National Consumer Council (1988) *Consumers and the Common Agricultural Policy* (HMSO, London)

Organisation for Economic Cooperation and Development (1987) *Historical Statistics 1960–85* (OECD, Paris)

Ritson, C. (1997) 'The CAP and the Consumer', in Ritson, C. and Harvey, D. (eds), *The Common Agricultural Policy*, 2nd edn (CAB International, Wallingford)

Part III
People, Workers and Welfare

10

Caring and Working: The Market, the State and the Care Economy

Sue Hatt

Introduction

Women and men are employed as different kinds of workers throughout the European Union. Women characteristically work in the public sector, in service occupations and on a part-time basis while men, on the other hand, are more often in full-time employment, remain in the labour force throughout their working lives and account for the majority of employees in manufacturing industry. In every member state, men are better rewarded for their employment than women. Within the household too, the work which women and men undertake differs considerably both in its nature and its extent. Despite an increase in men's participation in the domestic sphere, women spend longer than men on unpaid tasks even when they are engaged in full-time employment and the extent of their involvement in the domestic sphere restricts their ability to participate in the labour market. This chapter will explore the reasons why women have not just been a different kind of worker, but have also been disadvantaged workers in the European Union.

At the EU level, steps have been taken to improve the position of women in the labour market and to extend equality of opportunity but, since European integration was originally concerned with the establishment of an economic community, social policy has been narrowly focused on regulating labour markets. Consequently, it has been of limited value to those whose access to labour markets was restricted, either because of their age, their dependent status, their need to provide care for others, their sickness, their disability, or even their lack of appropriate skills. Unlike agriculture, where similar problems evoked a common policy response, the provision of welfare has been left largely to the member states, leading to considerable diversity in the policy regimes. The role of the EU has been confined to employment-related measures, such as the regulation of working time and the provision of maternity leave. These measures affect men and women differently depending upon the extent to which they participate in paid employment and, for women, their access to labour markets has been affected by the extent to which they are involved in the provision of care for other family members.

This chapter will first discuss the significance of domestic labour for the formal economy and will consider the interaction between domestic labour and paid employment. It will then examine the changing positions of women and men in European labour markets, with particular reference to Sweden, Italy and the United Kingdom. Whilst domestic labour underpins the ability of workers to participate in the formal economy, the interaction between the market and the family has implications for the economic well-being of women, especially in countries where the state plays a limited role in the provision of welfare. Finally the measures which have been taken at the EU level to promote equal opportunities for men and women in labour markets will be considered and their impact upon women in Sweden, Italy and the UK will be compared.

Domestic labour and the economy

The provision of care – especially childcare – has always been a central feature of women's lives, and this section will discuss the significance of this activity for the efficient functioning of the labour market. Within the domestic sector, a range of services are provided that are vital for the effective operation of the formal economy. Some of these services involve routine household and personal maintenance tasks, like making beds, cooking meals and washing clothes, and the provision of these services keeps workers physically prepared for employment. Domestic labour also involves providing 'highly personalised services of a kind that are distinct in terms of social relations from the services that might be provided through the market' (Gardiner, 1997 p. 241). Childcare and eldercare provide examples of these personalised services. Childcare is a complex and demanding process of recognising and responding to children's needs, making them feel secure, loved and respected as a person. Parent–child relationships can form the basis for trust and understanding, for developing social skills and for learning culturally appropriate responses. In these ways, the domestic sector builds the capabilities of workers, equipping them with a range of skills and enabling them to operate effectively as workers and citizens in the public world beyond the household (Gardiner, 1998). Children who do not receive proper care may well fail to mature into law-abiding citizens able to make a positive contribution to society.

In Europe, the labour input in the domestic sector has been provided predominantly by women. Evidence from time-use studies in the United Kingdom in 1995 showed that unpaid work, such as food preparation, care of the family or household, care of the home and shopping took 295 minutes per day for women but only 155 minutes per day for men (Office for National Statistics, 1997). In Sweden, the evidence for 1990 showed that, for those with older children, household tasks occupied 20 hours per week for men but 33 hours for women (Nyberg, 1998). In both countries, there was a strong division of labour by gender, with tasks such as washing, ironing and the care of young children being 'women's jobs' whilst men concentrated on car maintenance and do-it-yourself (DIY) activities. Changes in social attitudes have reallocated domestic labour to some extent and men's contribution to the household has increased whilst women's has fallen. However, the shares have remained distinctly unequal, with women spending far longer than men on unpaid domestic tasks, even when they are in full-time employment.

As other chapters have shown, technology has changed production methods in many sectors of the formal economy. The domestic sector, too, has been affected by technological innovation, bringing labour-saving devices, such as the vacuum cleaner, the automatic washing machine and the microwave oven, all of which have made one hour's housework far more productive than it used to be. Recent decades have also witnessed the growth of market-produced substitutes for domestic goods and services. As technological change in production methods has reduced product prices, children's clothes have been purchased rather than made at home, disposable nappies have reduced the time spent washing and take-away pizzas have provided easy alternatives to home-cooked meals. Consequently, the total time spent on routine domestic work in Europe has fallen.

However, technology has provided no substitute for the interpersonal care and the social relationships which form a pivotal part of domestic labour. The amount and the type of care which children need varies, depending on their age, their state of health, their emotional requirements and so on but, if children are to become effective members of society and the future workforce, then a very substantial investment must be made in their care. Small babies require continuous care throughout the day and night whilst toddlers and pre-school children need the presence of a responsible adult to assist with personal needs and to develop their interpersonal skills. School-age children want help with their homework and someone with whom they can 'talk issues through'. As Gardiner (1998) says: 'if these processes are effective, the outcome will be mature people who are physically and psychologically healthy and equipped with a range of skills, knowledge and values, the capacity to work and develop further' (p. 216).

Throughout Europe, this work which is known as emotional labour has been regarded as women's work. If this care is not provided, then the formal economy suffers (Gardiner, 1998). Poor health leads to absenteeism, and inadequate parenting contributes to truancy, juvenile crime and underdeveloped interpersonal skills, all of which affect employment and the extent to which workers can contribute to the economy and society. In some respects, the role of the domestic sector as a shock absorber for the formal economy has become more significant in recent decades as restructuring in the labour market, for example, has led to higher levels of redundancy and unemployment (Elson, 1998). The limits on public expenditure have also led to a decrease in the provision of public services and a consequent accommodation by the domestic sector. In the UK, for example, cutbacks in the school meals service has meant that more children rely on sandwiches made at home (Crompton and Sanderson, 1990). The domestic sector is not insulated from the rest of the economy; it has always been, and will remain, fundamental to its success.

Parenthood, paid employment and the welfare state

Parenthood affects men's and women's economic lives in different ways. While fathers have spent as long, or longer, than childless men in paid employment, motherhood has reduced a woman's hours of paid work. Domestic labour has underpinned the labour market, assisting men's full-time participation while, for women, providing services at home has constrained their activity in the formal economy. However, the extent of this constraint and its consequences for women have varied across Europe, depending upon the family structures, the social expectations of motherhood and the welfare provisions established at the national level. This section will consider the differences in women's and men's age-related economic activity rates in Italy,

Sweden and the United Kingdom, three member states with very different welfare regimes.

In many EU member states, the establishment of the postwar welfare state rested on the assumption that care for men, as breadwinners, and for children and the elderly, as dependants, had always been, and would always be, provided by women 'behind the scenes' of the market-based economy. The following statement from the Beveridge Report (1942) in the UK made this point very explicitly:

> The attitude of the housewife to gainful employment outside the home is not, and should not be the same as that of the single woman. She has other duties...Housewives as mothers have vital work to do in ensuring the survival of the British race. (Cmnd 6404)

During the postwar years, however, women have been increasing their participation in 'gainful employment'. Care for dependants can be provided by the family, by the state or by the market, and each of the EU member states has developed a different combination of these three strands to accommodate the provision of care. These regimes have varied considerably both in the extent of their provision and in the principles which underpin them. Esping Andersen (1990) classified welfare regimes as clustering around three basic models: the conservative, the liberal and the social democratic. In the conservative regime, traditional institutions, such as the family – especially the extended family – the church and charities, play a significant role in the provision of care, leaving the state providing compensation to even out the undesirable inequalities produced by markets.

The conservative regime, of which Italy provides an example, has tended to favour the 'male breadwinner' family structure and has done little to facilitate women's participation in the labour market. The liberal regime, on the other hand, has treated everyone as a breadwinner, encouraging participation in the labour market, but ignoring the differences between workers' ease of access to the labour market. The UK welfare regime has moved towards this model and female labour market participation has been high, but has been on terms which have been distinctly disadvantageous. Finally, the social democratic regime has socialised the costs of care by providing extensive childcare, healthcare and eldercare services. This regime, evidenced most nearly in Sweden, has facilitated the labour market participation of women as well as men.

In Italy, the role of the family has been extensive. Finance for house purchase or starting a business has often come from family sources (Bettio and Villa, 1998) whilst, in the formal economy, the service sector has not provided as large a share of total employment as it has in the northern member states. In Italy in 1997, 62 per cent of employment was in the service sector whilst, for Sweden and the UK, it accounted for 71 per cent of total employment. The weak and fragmented nature of state welfare services, the strong reliance on the family and the persistence of patronage within the benefits system have been identified as particular features of the welfare model in southern Europe (Ferrera, 1996). The consequences of the underdeveloped service sector and the emphasis on the family have made it hard for women to combine motherhood with paid employment and, in 1999, Italian women had an economic activity rate of 46 per cent which was the lowest in the European Union (European Commission, 2000). They entered the labour force as they left full-time education and 60 per cent of women in their late twenties were economically active in 1997 but, for every subsequent age group, the activity rate declined, depicting a pattern of labour market withdrawal as domestic responsibilities increased. This pattern of activity has been distinctly different from that of men, over 90 per cent of whom were economically active between the ages of 30 and 50, as Figure 10.1 shows.

Whilst high fertility rates have usually accompanied low labour market participation, Italy is unusual in that low labour market participation for women has been accompanied by the lowest fertility rate in

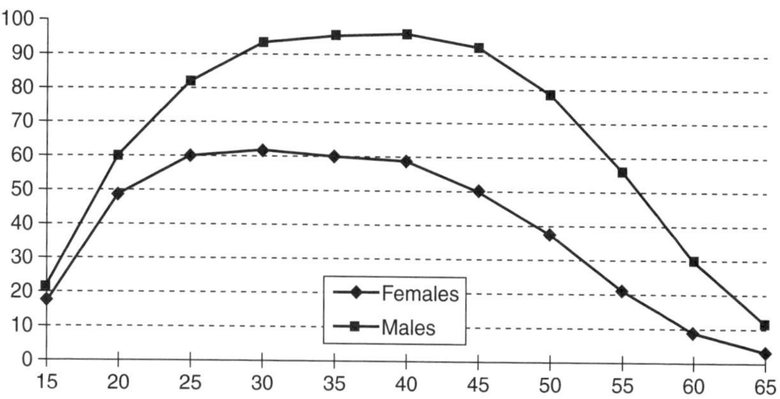

Figure 10.1   Age-related economic activity rates in Italy, 1997
Source: Eurostat (1999) *Labour Force Survey 1997*.

the EU. The 'arrested development' of the service sector has limited the demand for women's labour whilst the emphasis on the family has restricted the female labour supply. At the same time, rising youth unemployment has extended the duration of family support, increasing the cost of the investment which parents have been expected to make in their children (Bettio and Villa, 1998). These factors have contributed to the fall in the fertility rate, with consequences for the worker-dependency ratio and for pensions provision, both of which will be explored in Chapter 12.

In countries such as the UK where, until the late 1990s, the state has done little to facilitate women's employment and publicly funded childcare has provided places for a lower percentage of pre-school children than in any other member state, motherhood has marginalised, but has not debarred, women from employment. In the UK, only 35–40 per cent of pre-school children have been in publicly funded childcare (Moss, 1990) and working mothers have either turned to the private market or to informal childcare arrangements, provided by other family members. Well-qualified women have made most use of professional childcare services, employing a nanny or an au pair, or placing their children in a private day-care centre. However, these services are labour-intensive, and hence expensive, placing them out of reach of women with few qualifications who have relied on informal childcare arrangements with family or friends (Brannen *et al.*, 1994). This has restricted them to part-time employment, reducing their earnings, their career prospects and their pensions entitlement.

In the UK, the age-related activity rates for women have differed from men's and from those of Italian women, as Figure 10.2 shows. A high activity rate of 74 per cent in their early twenties dipped slightly for women in their early thirties and then rose again for those in their late thirties and early forties. Motherhood would seem to have been the biggest factor affecting British women's economic activity. Whilst 75 per cent of all women were economically active in 2000, only 67 per cent of married women with a pre-school child were economically active and, for lone mothers with a pre-school child, the activity rate fell as low as 40 per cent (ONS, 2001).

In Sweden, due to generous entitlements to parental leave, it has been possible for mothers with pre-school children to remain in the labour market. In 1997, over 80 per cent of women between the ages of 25 and 55 were economically active and the male and female age-related patterns of activity for women were very similar, as Figure 10.3 shows. Although Swedish women remained economically active, the

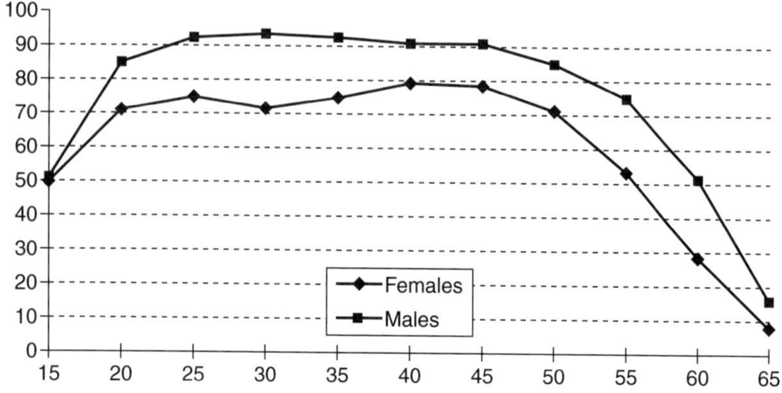

Figure 10.2   Age-related activity rates in the UK, 1997
Source: Eurostat (1999) *Labour Force Survey 1997.*

average hours of paid work for women with pre-school children were lower than for those without children. Mothers with pre-school children worked, on average, 15 hours per week in 1994, whilst those without dependent children spent 25 hours per week in employment (Nyberg, 1998). In the Nordic countries, the government has intervened actively to facilitate the labour market participation of women by providing childcare facilities, by introducing individual taxation and by offering generous maternity and parental leave entitlements. High rates of female participation have been accompanied by lifelong participation in the workforce.

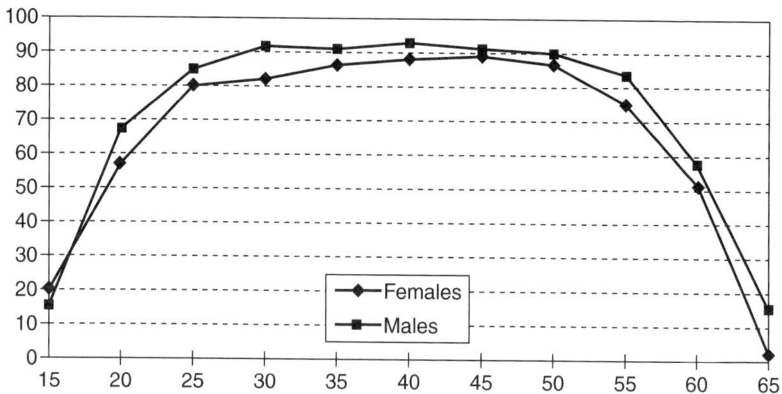

Figure 10.3   Age-related economic activity rates in Sweden, 1997
Source: Eurostat (1999) *Labour Force Survey 1997.*

In these three countries, the labour market opportunities for women interacted in different ways with their expected role within the family and the state's welfare policies. Consequently, the extent to which women of different ages participate in paid employment has varied considerably between member states and has been distinctly different from men's age-related activity rate. For men, the pattern is far more uniform across the member states, with continuous, full-time labour market participation being the norm for those between the ages of 20 and 55.

Women and men in European labour markets

This section will consider the changes that have taken place in European labour markets in recent decades and will outline the consequences of these developments for women's and men's employment, unemployment and earnings in the member states.

Changes in employment

Since the Treaty of Rome was signed, European labour markets have undergone significant changes. In 1960, two workers in every ten were employed in agriculture, four out of ten in manufacturing, whilst the remaining four were in the service sector. By 1996, these figures had changed considerably with a decline in employment in agriculture and manufacturing but a considerable increase in the percentage employed in the service sector, as Table 10.1 shows. European Commission (2000)

These changes have not affected men and women in the same way – nor indeed have they applied equally in each member state. Since men predominated as employees in agriculture and in the manufacturing industry, the demand for male labour has fallen. At the same time, however, the male labour supply has fallen. The introduction of new technology has placed an increasing emphasis on qualifications and men have been remaining in education until their early twenties,

Table 10.1 Employment in Europe, EC12 (percentage)

	1960	1999
Agriculture	21	4
Manufacturing	40	29
Services	39	63

Sources: The Agricultural Situation in the Community; European Commission (1961).

delaying their entry into the labour market. At the other end of their working life, men in their late fifties have been withdrawing from the labour market rather than continuing to seek employment until they reached retirement age. This combination of a reduction in the demand for male labour, accompanied by a fall in supply, has reduced male employment throughout the European Union.

For women, the changes in the labour market have had a different impact. During the latter half of the twentieth century, women's participation in the labour force rose just when the demand for their labour was increasing. The service sector has expanded and women have accounted for the majority of service sector workers in all member states. They have been strongly represented in public administration, hotels and restaurants and financial intermediation (Eurostat, 1999) while they accounted for over 70 per cent of all those employed as clerical workers in France, Denmark, Sweden, Finland and the UK and over half in all other member states. The expansion in employment opportunities in the service sector of the economy has increased the demand for female labour whilst changes in social attitudes have facilitated an increase in women's labour supply. Between 1991 and 1999, women's employment in the EU15 rose by 6.3 per cent, an increase of nearly 4 million workers (European Commission, 2000).

The nature of employment in Europe has also changed, as firms have sought to cut costs by using labour more flexibly. Many of the new employment opportunities have been for part-time, or temporary, workers or for those prepared to accept unsocial hours of employment. Between 1983 and 1994, 82 per cent of the new jobs created in the European Union were for part-time workers (Rubery *et al*, 1998). The extent to which these atypical working practices have been introduced has varied between member states, depending in part on the extent to which the policy regime has accommodated these changes. In those member states, such as the UK, with high proportions of part-time employment, nearly 70 per cent of all new jobs have been part-time while in Italy, where more than 90 per cent of the workforce were still employed on a full-time basis, only half of all new jobs were for part-timers.

However, in all member states, women predominated amongst the part-time workers with 34 per cent of women – but only 6 per cent of men – employed on a part-time basis in 1999 (European Commission, 2000). Consequently the changing opportunities in the labour markets have had a greater impact on women's than on men's employment. Figure 10.4 shows the difference between the proportions of women

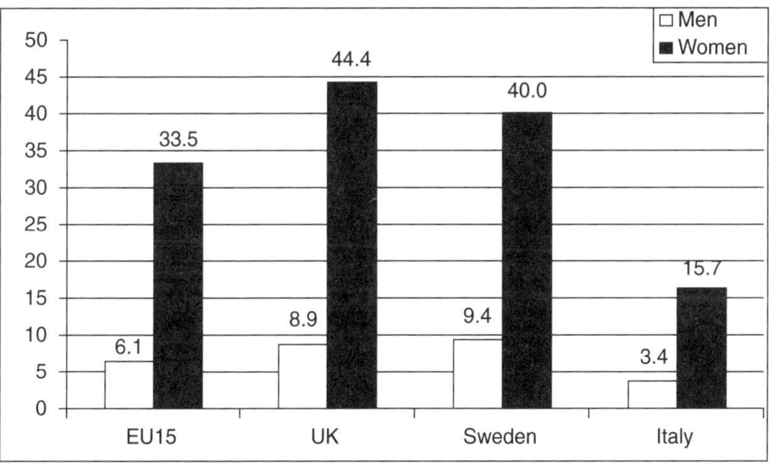

Figure 10.4   Part-time employment by gender, 1999
Source: European Commission (2000).

and men employed on a part-time basis in selected member states in 1999.

Changes in unemployment

Whilst women's employment has been rising, the decades since the establishment of the EEC have also seen an increase in the rate of unemployment in Europe. Restructuring of the labour market has combined with an increasingly open European marketplace and, as globalisation has brought competition from low-wage economies in East Asia, the manufacturing sector has shrunk and male jobs have been lost. Men's levels of employment have fallen and unemployment has risen. For women, the picture has been different in that the service sector has been expanding whilst women's participation in labour markets has been increasing. The overall result has been that, for women, both employment and unemployment have been rising.

Against this background of higher levels of unemployment, significant differences have persisted between men and women and between women in the different member states. In every country except the UK and Sweden, female unemployment has been higher than male unemployment and in Spain, for example, this discrepancy was quite considerable in 1997, with 28 per cent of women but only 16 per cent of men unemployed (European Commission, 1998). Furthermore, welfare regimes have tended to place more emphasis upon protecting men's incomes and fewer women than men have qualified for unemployment benefit.

Unemployment has posed particular problems for young workers just entering the labour market. In every member state, the unemployment rate amongst those aged between 15 and 24 has been higher than the average rate of unemployment, as Figure 10.5 indicates. The benefits entitlement for young unemployed people in search of their first job has varied between member states. In the UK, where youth unemployment remained at 30 per cent in 1997, 16-18-year-olds were one of the groups whose access to benefits had been curtailed. This extended the duration of their dependence upon family support. Although young job seekers have been entitled to some form of income maintenance in most countries in northern Europe, this has not been true in the Mediterranean countries where new entrants to the labour market have not been entitled to state support (Ferrera, 1996). In Italy, where youth unemployment stood at 37 per cent in 1997, young job seekers have been viewed as dependants whose families should support their needs. In 1990, 97 per cent of Italian 18–19 year-olds were living with their parents within a culture where parents sought to ensure that their children's living standards kept pace with their own (Bettio and Villa, 1998). The costs of parenthood in Italy

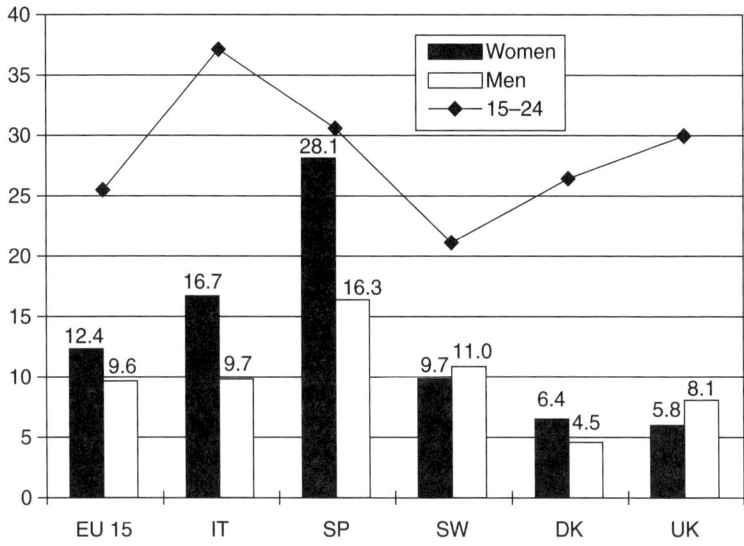

Figure 10.5   Unemployment by age and gender, 1997
Source: Eurostat (1999) *Labour Force Survey 1997.*

have been extended by the youth unemployment and the concept of the 'long-lasting family'. The implications for women's domestic labour of these young people remaining within the family home are considerable.

Men's and women's earnings

Although the gap between the proportions of women and men participating in the European labour force has been narrowing, their employment has remained segregated in different industries, occupations and sectors of the economy. Segregation in employment has had implications for career development, earnings and pensions. Since the signing of the Treaty of Rome, the real wages of both women and men have increased and the discrepancy between male and female wage rates has been reduced. Despite Article 119 committing member states to equal pay for men and women doing work of equal value, men's employment has remained better rewarded than women's, as Table 10.2 shows.

Although the gap between men's and women's earnings has varied in size between the different member states, it has remained apparent even in countries like Sweden with high rates of female labour force participation. Women's average earnings have been depressed by their segregation in the lower paid-sectors of the economy, by their greater involvement in part-time work and by the discontinuity of their employment. One study in the UK (Joshi and Davies, 1993) indicated that a mother with two children born in her late twenties could forgo as much as 57 per cent of her lifetime earnings compared with her childfree counterpart. Many of the factors depressing women's earnings are related to their extensive involvement in caring labour. Even in Sweden, women earned less than men in 1995, largely because they

Table 10.2 Women's average hourly earnings in industry as a percentage of men's, 1995

Sweden	83
Luxembourg	81
Denmark	79
Netherlands	69
Greece	68
United Kingdom	66
EU15	73

Source: European Commission (1998).

sought employment in the poorly paid public sector. They avoided the private sector because the 'caring deduction' – that is, the reduction in earnings due to absences from the labour market – was higher there than in the public sector. In the private sector, where Swedish men's employment has been concentrated, workers have been better remunerated and this gender segregation has confirmed the pattern of lower earnings for women (Hansen, 1997). Although caring is an important activity with significant implications for the future of the economy and society, yet the provision of care has meant that women have not only been 'different kinds of workers', but that they have also been disadvantaged workers in the European economy.

Social policies

This final section will consider the measures which the EU has implemented in the field of social policy to extend equality of opportunity in the labour market and it will examine their impact upon women in Italy, the UK and Sweden. European integration within the EU has promoted competition to raise living standards by encouraging firms to take advantage of economies of scale and increasing the productivity of labour. Whilst these changes should result in lower prices and benefits to consumers, the implications of integration for workers were likely to be more complex. The advent of the single market in the 1990s extended the opportunities for businesses to locate production anywhere in the EU. The employer pays a substantial proportion of the cost of social protection in many member states. Those countries with high levels of social protection for their workers feared that firms, seeking to cut costs, might locate where social benefits were lowest. Against this background, measures to establish a 'social Europe' seemed vital, and the signing of the Social Charter was a symbolic gesture, signalling an attempt to avoid a 'race to the bottom' with respect to workers' rights and conditions of employment.

Progress on converting the symbol into reality has been slow. Even though a social dimension has been on the agenda from the very beginning of the EEC, it has proved particularly difficult to establish a common approach to social issues since the welfare regimes in the member states have diverged considerably in both their scope and their underlying philosophy. In all member countries, the state has taken some responsibility for mitigating the adverse effects of economic change and labour market restructuring through the pursuit of active labour market policies but, beyond this basic level of commonality, there is considerable disagreement about the 'proper' remit of social policy.

The Treaty of Rome and the Single European Act both interpreted social policy narrowly, as relating to employment rather than to the wider concept of citizenship. Article 119 of the Treaty of Rome gave women the right to equal pay for work of equal value, but it took over twenty years before compliance was required. More recently, EU directives on maternity leave, parental leave and working time have again focused on the labour market. These measures have affected women in different ways in the member states because they have been implemented against the background of the provisions of the national welfare regimes.

Nevertheless, the EU has begun to develop a common social framework with respect to labour markets and employment. Through the Maternity Leave Directive of 1992, the EU has acted to provide a minimum entitlement so that women in any member state may be absent from employment without risk of dismissal following the birth of their child. To help women and men to reconcile their professional and family responsibilities, the EU introduced a directive on parental leave and leave for family reasons in 1996. This measure gives parents an individual entitlement to leave and, at the end of their period of leave, they have the right to return to the same job, or to an equivalent position. The response of employers to these changes has been mixed. Larger firms have tended to accept the enhancement of employment rights but small and medium-sized enterprises have stressed the practical difficulties where the number of employees is low.

More recently, parental leave has become available to both men and women, but the provision of benefits has been left to the discretion of member states. Evidence from other countries suggests that the lack of benefit will considerably reduce take-up of leave and some governments, in the UK for example, have not made any provision for the payment of benefit. Under these circumstances, the impact of the measure is likely to be reduced.

Women in employment have benefited from the maternity leave provisions. Before the introduction of maternity leave women often had no option but to leave their employment when they became pregnant. The right to take leave when their children were born and to return to their position after childbirth has been a significant gain, protecting mothers from occupational downgrading and from the adverse effects of discontinuous employment. Evidence from the UK has suggested that women who took maternity leave were likely to experience a smaller gender gap in their earnings than those women who interrupted their careers around childbirth (Joshi *et al.*, 1996). The provision of maternity leave has also strengthened the incentive for young women to participate in the labour market in order to accumulate a continuous work record which is necessary for leave entitlement.

The directive has been significant in the UK, as it superseded national provisions. The UK legislation, dating from the 1970s, limited eligibility for maternity leave to those women who had been with their employer for more than two years and this provision served to exclude nearly half the potential beneficiaries. A ruling from the European Court of Justice forced the UK to extend its legislation in line with EU requirements. Although British women have benefited from the EU directives, the impact on women in Italy and Sweden was more limited. In Italy, female economic activity rates have been low – as indeed birth rates have been – and so the directive has only affected a minority of women. In Sweden, the national provisions were more extensive than those of the EU and so the directives have done little to improve the position of women. Sweden remodelled its welfare state in the 1970s to encourage all women into the labour force and women's social entitlements were adjusted to treat them as workers in their own right (Lewis, 1992). The 'weak breadwinner' model recognised women's right to be compensated for unpaid work, the larger share of which they continued to perform.

The role of the EU in helping men and women to reconcile their parental and employment responsibilities has thus been constrained by the welfare regimes in the member states. The emphasis on economic integration has limited the EU's role to one of regulating labour markets, rather than considering the wider social issues which affect the ease with which women and men have participated in paid employment. Nevertheless, some of the measures introduced at the EU level have made a significant difference to women's entitlements and access to labour markets, especially in the more recalcitrant states such as the UK. The ECJ rulings on equal pay for men and women undertaking work of equal value, on occupational pension rights for part-time employees and on eligibility to maternity leave have improved the benefits offered under UK legislation. Since European law supersedes national legislation, the EU could, potentially, be significant in promoting greater equality between men and women. To date, however, its role in this sphere has been limited.

Conclusion

This chapter has shown how the economic well-being of women and men in Europe has been affected in different ways by the interaction of markets, states and households. For women, the extent of their involvement in domestic labour has restricted their ability to participate in labour markets. This, in turn, has adversely affected their earnings which have remained lower than men's in every member state. In recent decades, the changes in the economies and in labour markets have affected the employment of men and women in different ways, increasing women's participation and employment while men have been facing dwindling job opportunities and a fall in their participation rate. Despite these changes, women have remained disadvantaged in that their employment has been less well-rewarded than men's and more likely to be part-time, temporary and insecure.

The role of national governments in regulating and mitigating these labour market inequalities has varied. In some states, an emphasis on the free market has limited government intervention to negative measures, such as those designed to outlaw the most obvious forms of discrimination, while other member states have adopted a more positive approach. At the EU level, directives have been introduced to provide a common framework and to regulate labour markets. In countries such as Sweden, the impact of the European Union's directives has been minimal, since their existing legislation provided greater protection than the European Union requires. In Italy too, EU directives have been of limited benefit to women, many of whom are not in the labour market. In countries like the UK, however, the European Union's rulings have brought women more extensive benefits as they have extended their rights to equal treatment and to leave.

This chapter has argued that the domestic sector and the formal economy interact in significant ways and that, as women participate more extensively in the labour market, this interaction is beginning to raise fundamental questions about the current and future well-being of the people of Europe. Whilst domestic commitments constrain women's activity in the formal economy with adverse implications for equality of opportunity and their earnings, nevertheless, as more women enter the labour market, it has become hard to maintain the quantity and quality of unpaid labour in the domestic sector. So far, policy initiatives have been directed at issues of gender equality within the labour force but, in future, the issue of quality within the provision of care may become significant. Care is of fundamental significance for the economy and, in the absence of appropriate policies, the outcomes for economic prosperity and social stability in Europe are likely to be unsatisfactory. As the twenty-first century opens, the EU faces the challenge of ensuring that economic integration is accompanied by policy measures which support and develop equality of opportunity for all its citizens – both young and old, sick and healthy, male and female.

References

Bettio, F. and Villa, P. (1998) 'A Mediterranean Perspective on the Breakdown of the Relationship Between Participation and Fertility', *Cambridge Journal of Economics* vol. 22, pp. 137–71

Beveridge, W. (1942) *Social Insurance and Allied Services* Cmnd 6404 (London, HMSO)

Brannen, J., Meszaros, G., Moss, P. and Poland, G. (1994) *Employment and Family Life: A Review of Research in the UK 1980 – 1994*, Employment Department Research series no. 41 (University of London, Institute of Education)

Crompton, R. and Sanderson, K. (1990) *Gendered Jobs and Social Change* (Unwin Hyman, London)

Elson, D. (1998) 'The Economic, the Political and the Domestic: Businesses, States and Households in the Organisation of Production', *New Political Economy*, vol. 3, no. 2 (July) pp. 189–208

Esping Andersen, G. (1990) *The Three Worlds of Welfare Capitalism* (Polity Press, Cambridge)

European Commission (1961) *The Agricultural Situation in the European Community* (Brussels)

European Commission (1998) *Earning Differentials Between Men and Women; Study Based on the Structure of Earnings Survey* (Brussels)

European Commission (2000) *Employment in Europe 2000* (Brussels)

Eurostat (1999) *Labour Force Survey 1997* (Brussels)

Ferrera, M. (1996) 'The Southern Model of Welfare in Social Europe', *Journal of European Social Policy*, vol. 6, no. 1, pp. 17–37

Gardiner, J. (1997) *Gender, Care and Economics* (Macmillan – now Palgrave, London)

Gardiner, J. (1998) 'Beyond Human Capital: Households in the Macroeconomy', *New Political Economy*, vol. 3, no. 2 (July) pp. 209-21

Hansen, M. N. (1997) 'The Scandinavian Welfare State Model: The Impact of the Public Sector on segregation and Gender Equality', *Work, Employment and Society*, vol. 11, no. 1, pp. 83–99

Joshi, H. and Davies, H. (1993) 'Mothers' Human Capital and Childcare in Britain', *National Institute Economic Review*, November, pp. 50–63

Joshi, H., Pacci, P. and Waldfogel, J. (1996) 'The Wages of Motherhood: Better or Worse?' London School of Economics Discussion Paper WSP/122

Lewis, J. 'Gender and the Development of Wellan Regime' *Journal of European Social Policy*, vol. 2, no. 3, pp. 159–73

Moss, P. (ed.) (1990) *Childcare in the European Community 1985–1990* (Brussels)

Nyberg, A. (1998) *Women, Men and Incomes: Gender Equality and Economic Independence* (Fritzes, Stockholm)
ONS (1997) 'A Household Satellite Account for the UK', *Economic Trends*, no. 527, pp. 63–71
ONS (2001) *Social Trends*, no. 31 (London, HMSO)
Rubery, J., Smith, M. and Fagan, C. (1998) 'National Working Time Regimes and Equal Opportunities', *Feminist Economics*, vol. 4, no. 1, pp. 71–101

11
People in Search of Work: Albanian Migrants in Greece

James Korovilas

Introduction

The last decade of the twentieth century witnessed profound changes in the political and economic landscape of Europe. Between 1989 and 1991 the states of Eastern Europe, which had previously been run according to the principles of communism and central economic planning, embarked upon a process of reform which would see them establish Western-style democratic political systems and market-orientated economic systems. Under the old communist system citizens of most East European states were prevented from travelling to Western Europe, therefore migration flows between Eastern and Western Europe before 1989 were minimal.

One of the key reforms which took place in the early 1990s was the lifting of travel restrictions. This, together with wars in the former Yugoslavia, led to a significant increase in migration out of Eastern Europe and into the more prosperous countries of Western Europe. Table 11.1 lists the total number of migrants from Eastern Europe resident in a selection of West European countries in 1998. In order to appreciate the impact of these inflows upon each West European country, the table also includes the number of East Europeans as a proportion of the total population.

The accuracy of the figures in this table depends largely upon the ability of the West European countries to collect reliable data on the numbers of migrants in their respective country. This in turn is dependent upon the ability of the host country to register its immigrant population, since illegal immigrants who are not registered are unlikely to appear in official figures for the total immigrant population.

Table 11.1 Migrants from East European countries in West European states

Country	Total number of EE immigrants	Immigrants as % of total population
Switzerland	330 288	4.6
Germany	2 881 893	3.5
Sweden	129 837	1.5
Denmark	42 301	0.8
Finland	32 912	0.6
Norway	23 492	0.5
Greece	41 834	0.4
Spain	10 870	0.03

Source: European Commission (2000) own calculations.

The figures in Table 11.1 indicate that Germany and Switzerland have the highest inflows of migrants from Eastern Europe, both as a proportion of the total population and in absolute terms. The reasons why these countries have attracted a high number of migrants from Eastern Europe are twofold. First, these two countries have features which attract potential migrants, such as high wage levels and the existence of established ethnic communities which help to facilitate the integration of new arrivals. Second, Germany and Switzerland have been successful at registering migrants from former communist countries. This is in direct contrast to the figures for Greece, which grossly understate the number of migrants.

The main reason for this inaccuracy is the fact that up until 1997 the majority of immigrants in Greece from Eastern Europe were undocumented, and therefore do not show up in the figures collected by Eurostat. Figures published by the Greek Institute of Labour in 1999 put the number of immigrants from Eastern Europe at 700 000 – many times higher than the Eurostat figures. The majority of these, almost 400,000, come from Albania (Greek Institute of Labour, 1999). The accuracy of these figures is not in doubt; estimates on the number of East Europeans, and especially the number of Albanians in Greece, are available from several reliable sources which all give similar figures. When we use this larger and more reliable figure for the total number of East European migrants in Greece, we can see that, as a proportion of total population, the number of East European migrants in Greece is 6.5 per cent. This then paints a different picture of the flow of migrants from East to West Europe, with Greece having the second highest level in absolute terms, and the highest level when measured as a proportion of the total population.

The purpose of this chapter is to examine the flow of migrants into Greece, with particular emphasis upon Albanian migrants. During the autumns of 1998 and 1999, interviews were conducted with a large sample of the Albanians working in a small town in south-west Greece. This chapter will draw upon that interview material to consider the motives for migration and the experiences of the migrants. The implications for other EU member states will also be discussed. Most prominent amongst these is the concern that Albanian and other East European migrants in Greece might attempt to take advantage of the opportunity for free travel within the EU as laid out in the Schengen Agreement and move on to other EU member states.

Greece and immigration

For Greece, the experience of mass inward migration in 1991 was unusual. Between 1955 and 1975 Greece was a net exporter of labour, experiencing large-scale emigration to countries such as Australia, Canada, the USA and West Germany. This flow of essentially economic migrants out of Greece can mainly be explained in terms of standard 'push' and 'pull' factors. Whilst Greece was experiencing low levels of economic growth and limited employment prospects, and thus generating a push factor, the recipient countries were experiencing high levels of economic growth, high wage levels and labour shortages, creating the pull factor. Migrant labour was attracted and the recipient countries easily absorbed 1 200 000 Greeks (Lianos *et al*, 1997). During the 1980s levels of net migration stabilised, with modest levels of outward migration being balanced by a steady inflow of both Greeks returning from previous outward migrations and a new inflow of economic migrants from countries in South East Asia, for example the Philippines (Lianos *et al*, 1997).

Greece had traditionally seen itself as an exporter of labour and up until 1991 had not previously experienced the economic and social tensions associated with large-scale immigration. This absence of inward migration pressures prior to 1991 meant that Greece had no reason to impose either restrictive immigration policies or tough border controls. Therefore, Greece, was a 'porous' country, into which illegal migrants could easily flow. The collapse of communism in Albania in 1991 produced a mass exodus of Albanians, with the majority of them opting simply to walk over Albania's southern border into

Greece. This event was the main influence in prompting Greece to tighten up its immigration policy and, in 1991, new legislation was introduced which made infringements of immigration law, such as illegal entry, a criminal offence punishable with imprisonment. Despite these legislative measures coupled with the deployment of armed troops along its northern border, Greece was unable to stop the inflow of economic migrants.

The first wave of Albanian migrants arrived in Greece in 1991. This initial inflow of migrants consisted mainly of young men who initially found casual work in construction and agriculture. During the mid-1990s, they were joined by an increasing number of younger and older men, together with a large number of women. The pattern of migration among Albanian women, who now make up 40 per cent of the Albanian population in Greece, differs from that of Albanian men in several respects. All Albanian men are economically active. With a few exceptions, all Albanian men are either in work or actively seeking work. In contrast to this, some Albanian women are engaged in unpaid work, such as managing the home and childcare.

The other main difference between Albanian men and women is in their chosen lines of work. In contrast to Albanian men who tend to find work in agriculture and construction, many Albanian women find work in sectors which would not attract Albanian men, such as domestic cleaning and housekeeping. Although most Albanians in Greece are engaged in legitimate economic activities, a sizeable minority of Albanians are engaged in illegal activities such as drugs, arms smuggling and prostitution. A clear gender division exists amongst Albanians engaged in illegal activities – women are involved in prostitution and men dominate all other areas.

The vast majority of Albanians in Greece were attracted by the lure of greater economic prospects. The experience of Albanian migrant workers in Greece has been very mixed, with some managing to achieve a relatively high standard of living, whilst others have only just managed to survive on subsistence wages. Extended interviews with Albanian workers provided a rich source of qualitative material on which to draw. One group of three Albanian men described their circumstances as both comfortable and prosperous. They were all regularly employed as stonemasons and possessed a high degree of skill in this trade, a skill which had been largely lost by the local Greeks, since building in stone had been replaced by the availability of cheap, but aesthetically dull, concrete. Albanians were initially able to offer stone construction at a competitive price and were readily employed by local

Greeks who were keen to use stone as an alternative to the omnipresent reinforced concrete.

For the first two years, these three Albanians worked for a fixed daily wage. However, as the demand for their work grew, they became more ambitious and started to accept work on a price-per-job basis. This gave the Albanians an incentive to work more efficiently, get more work done on time and therefore earn more money. In terms of their average daily wage, this represented an increase in income of over 50 per cent. For the Albanian stonemasons, this level of income, together with the security of continuous work, enabled them to live comfortably in Greece and send a significant amount of money to their families in Albania. These stonemasons represented one of the success stories of Albanian migrant labour in Greece; in contrast, other Albanian migrants were not so fortunate and only managed to find poorly paid work where they were vulnerable to exploitation.

In the same town as the three successful stonemasons was an 18-year-old Albanian man who had been working in Greece for two years. During this time he had only managed to find badly paid work and was often exploited by his employers. For example, if he was asked to dig a trench, a daily rate would be negotiated but this would only be paid at the end of the job. When the job was finished the employer would simply refuse to pay him the full amount, claiming that the job had not been done properly. With only a limited income, this particular Albanian migrant could not afford to rent a place to live and was reduced to living in a disused chicken coop. Although his situation was far from comfortable, he insisted that his current life in Greece was better than the one he had left behind in Albania and he could even send some remittances back to his parents.

The response of the Greek government to illegal immigration

At the practical level, the response of the Greek government towards the inflow of migrants from Eastern Europe has been threefold. First, new legislation was introduced which imposed severe penalties upon illegal immigrants. However, there is little evidence that sanctions have been effective in reducing the inflow of illegal entrants. There are practical limitations which prevent imprisonment from being an effective deterrent to illegal migrants. Greece has a very small prison population with only limited facilities for detaining large numbers of illegal immigrants. The precise number of illegal aliens in Greece can at best only be estimated; however, various sources indicate that the number of Albanians in Greece is in the region of 400 000 (Lazaridis, 1998).

If we assume that a significant proportion of these Albanians are classed as illegal aliens, since they do not have either work permits or visas, this then gives us a clear indication of the difficulties that would be encountered by the Greek state if they insisted upon the arrest and imprisonment of all illegal aliens. It is clear that the necessary facilities for incarcerating all illegal aliens in Greece do not exist. The 1991 immigration law was impossible to implement. The deterrent value of a long prison sentence is lost when illegal immigrants are aware of the fact that they are not likely to be imprisoned for breaking immigration laws.

The authorities have been unable to prevent illegal immigration through effective use of legal sanctions such as imprisonment. The main alternative to imprisonment has been the widespread use of forced deportation. Greece and Albania share a common border. Illegal immigrants can be quickly and cheaply transported back to Albania by simply loading them on to a bus and driving them up to the Albanian border. Between 1991 and 1995, the Greek government deported just over one million illegal Albanian immigrants. Although the use of road transport is relatively cheap compared with air transport, the sheer volume of Albanians being deported and the relentlessness of the task inevitably meant that this became a very expensive operation. Between 1991 and 1995, £16 million were spent on apprehending and deporting Albanians (Droukas, 1998).

The migrants' response to deportation

A policy of mass deportation can only be sustained in the long term if it is successful in achieving its intended objective. With the benefit of hindsight it is clear that this policy of forced deportation was not effective in reducing the number of illegal immigrants in Greece. The main problem with forced deportation is that there is no guarantee that the deported Albanians will not simply return to Greece at the next available opportunity. Indeed, the fact that the total number of Albanians deported is greater than the total number of Albanians in Greece proves that many deported Albanians were returning to Greece only to be deported again. Such a policy of forced deportation can only succeed in significantly reducing the number of illegal immigrants if either the cost of reentry is intolerably high, or the act of deportation is sufficiently unpleasant to deter people from taking the risk of being caught and deported in the future.

We can consider the deterrent value of the financial loss which results from being deported. An illegal entrant who is deported will suffer financially both through loss of income and through having to incur the cost of reentry into Greece. With respect to the costs of re-entry, a fraudulently obtained visa for Greece can be bought for approximately £240. Alternatively, £200 can be paid to criminal gangs who specialise in smuggling people into Greece. As for loss of wages, it is often the case that deported Albanians return to Greece within one or two days and therefore will not lose many days' work. However, Albanians may be held by the police for several weeks before being deported, in which case they would lose a significant amount of potential earnings.

The average daily wage for Albanians working in Greece is £15 and therefore the loss of income from being deported can range from £30 to £200. In a worst-case scenario, an illegal entrant who is deported back to Albania will have to face an extra cost of £440. This is a substantial sum for an Albanian migrant worker earning £15 per day. However, with continuous work the amount lost can be made up within 30 days. A deported Albanian who returns to Greece immediately can only recover financially if he is able to remain economically active without further interruption. By looking at the number of deportations between 1991 and 1995 (just over one million) and taking into account the average number of Albanians in Greece at this time (350 000), we can easily calculate the average number of times that each Albanian was deported. If all 350 000 Albanians were deported three times over in this five-year period, this would give us a figure of just over one million deportations.

Therefore, each Albanian could on average expect to be deported once every 20 months. This does not tell us how often any individual Albanian migrant worker will be deported, since some Albanians were deported as many as twenty times, whilst others have managed to avoid deportation completely. However, this 'deportation interval' of 20 months gives us a clear indication of the perceived risk of deportation for an Albanian working illegally in Greece. An Albanian returning to Greece after being deported will, on average, expect not to be redeported for some time and will therefore expect to recover from the financial setback. The clear implication of this analysis is that the policy of mass deportation has not been effective as a means of significantly reducing the number of illegal Albanians in Greece, since it is generally regarded as only a minor inconvenience and does not dissuade them from returning to Greece.

A precarious equilibrium?

The Greek state has been unable to prevent illegal Albanian migrants from entering the country and has also been unable to force their return to Albania. The penalties for breaking immigration laws and the threat of deportation have both proved to have insufficient deterrent value. In 1997 the Greek parliament passed a presidential decree, PD358-359/97, which called for the registration of all illegal immigrants. This represented a significant change in the nature of Greek immigration policy, away from the coercive policies of incarceration and deportation and towards a more immigrant-friendly approach aimed at the integration rather than the exclusion of illegal immigrants.

The registration of illegal immigrants involved issuing them with residence permits valid for one, two or three years and has so far involved the registration of nearly 400 000 illegal immigrants. Of this number, 52 per cent were Albanian nationals (Greek Ministry of Public Order, 1999). The process by which illegal Albanian immigrants were registered and issued with residence permits is as follows: most Albanians were issued with either a six-month residence permit known as a white card, or a one-year residence permit known as a green card. Albanians who could prove that they had either filed a tax return or had paid national insurance contributions for 40 days were given a one-year residence permit. Those who had never paid tax and made no national insurance contributions were given a six month residence permit which could be extended for a further six months if the applicant could prove that they had made at least 40 days' worth of national insurance contributions during the first six-month.

Although these attempts to register and legitimise illegal economic migrants have been reasonably successful, some 200 000 Albanians remain unregistered because many Albanians are employed on an informal basis. Their employers are unwilling to declare that they are employing them, making it impossible for either the Albanians or their employers to pay tax or national insurance on their earnings. A further reason why so many Albanians have avoided registering for residence permits is that a large number of them are involved in some kind of criminal activity and therefore avoid any contact with the Greek state. This is especially true of those who have been convicted and deported in the past, since they are now registered as undesirable aliens, who if caught will be immediately redeported.

The incentive to migrate

There are two main theories of migration which can be used to explain the nature of the migration patterns between Albania and Greece. Neoclassical economists assume that individuals will attempt to maximise their utility. In terms of migration theory, the neoclassical position holds that an individual will decide whether to migrate to a particular country by weighing up the relative costs and benefits of migrating. The benefits of migration are seen in terms of push and pull factors. Push factors are those aspects of the donor country which are not good and therefore push the individual to consider moving to a country which does not have these disadvantages. Common push factors in donor countries are overpopulation, low living standards, lack of economic opportunities and political repression. Pull factors are those aspects of the recipient country which make it attractive to a potential immigrant, such as relatively high demand for labour, availability of land, good economic opportunities and political freedom.

The push–pull theory of migration can be used to explain why the majority of people chose to leave Albania and work in Greece. The figures in Table 11.2 demonstrate the collapse of the Albanian economy in the early 1990s and the strength of push motives for migration.

The very high levels of unemployment in the Albanian economy between 1992 and 1995 are mainly the result of the collapse in output

Table 11.2   Push factors affecting Albanian migration, 1990–8

	Albanian unemployment	Change in Albanian GDP (%)
1990	9.5	−10.0
1991	8.9	−27.0
1992	27.9	−7.2
1993	29.0	9.6
1994	19.6	9.4
1995	16.9	8.9
1996	12.4	9.1
1997	14.9	−8.0
1998	–	12.0

Sources: IMF 1997; EIU 2000; OECD 1999; EBRD 1998; OECD 1998.

which occurred in the early years of transition to a market economy. Table 11.2 also shows a recovery in the mid- to late 1990s which is associated with a reduced level of unemployment in the Albanian economy, although unemployment in Albania has been consistently higher than in Greece. This disparity in unemployment levels between the two countries generates a set of push–pull factors which encourage migration. Lack of job opportunities in Albania create the push factor, encouraging workers to leave in order to find work, whereas the relative abundance of work in Greece creates the pull factor which attracts the Albanian migrants.

Unemployment levels in Albania and the demand for cheap labour in Greece have been important factors in the push–pull motives for migration between the two countries. However, we also need to consider other economic disparities between the two countries and their influence upon the migration process.

The wage differential between the two countries is an important factor in this respect. In 1993, when the flow of migrants into Greece was at its peak, wages in Greece were ten times as high as those in Albania. On average, an Albanian migrant worker only needed to find two days' work in Greece in order to earn the equivalent of one month's work in Albania. The prospect of earning significantly more in Greece than in Albania is a clear 'pull' factor. However, this must not be seen as just a case of people opting for higher wages and therefore a better lifestyle. The wage levels in Albania were often insufficient to provide people with even their basic needs, such as food. Therefore, the wage differential between the two countries also contains a 'push' factor, where migrants are forced to leave home in order to escape absolute poverty.

Although the push–pull theory of migration can explain why Albanian migrants initially chose to work in Greece, subsequent waves of migration are explained in other ways. Albanians in Greece live in migrant communities which contain other members of their family, usually brothers or cousins. When asked why they chose to migrate, many stated that they left because of poverty in Albania and were attracted to Greece because of its relative prosperity. They often said that they chose to work in that particular part of Greece as they were following the lead of other members of their family. Some migrants are dependent upon family and community networks to the extent that without them they would not have left Albania in the first place. Although this is the case for very young and very vulnerable migrants, it is also true for those who lack the necessary confidence to face the risks of migration without support from existing migrant networks in the host country.

This process of migration, whereby the integration of new migrants is facilitated by existing networks, is in keeping with the theory of chain migration. Although chain migration theory is useful in helping us to understand how existing networks facilitate the flow of new migrants into Greece, it does not help us to understand the initial causes of migration. We must therefore rely upon the neoclassical theory of push–pull migration, although a more complete model would incorporate elements of chain migration theory as well.

Albanians in Greece: implications for the EU

There are two key aspects of the migration of Albanians into Greece which have implications for the European Union. First, the majority of Albanians in Greece are effectively economic migrants, who have chosen to work abroad in order to improve their economic prospects. Second, the Greek state has been forced to accept the presence of almost half a million Albanian migrant workers because neither imprisonment nor deportation is effective.

Since we have assumed that the majority of Albanian migrants were attracted to Greece by economic factors such as higher wage levels, it is likely that they might be tempted to move on to other EU states which appear to offer significantly better economic prospects. For an Albanian migrant who is thinking of moving on to another country, the obvious country to choose would be Italy. Although Italy does not share a common border with Greece, there is a significant flow of both goods and people between the two countries, since Italy is Greece's main trading partner (Economist Intelligence Unit, 1999). The cheapest and easiest way of reaching Italy from Greece is by ship, with many daily crossings connecting Patras, on the west coast of Greece, with a range of cities on the east coast of Italy. A 'deck class' one-way ticket to Italy can be obtained for as little as £20, which is equivalent to between one and two days' wages. When interviewed, 25 per cent of Albanian migrants in Greece were prepared to admit that they were actively planning to move on to other EU countries, especially Italy. There are good reasons to believe that this figure is an underestimate since the interviewed Albanians were reticient about their future plans. Those who admitted to being illegally resident in Greece were usually unwilling to reveal precise details about their activities and, in the interview sample, they never admitted the intention of entering other

EU countries. This reticence can be explained by the simple fact that an illegal alien in Greece can only hope to enter another EU country by doing so illegally and may well be unwilling to admit this intention. In the interview sample, 25 per cent were illegally resident in Greece.

Taking the reticence into account, the proportion of the sample wishing to move on to another EU country could be as high as 50 per cent. If this sample is in any way representative of the total population, it follows that a significant proportion of the Albanian population in Greece is considering a move to other EU countries. Albanians in Greece represent a potential flow of new migrants into Western Europe. In order to understand why to date Albanians have not tended to move on, we need to look more closely at the immigration status of Albanians in Greece. We must also consider whether there are legitimate ways in which they could travel to other EU member states.

Greece and the Schengen Agreement

Membership of the European Union has involved the removal of previous restrictions on the free movement of people and goods between member states. For citizens of EU member states, there are no legal restrictions upon their movement within the EU, or upon their activities within the EU. A citizen of any EU member state can travel to, work in and take up permanent residence in any other member state. This would suggest that there is no need for EU member states to impose checks on internal borders. However, the process of removing checks on internal borders is not yet complete, with some member states still feeling the need to restrict the entry of people travelling from other member states. The main obstacle to the complete removal of border controls between all EU member states is the as yet unresolved issue of third country nationals. Migrant labourers and asylum seekers, resident in the EU but not citizens of an EU member state, are seen as problematic.

In order for the complete abolition of internal border controls to take place, there first needs to be common agreement about asylum and immigration. A uniform immigration and asylum policy would ensure that each member state was confident about the nature of new inflows of people into other member states, and thus would not feel the need to impose extra border controls. For example, a country which runs a tight immigration and asylum policy might have reservations about relaxing its border controls whilst other EU countries are permitting relatively large inflows of migrant labour and asylum seekers. The Schengen Agreement, which came into force amongst the first wave of members in 1995, addresses this need for a common asylum and immigration policy and has helped to facilitate the removal of border controls between nine EU member states.

For Schengen members, who have removed their border controls, there are several benefits to be gained. Open borders will enhance the free movement of people and goods between Schengen members, leading to an increase in the volume of trade and increased labour mobility. These benefits have in general been rather small, since intra-EU trade was not significantly restricted by internal EU border controls and therefore can only be slightly enhanced by the removal of border restrictions. As for the mobility of labour, this also has not been significantly enhanced by the removal of border controls. For EU citizens, mobility of labour between member states is relatively low and is far exceeded by the relatively high labour mobility of non EU citizens, both in terms of intra-EU movements and the inflow of labour from non-EU countries. Schengen membership also has the key benefit of enabling its members to participate in the process of determining EU immigration and asylum policy. This in turn aims at keeping inward migration at modest levels and therefore minimises the need to monitor internal EU borders.

As Box 11.1 shows, although Greece has signed and ratified the Schengen Agreement, the abolition of border controls has not yet taken place. The presence of a large immigrant population has been one factor. Another important consideration is that the Greek–Turkish border is a popular crossing point for illegal immigrants from the Indian subcontinent. For these reasons Greece and Italy continue to monitor the movement of people passing between their two countries.

Box 11.1   The signatories to Schengen

The following countries are signatories to the Schengen Agreement and have removed border controls:

- Austria, Belgium, France, Germany, Italy, Luxembourg, Netherlands, Portugal and Spain

  The following countries have signed and intend to abolish border controls at a later date:

- Denmark, Finland, Greece, Iceland, Norway and Sweden

Greek immigration law empowers the police to check all persons entering and leaving the country, enabling them to ensure that Albanians attempting to leave Greece for Italy possess the appropriate travel documents and visas. Since these border controls are still in place, we need to consider whether there are any legitimate ways for Albanian migrants to enter Italy.

The Schengen Agreement has cleared the way for a uniform visa to be issued to visitors from a third country wishing to enter a country covered by the agreement. This uniform visa will allow a visitor unrestricted access to any member country for the duration of the visa, usually three-months. Many Albanians enter Greece on a three-month tourist visa. At the end of the three months they return to Albania to obtain another visa and, by continually renewing their visas, Albanian migrant workers are able to work in Greece for up to eleven months a year. It is difficult to establish how many Albanians are entering Greece on tourist visas, since many tourist visas are obtained fraudulently, rendering official figures grossly inaccurate. A sample of Albanian migrant workers in Greece during 1998 and 1999 showed that a quarter of them were in possession of a tourist visa.

As a Schengen country, Greece could issue Schengen visas to Albanians. However, Albanians are denied access to Schengen visas, being issued instead with visas only valid for Greece. The option to issue a restricted visa is available to Schengen members where a visa applicant fails to meet the criteria in Article 5 of the agreement, including proof that the applicant has sufficient means to support themselves for the duration of their stay. Since most Albanians who apply for visas do so because poverty has forced them to work abroad, it is therefore unlikely that they could demonstrate the ability to support themselves for the duration of their stay. Greece, by issuing restricted visas, has prevented Albanian migrants from gaining legal entry into other EU countries.

Albanians in Greece with residence permits represent a far greater potential problem than those with tourist visas. According to the most recent figures, they outnumber those with visas by three to one. The Greek Ministry of Public Order estimates that there are approximately 300 000 Albanians with residence permits. The significance of this figure becomes apparent when we consider that according to Article 21 of the Schengen Agreement, an alien holding a residence permit issued by a Schengen country may move freely within the territories of other Schengen members. This would suggest that since the majority of the Albanian population in Greece possess residence permits, they are therefore permitted to enter other Schengen countries. Although there is evidence that a significant proportion of Albanians wish to enter the more prosperous countries of Western Europe, there is no evidence of a large-scale movement having taken place. The main reason why Albanians with residence permits for Greece do not take advantage of the provisions laid out in the Schengen Agreement is because border checks are still applied between Greece and Italy. In Article 21 Schengen states that when aliens cross internal borders with a valid residence permit for a member country, they must provide evidence of means to support themselves for the duration of their stay. This provision enables Greece and Italy to prevent Albanians from entering Italy, without contravening the Schengen Agreement.

The motive for Greece joining the Schengen area appears to be rather different from the motives of other Schengen members. Schengen has enabled most of its members to benefit from free movement of goods and people between member countries. However, Greece has not realised these potential benefits. For Greece, joining Schengen was a strategic move with the aim of ensuring that Greece's external borders would be accepted as the external borders of the EU. By joining Schengen, Greece has gained support from the EU in its fight against both drug trafficking and illegal immigration (Baldwin-Edwards and Fakiolas, 1998).

Conclusion

During the 1990s there was a significant flow of economic migrants out of the former communist countries of Eastern Europe into the more stable and prosperous countries of Western Europe. Greece has absorbed the second largest number of total migrants and the largest number as a proportion of its own population. It is clear that the majority of these migrants have entered Greece in order to improve their economic prospects. A significant proportion of them are actively considering moving on to other more prosperous West European countries. Although Greece has signed and ratified the Schengen Agreement, this has not created an open border situation enabling Albanians legally to enter other Schengen member countries. The continued imposition of border controls between Greece and Italy has ensured that the vast majority of Albanian migrant workers are confined to Greece. Entry into Italy, and therefore other Schengen members, is only available to most Albanians through illegal means.

References

Baldwin-Edwards, M. and Fakiolas, R. (1998) 'Greece: The Contours of a Fragmented Policy Response', *South European Society & Politics*, vol. 3, no. 3, pp. 186–204

Biberaj, E. (1998) *Albania in Transition* (Westview Press, Oxford)

Castles, S. and Miller, M. (1993) *The Age of Mass Migration* (Macmillan – now Palgrave, London)

Clarke, S. (1999) 'Splitting Difference: Psychoanalysis, Hatred and Exclusion' *Journal for the Theory of Social Behaviour*, vol. 29, no. 1 (March) pp. 21–36

Clunies-Ross, A. (ed.) (1998) *Albania's Economy in Transition and Turmoil* (Ashgate, Aldershot)

Droukas, E. (1998) 'Albanians in the Greek Informal Economy' *Journal of Ethnic and Migration Studies*, vol. 24, no. 2 (April) pp. 348–65

Economist Intelligence Unit (1999) *Greece*, Country Profile, 3rd Quarter (EIU, London)

Economist Intelligence Unit (1999/2000) *Greece*, Country Profile (EIU, London)

European Bank of Reconstruction and Development (1998) *Transition Report* (EBRD, London)

European Commission (2000) *European Social Statistics* (Luxembourg)

Fassmann, H. and Munz, R. (1994) *European Migration in the Late 20th Century* (Edward Elgar, Aldershot)

Greek Institute of Labour (GSEE) (1996) *Enimerosi*, Issue 16 (July–August)

Greek Institute of Labour (GSEE) (1999) *Enimerosi*, Issue 48–9 (June–July)

Greek Ministry of Public Order (1999), Fax from Greek Ministry of Public Order 16/8/99.

Guild, E. (1998) 'Competence, Discretion and Third Country Nationals: The European Union's Struggle with Migration' *Journal of Ethnic and Migration Studies*, vol. 24, no. 4 (October)

International Monetary Fund (1997) 'Albania – Recent Economic Developments', *Staff Country Report*, No. 97/21 (IMF, Washington DC)

King, R., Iosofides, T. and Myrivili, L. (1998) 'A Migrant's Story: From Albania to Athens', *Journal of Ethnic and Migration Studies*, vol. 24, no. 1 (January) pp. 159–75

Korovilas, J. (1999) 'The Albanian Economy in Transition: The Role of Remittances and Pyramid Investment Schemes' *Post Communist Economies*, vol. 11, no. 3 (September) pp. 399–415

Layard, R. (ed.) (1992) *East West Migration* (MIT Press, London)

Lazaridis, G. (1998) 'Albanian and Polish Undocumented Workers in Greece', *Journal of European Social Policy*, vol. 8, no. 1 (February) pp. 5–22

Lianos, P., Sarris, A. and Katseli, T. (1997) 'Illegal Immigration and Local Labour Markets: The Case of Northern Greece' *International Migration*, vol. 34, pp. 449–84

Organisation for Economic Cooperation and Development (1998) *Economic Outlook* (OECD)

Pirounakis, N. (1998) *The Greek Economy* (Macmillan, London)

Simon, J. (1989) *The Economic Consequences of Migration* (Basil Blackwell, Cambridge, Mass)

Stark, O. (1991) *The Migration of Labour* (Basil Blackwell, Oxford)

Vaughan-Whitehead, D. (1999) *Albania in Crisis* (Edward Elgar, Cheltenham)

12
Europe's Demographic Time Bomb: The Challenge for Public Pensions

Martin Sullivan

Introduction

On 12 October 1999, the population of the planet was officially declared by the United Nations Population Fund (UNPFA) to have reached six billion. Since no one actually knows for certain when the six billion point was reached, this announcement was entirely symbolic. It was, however, symptomatic of a growing preoccupation among academics and policy-makers with demographic issues in general and the problems posed by an ageing population in particular. When addressing the theme of 'people', nothing can be more basic than to examine the demography of the EU and to do so within a global setting. Peterson (1999) suggests that demographic changes, of which the ageing of Europe's population is but a small part, might actually represent a greater threat to the world than the proliferation of nuclear or chemical weapons or extreme climate change. For this reason, it is entirely appropriate that a book about the people of Europe should include a chapter about demographic change and its consequences for policy-makers.

It should be clearly stated at the outset that demography is not an exact science and population projections are not precise predictions of what will happen. They are merely forecasts, statements of what is expected to happen if assumptions about future trends in birth, death and migration rates prove to be well-founded. In this respect, demography is like all social sciences. There is, however, a crucial difference between demography and other social sciences in that the publication of population data may well have an effect on the way people think and behave. Above all it might affect the climate of opinion in which policy-makers deal, not only with population questions, but also with

Table 12.1   Projected EU population shares (percentages) by broad age group, 2000–50

	2000	2010	2020	2050
Children	23.1	21.8	20.6	19.3
Workers	60.8	60.3	58.9	53.1
Elderly	16.1	17.9	20.5	27.6

Sources: Eurostat (1996); own calculations.

such issues as pensions and migration. As Jackson (1998) shows, changes in government policy in respect of families have the potential to influence fertility rates; tax breaks for working parents and generous public provision of childcare facilities might affect people's decisions about family size.

The population of the world is growing but, within this global picture, there are marked regional variations. In Europe, population ageing has already begun, as Table 12.1 demonstrates. In developing countries the situation is very different. To put it in crude economic terms, it still pays parents in these countries to have many children because the cost of bringing up children is low and there are consider-able benefits to parents in their old age from having grown-up children to look after them. Pension income is a well-understood feature of developed economies but, in developing countries, one looks to one's family to provide for one's declining years.

From the second half of the 1980s, a series of high-profile reports appeared (OECD, 1988; World Bank 1994, Taverne, 1995; Bank for International Settlements, 1998) pointing to the consequences of demographic ageing for the public pension systems of developed coun-tries. Gradually, the idea took hold that Europe was facing a demo-graphic time-bomb, where the 'grey generations' would increasingly come to dominate social and political life and absorb an ever larger share of society's resources. The most extreme versions of the demo-graphic time bomb scenario envisage the ossification of society, as the interests of the conservative old take precedence over those of the more dynamic young. Europe was thought to be particularly suscepti-ble to this time-bomb effect.

In Europe, it was argued, the problem would be especially difficult because of the heavy reliance on the so-called Pay-As-You-Go (PAYG) public pension arrangements. Concern began to grow that there was a time bomb ticking away beneath the public finances of many of the

Table 12.2   Projected old-age dependency ratios in the EU, 2000–50

	2000	2010	2020	2050
Austria	24.8	28.1	29.1	48.4
Belgium	28.0	29.6	35.8	48.0
Denmark	24.0	27.0	33.3	41.7
Finland	24.2	27.2	38.5	46.3
France	27.1	28.1	35.9	51.1
Germany	25.4	31.9	34.6	51.0
Greece	28.3	31.8	35.6	53.0
Ireland	20.6	22.8	32.4	73.2
Italy	28.7	33.5	38.7	60.8
Luxembourg	23.8	25.9	30.9	41.8
Netherlands	22.0	24.8	32.8	45.0
Portugal	25.0	26.6	30.0	48.8
Spain	27.1	28.6	32.5	61.8
Sweden	29.4	31.2	36.8	41.8
UK	26.5	27.3	32.7	47.1
EU15	26.5	29.6	34.7	51.9

Source: Eurostat (1996).

states of Europe because pension liabilities were going to become heavier and heavier in the future.

The scale of the problem appears in Table 12.2 which gives projections of the old-age dependency ratios for various countries. The old-age dependency ratio is the ratio of the people aged 65 and over to those aged 20 to 64. In all EU countries the dependency ratio is expected to increase considerably over the first half of the twenty-first century. Ireland presents the issue in a particularly acute form. In 2000 its dependency ratio was 20.6 but by 2050 it is projected to increase to 73.2. To illustrate the nature of the problem which these figures present, the next section will examine the structural features of the major types of pension provision that have been created in industrial societies. The reasons why ageing populations present a political and economic challenge to EU government will next be discussed, followed by an evaluation of the alternatives to current Pay-As-You-Go schemes to conclude the chapter.

Types of pension

While there are all sorts of schemes for spreading income over a longer period than the normal working lifetime, only three arrangements are sufficiently common in Europe to merit description here. The first is the Pay-As-You-Go system (PAYG). The second is the prefunded money purchase scheme (PMPS) and the third is the occupational pension based on final salary (OPFS). These pension arrangements emerged in the late nineteenth and early twentieth centuries as part of the social security arrangements that became essential for industrial societies. Friendly societies, mutual funds, insurance and assurance companies and, of course, the state itself began to provide security for people who were now better off materially as a result of economic development, but still faced the uncertainties of unemployment and ill health.

Public pension provision was an integral part of the social insurance schemes introduced by European states in the late nineteenth and early twentieth centuries. Although presented as an insurance fund into which all citizens contributed, the reality was that benefits were paid from general taxation. From the very start, there was no true 'fund' which carefully balanced contributions against benefits according to sound actuarial principles. From the earliest origins of state-financed national social insurance, benefits were paid out to people who had not made enough contributions to justify the benefits that they received. Everything depended on the power of the state to levy taxes – so the schemes became 'pay as you go' in the sense that each new generation of pensioners depended on a new generation of workers and taxpayers for their income.

There were other schemes that worked very differently. Prior to state action some people had formed Friendly Societies. Insurance companies came into existence and some employers began to provide pension arrangements to secure the loyalty of the workforce. These pension structures fell into two main categories. The first was an institutional structure for gathering small but regular savings so that they could be invested in property, bonds and shares to provide a fund of assets from which pension payments could be made. This set of financial institutions developed into what we now see as 'fund managers' whose expertise is to manage the investment of vast sums so as to provide the resources from which money purchase pensions are paid. Members of these schemes build up a fund during their working lifetime and use it to purchase an annuity on retirement from work. Such is the prefunded money purchase pension scheme (PMPS).

The most desirable sort of pension, which was only available to a small proportion of the population, was the occupational pension related to final salary (OPFS). Government employees and salaried workers in the larger private businesses with secure jobs could have regular deductions from their earnings put aside, usually together with an employer's contribution, in order to provide for a good income in retirement. The final pension would depend on the number of years of service and the level of contributions, but would also be related to their salary just prior to retirement. From the employee's point of view, this was a very attractive arrangement. For the employer, the pension scheme was a way of attracting and retaining a high-quality, loyal workforce.

Both the prefunded and the occupational pension schemes favour those who can save, can acquire assets, and can afford regular contributions out of their salary while maintaining an adequate standard of living. They are not an easy option for low-paid workers, for those with discontinuous employment, part-time workers and women whose care commitments interrupt their earnings. These categories would be much better served by PAYG systems because of the redistribution inherent in these schemes.

The PMPS and the OPFS differ from the PAYG schemes in several important respects. In the first place, they are private sector schemes outside direct government control, although regulatory and taxation rules govern their transactions. The state regards such arrangements as desirable in terms of social stability. Second, these non-government schemes were 'funded'. The contributions were invested in real assets within a managed portfolio in order to provide a balance between income and capital growth. Third, PAYG schemes were redistributive in that benefits were not related as closely and directly to the individual's contributions as in the other two schemes. If benefits are paid from a PAYG system financed in large part from progressive taxation, the effect is highly redistributional. Finally, the PMPS and OPFS funds, if honestly and competently managed, could deal with inflation; in principle, if not in practice, this meant that pension levels were safeguarded. The uprating of public pensions under PAYG is, of course, a highly political question.

The existence of a demographic time bomb in the form of an ageing population has drawn attention to the problems of a PAYG system. The problem, however, started much further back in time. Even when these schemes were first set up, benefits were granted to people who had not made contributions and this political approach to public pensions has continued ever since. There is a strong temptation, which politicians in search of electoral popularity rarely resist, to extend benefits to new and deserving sections of the population. The governments of Europe have gone down this path and the unfunded liabilities in terms of generous pensions promises are now just as much a part of the problem as the demographic time bomb itself.

Under PAYG, an ageing population implies a bigger and bigger intergenerational transfer from the working age groups to the ever larger pensioner population. Tax burdens must rise and, inevitably, much of this increased taxation falls on non-pensioner households. If nothing is done, the share of EU GDP absorbed by public pension payments, at the time of writing about 12 per cent, could grow to exceed 20 per cent over the next two or three decades. Cutting benefits or increasing retirement ages – or both – could reduce this rate of growth. Such changes are unlikely, however, in view of the increased electoral significance of the pensioner vote. There are other benefits to the economy from encouraging the growth of private savings associated with funded pension schemes. The savings provide a stock of funds for investment, promoting economic growth.

The alternative to raising taxes is to finance pension payments through government borrowing but here too there is a difficulty. Under the Treaties of Maastricht and Amsterdam strict budget deficit ceilings have been set and monetary union implies careful control of public debt. The authorities seem to be caught between a rock and a hard place – unpopular tax increases or failing to comply with treaty obligations. The issue is compounded since its incidence is uneven across Europe; most member states have similar problems, but some are more serious than others. The politics of easing public pension problems by allowing some member states to run larger budget deficits than others could be contentious.

There is a growing consensus, moreover, that a switch, sooner rather than later, from PAYG to prefunded private pensions is the only realistic way for Europe to avoid serious problems. Occupational pensions may well continue to provide for a small proportion of the population, but do not constitute a solution for the population as a whole. Yet the abolition of the national PAYG pensions schemes, and their replacement with PMPSs would be very difficult, and it is certainly arguable that the case for such radical change to Europe's pension arrangements is not yet proven. Perhaps the problems of PAYG have been overstated; perhaps the difficulties are not insurmountable.

Prefunded pensions are thought to be unaffected by demographic trends. This is because the value of the pension benefits depends on the savings of individuals over their working lifetime – and, of course, on the return earned by the fund – rather than on the ability of the government to extract more taxes from the shrinking workforce of a slowly growing economy. Whilst this argument is valid there are other difficulties with the PMPS approach which need to be evaluated first and I shall return to explore this argument in a later section of this chapter.

European demography

The underlying cause of Europe's increasing old-age dependency ratios is, as Grundy (1996) shows, the transition from relatively high to very low fertility rates during the latter half of the twentieth century. All EU countries experienced a sharp increase in their fertility rates during the two decades immediately following the Second World War. This 'baby boom' which peaked in the mid-1960s stood in marked contrast to the low birth rates of the interwar years. The high birth rates of the baby boom years mean that from 2010 onwards the number of elderly people in the EU will rise steeply. At the same time, a sustained downward trend in fertility since the mid-1960s means that too few children are now being born in the EU to maintain a stable balance between the working and the retired populations.

Changes in life expectancy also have an important impact on the future balance within the EU population. It is increases in the residual life expectancy, the life expectancy of people in middle or later life, that are relevant here. Improvements in the life expectancy of the middle-aged and elderly mean that larger numbers of individuals will survive to the age of 65 and beyond. As Table 12.3 shows, infant mortality has declined significantly in all EU countries since the 1970s. Portugal's record of reducing infant deaths from 55.5 to 6.8 per 1000 live births in just over 25 years is particularly remarkable. Infant mortality in the EU is now extremely low at 5.5 deaths per 1000 live births and any further reductions in infant mortality are, therefore, likely to be very small. By contrast, residual life expectancy has increased substantially in many countries since the 1960s, and, as Shiro (2000) shows, there is no reason to suppose that this trend is anywhere near exhausted. The vast majority of deaths occurring each year in the EU are among people aged 65 and over. With very low rates of fertility and child mortality, increases in residual life expectancy have become a major determinant of further population ageing.

One solution to the ageing problem is migration. As Korovilas demonstrates in Chapter 11, push and pull factors are moving Albanians into Greece quite rapidly and these migrants are nearly all in the working age groups. Considerable inward migration is already

Table 12.3   Infant mortality: deaths during first year per 1000 live births, 1970–96

	1970	1980	1990	1996
Austria	25.9	14.3	7.8	5.1
Belgium	21.1	12.1	7.9	5.6
Denmark	14.2	8.4	7.5	5.6
Finland	13.2	7.6	5.6	3.5
France	18.2	10.0	7.3	4.8
Germany	21.1	12.4	7.2	5.0
Greece	29.6	17.9	9.7	7.2
Ireland	19.5	11.1	8.2	5.6
Italy	29.6	14.6	8.2	6.0
Luxembourg	24.9	11.5	7.3	4.9
Netherlands	12.7	8.6	7.1	5.7
Portugal	55.5	24.3	10.9	6.8
Spain	28.1	12.3	7.6	6.0
Sweden	11.0	6.9	6.0	4.0
UK	18.5	12.1	7.9	6.0
EU15	22.9	12.3	7.7	5.5

Source: Council of Europe (1998).

easing some of the economic problems of the EU but it is also causing tensions within the social fabric. Large-scale immigration by young working-age people would immediately reduce the rate at which old-age dependency ratios are increasing. By contrast, rises in fertility rates and reductions in infant mortality only take effect two decades later.

Migrant workers are already used extensively in some EU member states, but mainly on a seasonal or temporary basis. Every summer, workers from India, Morocco and Russia come to pick, wash and pack vegetables on European farms before returning home in the autumn. Primary immigration, the permanent settlement of workers and their families, has, on the other hand, all but dried up in the EU. Britain and Germany, for example, both closed their doors to mass primary immigration during the first half of the 1970s. Yet, a study by the United Nations, reported in *The Economist* (2000), estimates that, on the basis of current birth and death rates, the EU would need to import 13.5 million workers annually, over the next 50 years, in order to maintain the current ratio of workers to retired people. The UK alone would need over a million new immigrants annually up to 2050. Such figures are unrealistic and so migration offers no viable solution.

The problems of current schemes

Nearly 90 per cent of all pension incomes in the EU are derived through national PAYG schemes. As Table 12.4 shows, in 1995, spending on pensions accounted for some 39 per cent of EU social protection expenditure, compared with 27.6 per cent spent on healthcare and 8.4 per cent on income replacement for the unemployed. The figures differ considerably between countries, with Italy spending over half of social expenditures on pensions while in Ireland the equivalent figure is only 20 per cent. The Italian and German schemes currently provide retiring people with a level of income replacement equal to around 90 per cent and 70 per cent of average earnings respectively. The UK scheme, by contrast, provides an income replacement rate of around 15 per cent of earned incomes.

Public pensions currently absorb around 12 per cent of EU GDP. However, a survey of projections of future pension expenditures carried out by eleven EU countries (European Commission, 1996) suggested that by 2030, the pensions burden, the ratio of public pensions expenditure to GDP, could be between 15 and 20 per cent in Belgium, Finland, France, Germany, Italy and the Netherlands, and between 10 and 15 per cent in Denmark, Sweden and Spain. Only the UK and the

Table 12.4   Pensions expenditure as a percentage of total social protection spending

	Pensions	Healthcare	Unemployment
Austria	37.7	25.6	5.6
Belgium	31.6	25.8	14.3
Denmark	37.6	17.8	14.7
Finland	28.9	21.2	14.3
France	36.5	29.0	8.2
Germany	40.3	31.1	9.1
Greece	42.1	26.0	5.9
Ireland	19.9	35.4	17.3
Italy	54.5	21.4	2.2
Luxembourg	30.6	24.3	3.0
Netherlands	32.0	28.9	10.1
Portugal	36.0	32.8	5.5
Spain	40.9	30.0	14.3
Sweden	34.7	21.6	11.1
UK	33.9	25.8	5.9
EU15	39.0	27.6	8.4

Source: European Commission (1999).

Republic of Ireland had projected pensions burdens for 2030 which were below 10 per cent. Of course, these are only projections; in the event of faster than anticipated economic growth, they might prove excessively pessimistic. Nevertheless, there is a general expectation that the shares of national GDP absorbed by public pension systems will rise substantially after 2010.

The probability that governments throughout the EU will face rising public pensions bills, the financing of which will prove politically difficult to sustain, has led to a number of member states implementing measures aimed at reducing the long-term growth of pension costs. These typically include increases in the official retirement age, measures to restrict future eligibility for a state pension and the introduction of less generous methods of indexing pension benefits. Although these parametric changes to scheme design will reduce the rate of growth of public pension costs, some commentators, for example Borsch-Supan (2000), suggest that they may not be sufficient by themselves.

An evaluation of prefunded schemes

The advocates of prefunding suggest that a number of important benefits would arise as a result of a move away from PAYG as the method of providing EU citizens with pensions in the future. First, they claim that the ability of prefunded pension schemes to provide people with adequate retirement incomes is less susceptible to changes in demographic conditions. A switch to prefunding would, therefore, defuse the demographic time bomb.

In addition, it is suggested that because pensions received from prefunded schemes are derived from a combination of saving and investment returns, prefunded schemes will deliver better retirement incomes than those available through public PAYG schemes. It is also claimed that prefunded schemes are not susceptible to the kind of politically motivated changes to benefit levels and/or scheme coverage which have, in the past, done much to drive up the long-term costs of some national PAYG pension schemes.

Prefunded pension schemes require people to save during their working lives in order to accumulate a stock of assets. Their fund is then used to purchase an annuity, which is simply an arrangement whereby an insurance company accepts the obligation to provide an individual with a specified level of income during their retirement in return for an upfront payment. Prefunded schemes can, in principle, be either publicly or privately administered. A public sector scheme based on prefunding could employ a mixture of compulsion and inducement to secure an appropriate level of contributions. For some people, public provision would seem more proper than handing over pension provision to private sector financial institutions. For others, however, the record of political interference would argue in favour of private sector involvement. In addition, if compulsion is to be a feature of prefunding, perhaps because people would not save enough voluntarily, contributions to a publicly managed scheme might be more acceptable to workers than enforced saving via private schemes. The literature on prefunding is characterised by a strong bias in favour of private saving for retirement. As Banks and Emmerson (2000) observe, this is possibly due to the high political risks attached to government-managed prefunded schemes.

The fact that prefunding through the private sector has attracted more attention than the publicly administered alternative may also reflect the reality that privately provided prefunded schemes are already a feature of the European pensions environment. Industry-based and employer-provided occupational pension schemes are available in northern Europe, although they are far less common in the EU's Mediterranean countries. These OPFS schemes, described earlier, which typically provide retiring workers with a level of pension benefit equal to a fixed fraction of their salary at retirement, are usually pre-funded from contributions made by workers, and often by their employers as well. In Germany, however, the overwhelming majority of occupational schemes are financed on a PAYG basis. Individual saving for retirement is also important in Europe – most notably in the UK. Britain has a much lower level of unfunded pension provision than most other European states.

In a switch to prefunded pensions, both final salary occupational schemes and private pensions could, in principle, substitute for public PAYG schemes. There are, though, a number of practical problems associated with salary-related occupational pensions, which cast doubt on their potential to act as an alternative to public PAYG schemes. These problems concern the coverage of occupational pensions and their tendency to impede labour mobility. Generous OPFS schemes are becoming more and more expensive to provide and, as labour markets restructure towards greater flexibility, this type of pension provision seems likely to 'wither on the vine'. Civil servants may soon become the only significant group with generous inflation-proofed OPFS pensions. High administration costs also mean that economies of scale are

some respects, the proposal to modify PAYG is an attempt to distance government from the hard decisions that have to be made. In the UK, which has low pensions by EU standards, there has been a demand to restore the earnings link for public pensions. In many other member states, where pension levels are higher, the problem of meeting the costs is even more serious. Governments need to take these issues on board and deal with a policy dilemma which faces all European states.

References

Bank for International Settlements (1998) *The Macroeconomic and Financial Implications of Ageing Populations: A Report by the Group of Ten* (BIS, Basel)

Banks, J. and Emmerson, C. (2000) 'Public and Private Pension Spending: Principles, Practice and the Need for Reform', *Fiscal Studies*, vol. 21, no. 1, pp. 1–63

Boldrin, M. Dolado, J., Jimeno, J. and Peracchi, F. (1999) 'The Future of Pensions in Europe', *Economic Policy*, October, pp. 289–320

Borsch-Supan, A. (2000) 'Pension Reform in Germany: To Fund or not to Fund', *World Economics*, vol. 1, no. 1 (January–March) pp. 81–101

Council of Europe (1998) *Recent Demographic Developments in Europe* (Strasbourg).

Davis, E. P. (1997) *Pension Funds: Retirement-Income Security, and Capital Markets* (Oxford University Press, Oxford).

The Economist (2000) 'Europe's Need for immigrants', 6 May

European Commission (1996) 'Public Pension Expenditure Prospects in the European Union: A Survey of European Commisssion (1999) *Eurostat Year book, A Statistical Eye on Europe 1998/9 edition* (Luxembourg)

National Projections', *European Economy*, No. 3, Directorate General for Economic and Financial Affairs

Eurostat (1996) *Demographic Statistics* (European Commission, Brussels)

Grundy, E. (1996) 'Population Ageing in Europe', in Coleman, D. (ed.), *Europe's Population in the 1990s* (Oxford University Press, Oxford) pp. 267–96.

Jackson, S. (1998) *Britain's Population* (Routledge, London)

Miles, D. (1998) 'The Implications of Switching from Unfunded to Funded Pension Systems', *National Institute Economic Review*, no. 163, pp. 71–86

Mullan, P. (2000) *The Imaginary Time Bomb* (I. B. Tauris, London)

OECD (1988) *Ageing Populations: The Social Policy Implications, Organization for Economic Cooperation and Development* (OECD, Paris)

Peterson, P. G. (1999) 'Gray Dawn: The Global Aging Crisis', *Foreign Affairs*, January/February, pp. 42–55

Shiro, H. (2000) 'Greater Lifetime Expectations', *Nature,* 15 June, pp. 744–5

Taverne, D. (1995) *The Pension Time Bomb in Europe* (Federal Trust, London)

World Bank (1994) *Averting the Old-Age Crisis* (Oxford University Press, Oxford)

13
Conclusion: Insiders and Outsiders

Frank Gardner and Sue Hatt

People, in their various guises, have been the focus of this book. As the EU has developed its activities during its first 50 years, the lives of the people in the member states have been affected, to a greater or lesser extent, by the policies enacted in Brussels. These changes have impacted differently in each member state depending upon factors such as the state of the economy, the degree of compliance and the existing national provisions. For example, Panah demonstrated in Chapter 4 that the arrival of Wal-Mart on the European scene brought advantages to those consumers and producers who were in a position to respond positively to the new climate. Small producers, however, fared less well. Similarly, the CAP has protected EU agricultural producers from the vagaries of world markets while increasing the instability for agricultural producers in the rest of the world as Hatt has discussed in Chapter 9. In both these cases, the 'insiders' have been the principal beneficiaries while the 'outsiders' have been less well served.

One topic has not received explicit attention within this book although there have been several passing references to it. There is no chapter on external relations and on enlargement; no specific analysis of the consequences for people outside. 'Europe' is all too often used in common speech instead of the correct term 'European Union'. There are Europeans outside the charmed circle. Beyond Europe too, there are other 'outsiders' – some rich and powerful rivals, others poor and dependent. It is to this theme of insiders and outsiders that some concluding remarks must now be addressed.

One of the most bitter criticisms made of the European project is that it is an exclusive club for privileged European people and the rich, white corporations who abide by one set of rules in their northern headquarters and exploit low-cost labour and low environmental stan-

13
Conclusion: Insiders and Outsiders

Frank Gardner and Sue Hatt

People, in their various guises, have been the focus of this book. As the EU has developed its activities during its first 50 years, the lives of the people in the member states have been affected, to a greater or lesser extent, by the policies enacted in Brussels. These changes have impacted differently in each member state depending upon factors such as the state of the economy, the degree of compliance and the existing national provisions. For example, Panah demonstrated in Chapter 4 that the arrival of Wal-Mart on the European scene brought advantages to those consumers and producers who were in a position to respond positively to the new climate. Small producers, however, fared less well. Similarly, the CAP has protected EU agricultural producers from the vagaries of world markets while increasing the instability for agricultural producers in the rest of the world as Hatt has discussed in Chapter 9. In both these cases, the 'insiders' have been the principal beneficiaries while the 'outsiders' have been less well served.

One topic has not received explicit attention within this book although there have been several passing references to it. There is no chapter on external relations and on enlargement; no specific analysis of the consequences for people outside. 'Europe' is all too often used in common speech instead of the correct term 'European Union'. There are Europeans outside the charmed circle. Beyond Europe too, there are other 'outsiders' – some rich and powerful rivals, others poor and dependent. It is to this theme of insiders and outsiders that some concluding remarks must now be addressed.

One of the most bitter criticisms made of the European project is that it is an exclusive club for privileged European people and the rich, white corporations who abide by one set of rules in their northern headquarters and exploit low-cost labour and low environmental stan-

some respects, the proposal to modify PAYG is an attempt to distance government from the hard decisions that have to be made. In the UK, which has low pensions by EU standards, there has been a demand to restore the earnings link for public pensions. In many other member states, where pension levels are higher, the problem of meeting the costs is even more serious. Governments need to take these issues on board and deal with a policy dilemma which faces all European states.

References

Bank for International Settlements (1998) *The Macroeconomic and Financial Implications of Ageing Populations: A Report by the Group of Ten* (BIS, Basel)

Banks, J. and Emmerson, C. (2000) 'Public and Private Pension Spending: Principles, Practice and the Need for Reform', *Fiscal Studies*, vol. 21, no. 1, pp. 1–63

Boldrin, M. Dolado, J., Jimeno, J. and Peracchi, F. (1999) 'The Future of Pensions in Europe', *Economic Policy*, October, pp. 289–320

Borsch-Supan, A. (2000) 'Pension Reform in Germany: To Fund or not to Fund', *World Economics*, vol. 1, no. 1 (January–March) pp. 81–101

Council of Europe (1998) *Recent Demographic Developments in Europe* (Strasbourg).

Davis, E. P. (1997) *Pension Funds: Retirement-Income Security, and Capital Markets* (Oxford University Press, Oxford).

The Economist (2000) 'Europe's Need for immigrants', 6 May

European Commission (1996) 'Public Pension Expenditure Prospects in the European Union: A Survey of European Commisssion (1999) *Eurostat Year book, A Statistical Eye on Europe 1998/9 edition* (Luxembourg)

National Projections', *European Economy*, No. 3, Directorate General for Economic and Financial Affairs

Eurostat (1996) *Demographic Statistics* (European Commission, Brussels)

Grundy, E. (1996) 'Population Ageing in Europe', in Coleman, D. (ed.), *Europe's Population in the 1990s* (Oxford University Press, Oxford) pp. 267–96.

Jackson, S. (1998) *Britain's Population* (Routledge, London)

Miles, D. (1998) 'The Implications of Switching from Unfunded to Funded Pension Systems', *National Institute Economic Review*, no. 163, pp. 71–86

Mullan, P. (2000) *The Imaginary Time Bomb* (I. B. Tauris, London)

OECD (1988) *Ageing Populations: The Social Policy Implications, Organization for Economic Cooperation and Development* (OECD, Paris)

Peterson, P. G. (1999) 'Gray Dawn: The Global Aging Crisis', *Foreign Affairs*, January/February, pp. 42–55

Shiro, H. (2000) 'Greater Lifetime Expectations', *Nature,* 15 June, pp. 744–5

Taverne, D. (1995) *The Pension Time Bomb in Europe* (Federal Trust, London)

World Bank (1994) *Averting the Old-Age Crisis* (Oxford University Press, Oxford)

a significant feature of final salary occupational pensions. Consequently, their availability tends to be restricted mainly to employees of large firms and to public sector workers. A survey of occupational pension provision in twelve OECD countries (Davis, 1997) revealed that, in the late 1990s, only in Australia and Switzerland, where employer-provided occupational schemes are mandatory, did coverage of such schemes exceed 50 per cent of the employed workforce.

Member states of the European Union are most unlikely to compel employers to provide their workers with pensions linked to final salaries. To do so would significantly reduce the competitiveness of many small and medium firms and damage their potential for job creation. In addition, it can be argued that because OPFS arrangements reward long stayers and penalise workers who change jobs frequently, they can act as a significant impediment to labour market flexibility. For these reasons, most attention was given to the prefunded money purchase mechanism. In a switch to prefunding, therefore, individually funded private pensions would represent the main mechanism by which the great majority of working-age people provided savings for their retirement.

The belief that a move to prefunding could provide future pensioners with better retirement incomes at a lower cost than PAYG stems, in large part, from the fact that PMPS contributions are invested in assets which include a substantial proportion of equity shares. In the countries of the EU, these assets have increased in value by around 10 per cent each year for most of the last two decades of the twentieth century. During a similar period, the growth of earnings, the chief determinant of pension increases under PAYG, has rarely exceeded 3 per cent per annum. It seems reasonable to assume that investment returns will continue to outstrip earnings growth in the foreseeable future. If this is indeed the case, then the level of future pensions could be greater and the cost of providing a given level of pension lower, were there to be a switch to prefunding. If investment returns were the only factor to be considered, then the case would be very strong.

There are, however, other issues at stake. The ability of people to make adequate contributions is very important. In order to build up a fund of sufficient size to purchase a reasonable retirement annuity, contributions must be made regularly over a long working life. Anything which interrupts the flow of contributions to the scheme will, therefore, reduce the value of the fund and, hence, the retirement income associated with it. Certain categories of workers would suffer;

late starters, the chronically sick, women with discontinuous careers and those who experience significant periods of unemployment will be poorly served. Low-paid and part-time workers will clearly do badly compared with full-time and well-paid workers because their contributions will be lower. Long-term sickness and any disabilities which affect participation in the labour market would become highly problematic if there were a general switch to PMPS which, unlike PAYG, has no redistributive element within its structure.

Financial market conditions at the time a pension is taken can also have a significant effect on the level of retirement income under PMPS. A slump which reduced the market value of the assets in the fund would reduce the sum of money available for the purchase of an annuity. It is, of course, the task of pension fund managers to avoid undue exposure to such an eventuality by investing in a broad range of assets, prudently managed. A more serious weakness of the PMPS is the timing of the annuity purchase. Changes in interest rates can make a considerable difference to the size of the annuity that can be purchased with a given sum. More flexible arrangements with respect to drawdown go some way to meet this problem which, at present, can upset even well-planned pension arrangements.

Much of the discussion of PAYG versus PMPS carries political overtones. The advocates of PAYG value the redistributive element because they do not wish to see people who have low or irregular incomes all their working lives condemned to penury in old age. For those who put a high value on the provision of broadly equal benefits, there is no alternative to public PAYG schemes. They see PMPS as an individualistic scheme which provides good pensions for those lucky enough to be able to afford it, but a scheme which does little for those who are less well off. Critics of PAYG, on the other hand, point to the increasing financial burdens that will be placed on future generations and deplore what they regard as the politicisation of pension issues. The critics of government-run PAYG may also claim that people will have a strong incentive to save if they see it as providing for their own old age.

The final issue concerns the transition from PAYG to PMPS. Europe's public PAYG schemes could not simply be dismantled and replaced by prefunding at a stroke. There would have to be a transition period during which public PAYG schemes were run down and private funds built up. If PAYG were simply discontinued, people in the last years of their working lives would not have sufficient time left in which to accumulate an adequate fund before retirement. There would, therefore, be considerable transition costs which, as Banks and Emmerson (2000) note, would have to be set against the longer-term savings.

The move from public PAYG to prefunding will create a double generational burden for people of working age during the transition. During the rundown, taxpayers will have to continue paying for the current generation of pensioners, as well as making contributions towards their own funds. Alternatively, governments could finance the outstanding PAYG, liabilities by borrowing, but this would only transfer the burden to future generations and at the cost of imperilling the Stability Pact. Those member states that have adopted the common currency find their freedom of action with respect to debt and deficits constrained by treaty obligations. It is thus very difficult to make some people better off by moving from PAYG, without making others worse off (Miles, 1998).

Pensions in Chile

The case of Chile is frequently held up as an example of how personal saving for retirement can be successfully introduced in place of a PAYG state pension scheme. The Chilean individual capitalisation pension scheme was introduced in 1981, requiring workers to contribute a minimum of 10 per cent of their monthly earnings to a privately managed pension fund. On reaching retirement age, workers can either use their entire fund to purchase an annuity, or set up an income draw-down plan, with or without the option to purchase an annuity at a later date. Competition between fund managers, made possible by low switching costs, is meant to keep management charges low, and individuals' funds are backed by a 100 per cent government guarantee. Annuities are also partially guaranteed by state support for the insurance companies from whom they were purchased. The security of savers' funds is further enhanced by stringent regulation relating to the investment practices of fund management firms and the flow of information between fund managers and their clients.

The apparent ease with which the Chilean government was able to introduce prefunded pensions is not likely to be replicated in the European context. The political situation in Chile, as well as the demographic structure, makes valid comparisons difficult. As Boldrin *et al.* (1999) point out, circumstances in Chile during the early 1980s were very different from those prevailing in EU member states at the beginning of the twenty-first century. The public pension scheme was relatively underdeveloped and there were very few elderly people in the population compared with young people. Consequently, it was politically possible to ease the double generational burden by reducing the value of pension benefits payable through the public scheme. Miles (1998) shows that the transitional costs associated with moving to private prefunded pensions will be much higher for countries where the population is ageing rapidly and where the value of pensions provided by the public PAYG scheme is generous.

Conclusion

Fears about the harmful effects of an ageing population are not new. In the UK, for example, a Royal Commission was established in 1944 to consider the implications of the low fertility rates of the interwar period and the increases in longevity that were becoming apparent. Furthermore, ageing is not the only determinant of pension expenditures. Indeed, some commentators, for example Mullan (2000), suggest that ageing alone will not significantly increase the cost of PAYG public pension provision in the EU. Just as important are changes to scheme coverage and increases in the level of benefits. The indexation of pensions either to the cost of living or to earnings has provided generous levels of benefit. Schemes have been extended to include groups like the self-employed and part-time workers. Although these changes have some immediate effect on the pension bill, the full effects take time to work through. These modifications are likely to be popular in the short term, but, in the longer term, the economic effects may be problematic.

In recent years, PAYG pensions have become a contentious agenda item for Europe's politicians. The strain that will be put on the public finances of many member states has led to proposals to adopt new structures. There are many problems associated with such reform and there may be other ways of dealing with the pension problem without such radical surgery. For example, policies to reduce unemployment and increase labour market participation in Europe would ease the financing problem by increasing the flow of contributions into national PAYG schemes. Much depends on the decisions to be made about uprating pensions. The debate in the UK is between linking pensions to the cost of living or linking pensions to earnings and allowing pensioners to share in the growth of the economy.

It is very difficult to see how these issues can be resolved without prolonged and heated political debate. As the number of pensioners grows larger, the politicians will take note of a new electoral factor. In

dards outside Europe. To illustrate these points one might begin by citing the case studies of Wal-Mart in Chapter 4 and the Albanian migrants in Chapter 11.

The insiders in each of these two cases are the citizens of the EU and the outsiders the workers and producers who live beyond the ring fence of 'Europe'. For Wal-Mart, there are two sets of producers. The first group is made up of the powerful outsiders – the Wal-Mart managers – corporate executives who bring capital and expertise from outside, stimulate competition and reap rich rewards when they exploit market opportunities within a Europe without borders. The second group is composed of powerless outsiders – the varied suppliers of products sourced from developing countries wherever wages and environmental standards are lowest. For the Greeks who employ Albanians as casual workers the insider–outsider situation is somewhat different. 'Outsiders' in this case live among an indigenous population as a migrant labour force on the fringes of the law. The liberation of market forces has been the driver of the European idea and has made possible a new set of economic opportunities for both insiders and outsiders. In making use of these opportunities, some people benefit more than others.

In its dealings with the people outside the area bounded by the member states and the associated states within the European Economic Area (EEA), three patterns of EU behaviour can be distinguished. The first is with the near neighbours, some of whom may be future members of the club. The second is with the powerful actors on the global stage – the United States, Japan, international institutions and the larger multinational corporations. The third is the heterogeneous group of developing countries, some of whom have colonial or linguistic ties with the states of the EU.

The situation is complicated by the fact that the member states of the EU retain much more autonomy in the conduct of foreign and security policy than in trade matters. Although the central institutions seek to expand their competence from the 'low politics' of trade to the 'high politics' of international relations in general, there is as yet little evidence of this sort of sovereignty being pooled and devolved to EU institutions. Member states retain their own diplomatic and consular services and jealously guard the recognition of their independence.

In the chapters dealing with the budget and the CAP, the importance of national economic interests within the enlargement debate was mentioned. There has been a clear contrast between intergovernmental bargaining at the practical level and *communautaire* rhetoric at the linguistic level. This distinction has nowhere been more in evidence than when the financial cost–benefit calculations are made with respect to enlargement and consequent CAP changes. It is clear that existing states view the prospect of new members primarily from a national financial perspective. The applicants from East Europe are viewed not so much as family to be reunited with their loved ones, but rather as poor relations in search of remittances. One must conclude, from the analyses of Ardy and Hatt in Chapters 6 and 9, that both the financial structure of the CAP and the budgetary redistribution mechanisms already in place will be under great stress as the enlargement discussions unfold.

A second aspect of the relationship with near neighbours is uncovered in Chapter 11 dealing with Albanian migrants within Greece. At present the workers of East and east Central Europe are outsiders and constitute part of the low-cost labour reservoir used by EU insiders. In this respect, the stonemasons and ditch diggers of Albanian origin resemble very closely the Slovak au pairs who look after the children of well-paid professional couples in south London and the Czech machinists who make parts not only for Skoda cars assembled in the Czech Republic, but also for Audi and Volkswagen cars assembled within the EU. The migration issue, related as it is to the economics of labour supply, lies at the very heart of policy dilemmas discussed by Sullivan in Chapter 12. It is not only that the cheapness, tractability and mobility of moderately skilled workers from the East is important in microeconomic terms, it is also that much wider questions such as population age structure, pensions and macroeconomic management within the EU call for attention when migration and labour market policy-making are discussed.

The analysis that Sullivan makes of the 'demographic time bomb' reveals with great clarity the dynamic forces driving migrants into the wealthy core of Europe. Rich Europeans are having fewer children, are living longer and are consuming more. Expectations about living standards after retirement and the problems of Pay-As-You-Go pensions in a geriatric EU begin to appear on political agendas. Some of Europe's near neighbours, especially those to the south, are poor and have large families. There is a very steep migration gradient. The outsiders would like to come in and enjoy the benefits of living inside. The youthful energy of migrants is valued as a labour input but indigenous Europeans frequently evince hostility towards immigrants as a social group. Neither the member states nor the EU have had the courage to confront the economic and social complexities of migration.

Migration is a contentious issue, giving rise as it does to racism and xenophobia. All too often politicians prefer to look the other way; this is unfortunate. People – both migrating people and resident people – are what government is supposed to be about, and to ignore the underlying dynamics of migration is very likely to make matters worse. The EU response to the formation of a new Austrian government following the election of a right-wing coalition in early 2000 highlights the sensitivity of these issues.

The analysis of the working of the Schengen Agreement in Chapter 11 is interesting in this respect. The movement of Albanians from Greece to Italy is prevented in principle by Article 21 of Schengen but in practice by the fact that border checks are carried out regularly – a procedure only made possible by the facts of geography. Having no land border with any other EU member state means that travel from Greece must be by air or sea. Border checks are practicable on ferries and at airports so passports are routinely demanded and the movement of people can be controlled. Article 21 cannot be implemented for states linked by road and rail because the effective monitoring of migrants hidden within legitimate, massive daily movements of EU citizens across member state boundaries is not possible without grave damage to the very concept of free movement of people.

Another group of people who are seen as would-be immigrants are the displaced persons in the poor countries of Africa and Asia who become victims of civic breakdown and violence and present themselves as refugees. The difficulties of distinguishing this group from the much larger number of desperate people who are victims of economic underdevelopment and would often be classified as economic migrants are very considerable. Both in principle and in practice the sieving of refugees from migrants is proving to be an almost impossible task. It is poverty that drives migration and only the spread of prosperity to the poorer countries can reduce migration pressures.

These practical concerns as well as the ethical case for giving development assistance are important within the ruling elites of the EU and its member states. The European Union concerns itself with human rights issues, trade, aid and economic development within many states in Africa, the Caribbean and Pacific (ACP) largely because of historical ties and some feeling of responsibility but also in order to project a European global presence. The gross inefficiency of the aid programmes administered by the EU was heavily criticised by British parliamentarians in the summer of 2000. The inevitable and predictable response was to point out that the EU agencies did not have enough staff to work effectively. A more serious criticism of EU involvement in aid provision is that it has not been accompanied by measures to foster self-reliance and has even in some instances damaged local economic activity. It has long been accepted (Hayter, 1971) that national governments have been guilty of misusing aid budgets to further their own economic interests rather than the welfare of the aid recipients, so it should not surprise us that the EU does likewise.

Overall, it is difficult to give much credit to the EU in its dealings with people outside. Perhaps we should expect nothing else. The EU is not an altruistic organisation. It was a hard bargainer on trade issues in the General Agreement an Tariff and Trade (GATT). This bargaining power has been used against both US-led multinationals and poorer countries. In the first case this may be legitimate but in the second it is highly debatable. All too frequently its member states insist on using EU power to further the economic interests of articulate insiders – people, pressure groups and firms within the current membership of the EU. Sectional and national interests are pursued using EU agencies and bureaucrats, largely because the political machinery of 'Europe' is open and responsive to well-organised lobby groups (Moravscik, 1998). The idealistic impulses of the early years, if indeed there ever were any, are long dead. Large corporations are happy with the new Europe and, in so far as they deliver economic benefits to consumers, the people of the new Europe are happy too. Bradley suggests that Euro capitalism, popular capitalism and globalisation are evolving into a new economic order, and Panah suggests that the most active agents for change in the 'brave new world' are the corporate strategists of big business. Sadly, the world's poorest people benefit little from globalisation and the institutions that preside over it.

There is a third pattern of interaction. It concerns contacts with the major world powers. It must be stressed yet again that this is an area where the largest of the member states have insisted on keeping matters very much in their own hands. World summits are composed of national leaders and the meetings of G7 or G8 remain the province of sovereign states. In security matters also, the long-running troubles in the Balkans demonstrate the continued importance of NATO as the command structure for the deployment of national armed forces. Ever since the demise of the European Defence Community in August 1954 it has been US leadership within NATO that has shaped defence issues in Europe, as Gardner has argued in Chapter 2.

In trade matters, the European Union takes centre stage. Even in this, its long-established field of action, it is now confronted by a new body, the World Trade Organisation (WTO). In future, the WTO may have a powerful impact on world markets for agricultural commodities. The Uruguay negotiations influenced the direction of the CAP as Chapter 9 noted. Hatt also pointed to the GMO issue as one among many where consumers are putting food standards on the agenda and begin to question the dominance of agribusiness interests within the structure of the CAP. Since the WTO can be used to resist attempts to regulate GMOs, claiming that this is 'protectionism in disguise', the EU may yet find itself defending European consumers against powerful multinational corporations. These organisations have begun to use free trade as a stick to beat the environmentalists and to defeat the guardians of local community interests.

Whether it is the banana war, where the USA is the spokesman for American-owned producers and the EU seeks to protect the smaller producers of the West Indies, or whether it is chemical additives in animal fodder, the Europeans expect their Union to give some protection against the economic power of the USA when it acts forcefully to further the interests of American multinational corporations. It remains to be seen whether or not consumers will gain an effective voice within the EU. At present 'people' – that is, real human-being-type people – are much less comfortable in the New Europe than legal 'persons' – that is to say, corporations, government agencies and the like.

By insisting within this book on a 'people' focus, we have sought to evaluate the contribution that European integration has made to welfare in general and the well-being of particular groups of people in particular. In nearly every case our first judgements look at economics. Are savers going to be better protected from fraud and mismanagement when regulations operate at the European rather than the national level? Will travellers get cheaper, safer airlines? To what extent does the CAP meet the goals of efficiency, stability and equity and to whom do the benefits flow – farmers, consumers or agribusiness? Does the EU budget function properly and will a single currency and a more cen-tralised monetary system begin to correct some of the weaknesses that have developed over the years?

These are the primary questions. But there are other deeper questions which arise immediately the economic issues are analysed. One set of questions, similar in some respects to the 'insider–outsider' theme dealt with above, is the complication posed when we consider a set of dichotomies which contrast the benefits and costs that the European project has produced for different sorts of 'insider'. For instance, the large Single Market favours the firm that thinks strategically and can grow to achieve economies of scale, as Chapter 4 has argued. Small firms are threatened by this process and some workers will be displaced. People unwilling or unable to move will suffer as the dynamic of newly released market forces takes hold. The EU increases career opportunities but only for those able to access them, and Chapter 10 outlines the issues facing those with care responsibilities. Notwithstanding the creation of TENs which were discussed in Chapter 8, the core–periphery dichotomy persists. In the centre, jobs and high incomes are seen as desirable but the concomitant crowding and pollution are unwelcome externalities. At the periphery, migration of young people leads to a loss of vitality. Perhaps the most difficult questions raised by this analysis concern the balance between local autonomy and central regulation. These questions matter in economics as well as in politics.

'Europe' in its current condition of integration is best described as a market without a state. Many chapters have pointed to unfortunate consequences in particular issue areas. The problem of a single market in financial services without a single regulatory framework in Chapter 7 is one of the clearest examples of this; Ardy in Chapter 6 points to the reluctance of member governments to give significant budgetary discretion to EU institutions; Hatt in Chapter 9 points out that food safety questions and animal health issues are becoming more and more important: yet responsibility for such critical issues is ill-defined as between member states, the EU and indeed the WTO. In Chapter 5, Cullen deals with one case where the centralising forces are clear and explicit – monetary integration and the single interest rate for the single currency – and another case in Chapter 8 where subsidiarity rules and local solutions to local transport needs must be fitted into cross-border trans-European networks.

There can be agreement on the analysis and yet passionate disagreement on the prognosis and the prescription. Enthusiasts for the European Project see every difficulty as a growing pain that will be solved by further integration. For Europhiles the idea is such a good one that progress towards a more perfect union is the only possible path forward. It was argued by Gardner in Chapter 2 that the end was essentially political and the means was economic. If this is indeed true and the great majority of Europeans feel this striving for unity to be valid in its own right, then economic judgements are not the most salient considerations in making policy.

Many people fear the loss of autonomy and democracy. Confusion can always be generated by drawing on the contrasting and persisting differences between member states in historical and cultural values, the nature of sovereignty and worries about linguistic pride and national identity. In arguing against any further deepening, critics of the federal ideal can and do use the economic failings of the existing imperfect confederation as evidence that the whole thrust of the project is misguided. Their strongest arguments centre around the concern for the welfare of the local community and the need to safeguard legitimate interests through effective democratic structures. These structures do not exist within the current arrangements of the EU. National Parliaments are unable to scrutinise EU legislation effectively while the European Parliament does not fill the gap. This is the infamous 'democratic deficit'. In so far as the economic failings of the EU are compounded by this deficit, the critics have a point.

The most serious failing of the EU in its fifty-year history lies in this failure to create a 'People's Europe'. In this collection, we have tried to show how some of the economics of integration have worked out. In so doing we do not come down on the side of the enthusiasts or on the side of the sceptics. What does appear, however, is the picture of an institution that must do much more to serve the welfare of its own people and conduct itself more circumspectly in international affairs. It may do this either by deepening and developing into a better federal institution or by going for the wider and weaker structure with a more limited role for the central bureaucracy and the emergence of a Europe of city regions respecting each other's differences while cooperating peacefully on matters of common concern. The future of the European idea is constantly being reshaped and it remains very much 'a journey to an unknown destination'.

References

Hayter, T. (1971) *Aid as Imperialism* (Penguin, Harmondsworth)
Moravcik, A. (1998) *The Choice for Europe* (UCL, London)

Index

6. The establishment of a protectorate over northern China from the Wall to the Yangtze River.

7. The encirclement of Mongolia and the establishment as far as Tibet of Japanese influence by means of Japanese instructors, this measure to establish a precautionary threat to Russia on the north and India on the south.

8. The acquisition of all islands in the Pacific, including Hawaii.

9. The eventual acquisition of Australia and New Zealand.

10. The establishment of Japanese control over all the yellow races, including the Malays. On this point the student had used a word that indicated the control was to be fatherly; Roosevelt was later unable to recall the word used.

The student said that through the execution of this plan, Japan would be able to threaten Europe.

Roosevelt was concerned about how Japan intended to fit the United States into this proposed expansion. The Japanese assured him that the United States need have no fear: Japan intended only to establish outposts in the New World. Probably Japan would establish one outpost in Mexico and another in Peru. Other than this Japan would not molest America, but the Americans must remember that the Japanese being a temperate zone people must have Australia and New Zealand to expand in.

Still a student at Harvard, Roosevelt, at 21, became engaged to Eleanor Roosevelt, a distant cousin. They married in 1905, after he had graduated from Harvard and become a law student at Columbia. Her